Also by Leo Spitzer

The Creoles of Sierra Leone:
Response to Colonialism, 1870–1945

Lives in Between: Assimilation and Marginality in Austria,
Brazil and West Africa, 1780–1945

HOTEL BOLIVIA

HOTEL BOLIVIA

THE CULTURE OF MEMORY IN
A REFUGE FROM NAZISM

LEO SPITZER

HILL AND WANG

A DIVISION OF FARRAR, STRAUS AND GIROUX

NEW YORK

Hill and Wang
A division of Farrar, Straus and Giroux
19 Union Square West, New York 10003

Copyright © 1998 by Leo Spitzer
All rights reserved
Distributed in Canada by Douglas & McIntyre Ltd.
Printed in the United States of America
Designed by Jonathan D. Lippincott
First edition, 1998

Library of Congress Cataloging-in-Publication Data
Spitzer, Leo, 1939-
    Hotel Bolivia : culture and memory in a refuge from Nazism / Leo
Spitzer.—1st Hill and Wang ed.
      p.   cm.
    Includes bibliographical references.
    ISBN 0-8090-5545-7
    1. Jews—Bolivia—History.   2. Refugees, Jewish—Bolivia—History.
3. Jews—Germany—History—1933–1945.   4. Jews—Persecutions—
Austria.   5. Spitzer, Leo, 1939–   —Childhood and youth.   6. Bolivia—
Ethnic relations.   I. Title.
F3359.J4S75   1998
984'.004924—dc21
                                        97–42416

For Alex, Oliver, Gabriel
for Mindy and Erik
for Jessica
and for Zoë

CONTENTS

PREFACE   ix

1. DESPERATE DEPARTURE
RECHNITZ   3
TWO PHOTOGRAPHS   8
TERROR UNCHAINED: 1938   11
"WHY DID YOU WAIT SO LONG TO LEAVE?"   24
GETTING OUT   31
ELLA   35
"AND YET WE WERE THE LUCKY ONES . . ."   45

2. THE CROSSING   47
THE ALBUM   49
"WE HAD ALL BECOME REFUGEES . . ."   56
EXITS, PORTS, AND CROSSINGS IN BETWEEN   60
THE *ORAZIO* TRAGEDY   66

3. INVISIBLE BAGGAGE
INHERITED RELICS   75
"THE MOON WAS MORE REAL TO US . . ."   81
"SO STRANGE, SO UNBELIEVABLY STRANGE . . ."   84
IMAGES OF DIFFERENCE   88
EL LÁPIZ DE SANDEN   99
APPEARANCES   104

4. "BUENA TIERRA"

DEEP IN THE JUNGLE . . .   107

JEWISH IMMIGRATION, AGRICULTURAL COLONIZATION   108

THE PROMISED LAND   122

A FADING DREAM   130

A MATTER OF *YEKKES* AND *POLACOS*   138

5. ANDEAN WALTZ   141

NOSTALGIC MEMORY   143

CRITICAL MEMORIES, LAYERED IDENTITIES   153

LOOKING BACK: THREE VIGNETTES   159

6. LOS JUDÍOS ALEMANES

THE ANAS   161

"AND THEY LOOKED AT US . . ."   163

BIG NOSES AND THE ELDERS OF ZION   165

NAZIS IN THE STREETS   175

APARTNESS WITHIN THE CONTACT ZONE   180

7. SURVIVING MEMORY

"HOTEL BOLIVIA"   183

MEMORY AND BOLIVIA AS EXPERIENCE   189

TRANSMISSION   193

POSTSCRIPT

NOTES FROM A RECENT RETURN   199

NOTES   203

PERSONAL SOURCES   225

INDEX   227

PREFACE

Desperate to escape the increasingly vehement persecution in their home-lands, thousands of refugees from Nazi-dominated Central Europe, the majority of them Jews, found refuge in Latin America in the 1930s. Bolivia became a principal recipient of this refugee influx by the end of the decade when Argentina, Brazil, Chile, and Mexico—traditional countries of choice for European immigration—closed their gates or applied severe restrictions to the entrance of newcomers. Indeed, in the panic months following the German *Anschluss* of Austria in March 1938 and *Kristall-nacht* in November of that year, Bolivia was one of very few remaining places *in the entire world* to accept Jewish refugees.[1] In the short period between then and the end of the first year of World War II, some twenty thousand refugees, primarily from Germany, Austria, and Czechoslovakia, entered Bolivia—more than in Canada, Australia, New Zealand, South Africa, and India combined. When the war ended, a second, smaller wave of immigrants, mostly Eastern European Holocaust survivors and displaced relatives of previous refugees, arrived in Bolivia. (Also in these postwar years, a small number of Nazis who were fleeing or had help escaping prosecution in Europe—the best known among them being Klaus Barbie—came to Bolivia.) The new immigrants settled primarily in La Paz, a city in the central Andean mountains, more than 12,500 feet above sea level, as well as in Cochabamba, Oruro, Sucre, and in small mining and tropical agricultural communities throughout the land.[2]

In Bolivia, the refugees began to reconstruct a version of the world they had been forced to abandon. Their own origins and social situations were diverse in Central Europe, ranging across generational, class, educational, and political differences and incorporating various professional, craft, and artistic backgrounds. Some of them had at one time been engineers, doctors, lawyers, musicians, actors, and artists; others were skilled and unskilled workers whose livelihoods had been interrupted by Nazi exclusionary decrees. Although most who came to Bolivia were Jews or were married to Jews, a significant minority were non-Jewish political refugees: Communists, Socialists, and others persecuted by the Nazi regime. Jews themselves differed greatly in the degree of their identification with their religion and its traditions. There were Zionists, atheists, Orthodox, High Holiday Jews, and nonpractitioners among them. They shared a common identity as Jews only in the sense, perhaps, that they had all been defined as "Jews" from the outside—that the Nazis had "othered" them as Jews.

No matter what their background differences had been in Europe, the vast majority of refugees arrived in South America in dire straits, with few personal possessions and very little money. This in itself had a leveling effect, cutting across their previous class distinctions. But other factors also helped to create a sense of collective identity among them, aiding in their adjustment and survival. Their common history of persecution was certainly one of these. Each and every refugee had been identified as undesirable, stripped of citizenship and possessions. Despite differences in the details of their particular experiences, they were all "in the same boat." The war back in Europe, and the fact that so many of them had relatives and friends from whom they had been separated, were ever-present realities of which they were collectively conscious and that bonded them together. They kept themselves and each other informed of news about the war from accounts in the press and radio, and they shared efforts to discover the fate of those left behind. In this regard, the German language (which they spoke at home and among themselves) was their vehicle of inquiry, information, and unity, allowing them to communicate intimately and to express themselves with a degree of familiarity that most could never attain in the Spanish language of their surroundings.

But ultimately, it was Austro-German Jewish bourgeois society, the cultural end product of nineteenth-century Jewish emancipation in Central Europe, that gave the new arrivals a model for emulation and a common locus for identification in their place of refuge. Indeed, at the very time when that dynamic social and cultural amalgam was being ruthlessly and systematically destroyed by the Nazis, the Jewish refugees in Bolivia tried to recall and revive a version of it in a land thousands of miles from their home; in a country that offered them a haven, but in which many of them felt themselves as mere sojourners.

Hotel Bolivia examines this particular episode as a point of entry for the exploration of an important but generally neglected aspect of the experience of group displacement—the relationship between memory and cultural survival during an era of persecution and genocide. Taking into account the inherently constructed nature of memory, my purpose is to analyze the social and ideological dimensions influencing individual and combined recollections, and the ways in which past experience is shaped, reorganized, transformed, and narrated to serve changing needs. In this sense, especially, this book is more than the historical presentation of a significant, yet not widely recognized, refuge from Nazi persecution. It contributes to, and is in dialogue with, a major objective of contemporary historical and cultural studies: the effort to document the life stories and reclaim the memories and discourses of ordinary persons who might otherwise remain hidden from history. And it is directly concerned with theoretical issues, increasingly evident in historical writing, having to do with the contextualization of memory and the interdependence—and tension—between memory and history. In reflecting on representations of remembered experiences, and on changes within these—over time and between people—I hope to contribute to the historical study of memory itself.

Alto Perú, the region that became Bolivia after gaining its independence from Spain in 1824, had once before been the refuge of people escaping religious intolerance and persecution in Europe. In the course of the sixteenth century, and during the extended, often brutal sway of the Spanish Inquisition, thousands of New Christians, or Marranos—persons of Jewish origin who had been converted to Christianity by force or prudent choice of their own—left the Iberian peninsula; clandestinely or openly, many sought haven in Spain's Latin American colonies. Bringing badly needed technical and entrepreneurial skills with them, a number of Marranos settled around the silver-mining areas of Potosí and in centers of trade and commerce like Chuquisaca (later Sucre), Santa Cruz, and Tarija. Over the years, some of these Marranos, or their offspring, intermarried with local Christians and were integrated into the Catholic establishment. In the process, the background religious "stain" that had made them identifiable as "outsiders" was blurred if not eradicated. But traces of their Sephardic ancestry survived—discernible both in family names and in customs of Jewish origin that were perpetuated for generations, despite the loss of their original meaning.[3] Until well into the first decades of this century, for example, it was the custom for women in some families in Santa Cruz to light candles on Friday evening, a Jewish ritual inaugurating the Sabbath, and for persons associated with some of the oldest and most distinguished "colonial" families in Sucre to maintain a semi-secluded seven-day deep mourning period for their dead that, in form if not substance, bore a great resemblance to the Jewish mourning practice *shivah*. Ancient candlesticks and silver objects of Sephardic origin, as well as incunabula inscribed in Hebrew, were passed down within some of Sucre's families for generations.[4]

But despite the early presence of Marranos in Bolivia's colonial past, and relics of Judaic practices and beliefs, few—if any—Jews seem to have emigrated to the country in the first century of its independence. In this respect Bolivia was quite different from its more accessible and economically attractive South American neighbors like Argentina and Brazil, whose governments had periodically encouraged "white settler" immigration from Europe, and which developed substantial Jewish communities in the course of the nineteenth and early twentieth centuries.[5] A few Eastern European Jews did trickle into Bolivia in the early 1900s, fleeing persecution in Poland, pogroms in Russia in the aftermath of the failed revolution of 1905, or after the Bolshevik Revolution of 1917. But before the rise of Nazism very few Jews, perhaps less than a hundred from Alsace, Poland, and Russia, had settled in this Andean land.

Indeed, had it not been for the special circumstances created in Europe by the ascendancy of National Socialism in Germany and Austria and the outbreak of World War II, it is highly unlikely that Bolivia would have been more than a remote tourist fantasy for most of the persons who found refuge there in the 1930s and early 1940s. Landlocked and relatively geographically isolated in the west-central part of the South American continent, Bolivia is a land of awesome natural beauty, challenging physical and climatic extremes, and immense cultural richness. Some two-thirds of its national land surface, near the equator, consists of tropical and semitropical lowlands containing virtually impenetrable rain forest and regions of potentially bountiful agricultural and mineral production. In contrast, the western one-third of Bolivia is defined by the colossal Andes mountains, which extend, spinelike, north to south, in two immense ranges, the Cordillera Real and the volcanic Cordillera Occidental, with numerous peaks rising to more than 21,000 feet. The highland plateau, the altiplano, stretches between these ranges—a vast plain of some 40,000 square miles, at an average elevation well over 14,000 feet above sea level. This is also the location of Lake Titicaca, the highest navigable lake in the world and the central sacred site of the great pre-Hispanic Tiahuanaco and Inca civilizations. Windswept, cold, and haunting, if not forbidding in the starkness and expansiveness of its landscape, the altiplano has nonetheless been the core site for human settlement for millennia—the place where many of the staple products and animals of the Andean peoples were domesticated and the area that, at the time of the refugees' arrival in the land, supported nearly 60 percent of Bolivia's population and most of its cities.

Although these awesome but extreme geographical features were certainly not an exclusionary barrier to the arrival and settlement of persons born and raised in more temperate Central Europe, they did constitute an impediment for the less fit, the elderly, and the physically impaired among the refugees. Many newcomers trying to settle in high-altitude locations or in the tropical lowlands faced daunting challenges to their physical adjustment, as well as dangers to their health. In the 1930s, moreover, Bolivia seemed to offer the refugees few cultural parallels to the lifeways and customs with which they were familiar. When they arrived, Bolivia was—as it remains today—culturally the "most Indian" of the American republics. Only between 5 and 10 percent of Bolivia's approximately 3.25 million native inhabitants in the mid-1930s belonged to the Spanish-speaking urban elite—the predominantly Catholic group that identified itself as "white," was educated in the ways of European culture, and had ruled the country politically and economically since its independence from Spain. A larger population of *mestizos*—people of Spanish and Indian parentage or descent, generally referred to as *cholos*—belonged to the urban lower-middle and lower classes, or were rural freeholders, and were on a much lower rung in the social hierarchy. They spoke Spanish as well as one of the Amerindian languages, received less formal education and inculcation in European cultural ways and outlooks, dressed in Western but also in a uniquely *cholo* style, and practiced a Catholicism strongly influenced by the belief systems and folk religion of the indigenous populations. But they identified themselves as apart and socially above the largely subordinated and exploited Quechua- and Aymara-speaking Indian majority, a group that comprised more than 70 percent of Bolivia's population and serviced the dominant groups as manual laborers, servants, workers, farmers, miners, and soldiers.

Most refugees entered Bolivia with little or no background knowledge about it other than from reports that it was among the least "Europeanized" of the South American nations, or from popular literature that represented its impoverished indigenous populations as "primitive," "wild," "uncivilized," or, conversely, as "noble" and "unfathomable." "The Indian women were sometimes beautifully dressed, even richly dressed," remembered one immigrant. "But they had no culture. They had no civilization." "We never had seen anything like them. Already on the train coming to La Paz, at stops, a real novelty: we looked at them and they looked at us."[6] These reactions attest to the bewilderment and sense of strangeness that many immigrants experienced, as well as the curiosity that often characterized their initial meetings with the Indians, and display stereotypical biases that inhibited more intimate contact and understanding.

But while the refugees' preconceptions brought from Central Europe impeded deeper cross-cultural exploration, cultural stereotypes also influenced the perceptions of *mestizo* and "white" Bolivians, and affected their relations with immigrant Jews. In the early 1940s, and occasionally after the end of the war, these stereotypical characterizations, some of them deriving from ancient Christian prejudices about Jews as "Christ killers" and "money grubbers," were employed by Nazi provocateurs and sympathizers in Bolivia to stir up anti-Semitic agitation against the refugees, and to seek their expulsion from the country. A Bolivian recalled:

> Outwardly, it was certainly difficult to tell the difference between an *alemán* [German] and a *judío alemán* [Jewish German]. They were different in the sense that the latter seemed ready to take almost any job—even to work doing hard manual labor. There were certainly many of them coming into the country. "Hordes of *judíos alemanes*" someone wrote in a newspaper at the time. But I don't know if we would really have paid much attention to them if it hadn't been for the scandals alleging that Jews had entered the country illegally, with invalid documents, and the vicious anti-Jewish agitation disseminated by a few newspapers and politicians sympathetic to the Nazi cause.[7]

The title of this book expresses the truth that for many German-speaking refugees Bolivia was indeed a transitory home—a larger version of a temporary resident "hotel"—which they eventually left after the war had ended. Although more Jewish immigrants arrived in the country in the postwar years, these newcomers were in the main Yiddish-speaking Eastern Europeans who had survived the Holocaust; they came to Bolivia to join family or friends who had managed to emigrate while there was still time, in the late 1930s. Most German-speaking refugees, in contrast, "checked out" of Bolivia, choosing not to settle permanently in this Andean nation. They generally reemigrated to neighboring countries like Argentina or Chile, which seemed "more European" and less physically and culturally daunting, or to the United States or Israel, or they returned to their countries of origin.

I was born in Bolivia ten days after the German invasion of Poland and the outbreak of World War II in September 1939. As a child of Austrian-Jewish immigrants who had fled there only months before, during the period of "panic emigration" from Central Europe, I have had a privileged connection to the refugee experience about which I write—one that has allowed me to combine a long-standing scholarly interest with the vantage of an insider's perspective. While this book is thus the work of a historian, personal memory is not only a component of its overall makeup but a key factor in its creation. As a work of history, it is grounded in many of the traditional sources of historical reconstruction: in documentary materials found in archives, repositories, and libraries in Bolivia, the United States, England, Austria, Germany, and Israel. It makes extensive use of written memoirs, letters, photographs, family albums, artistic representations, newspaper articles, and advertisements. But it is also in very large part based on videotaped accounts collected from the immigrants and witnesses—on more than one hundred and fifty hours of interviews with surviving refugees (now widely dispersed throughout the world), with Bolivians, and with members of the "second generation" who, like myself, were born in Bolivia or had entered the country as very young children. My personal background, and the Bolivian refugee history of members of my family, have certainly eased my access to the people I have interviewed, and established a bond of common understanding and experience between us that could not easily be attained any other way. One of the first people to respond to my notice (in the German-Jewish New York publication *Aufbau*) about this project and my interest in speaking with people who had emigrated to Bolivia, turned out to have been a kindergarten teacher of mine in La Paz; another, now living in Chicago, had worked in partnership with my father and uncle in the early 1940s on construction jobs and, before his own departure from Bolivia after the war, had been a close family friend. I discovered photos of both of them in our Bolivia albums; they had pictures of me, or of others in our family, in theirs.

Clearly, therefore, *Hotel Bolivia* is refracted through lenses of my own Bolivian childhood memories and the shadowed presence in my own life of my family's "lost Europe." My aim in its pages has been to be aware of, and responsive to, the advantages and possible pitfalls of my special relationship to the places, the subject, and the people about whom I write. My dual role, as historian and participant, is a visible element throughout this book.

The idea of writing about the thousands of Jewish refugees who fled to Bolivia from the Third Reich, and about the memory and transmission of this experience, has been with me for a long time. During the last half-dozen years in which I actively transformed the idea into the real project, I have been fortunate to receive invaluable encouragement, guidance, and information from many people, and have been helped and supported by many institutions and foundations. While I am, of course, solely responsible for any factual errors and interpretative flaws in this book, I wish to acknowledge my appreciation to them for their generosity and kindness.

I owe an immense debt of gratitude to all participants and witnesses of this immigration who welcomed me into their homes and allowed me to videotape them, entrusting me with accounts of their lives, with memorabilia and photographs, and with their recollections and feelings about the refugee experience. I have listed the names of people I interviewed and people who gave me access to family documents and artifacts, as well as individuals interviewed by others whose accounts I heard or read in transcript, at the end of the book.

Bolivians have been recognized all too little for their generosity in granting asylum to so many thousands of refugees and for permitting them to renew their lives. I hope this book makes some small rectification of this historical omission. My reentry and reconnection to Bolivia in 1991 after an absence of almost two decades was mediated and eased through the colossal generosity, friendship, and contagious good humor of Dr. David and Kathy Fringer, who invited me into their home and made me part of their family during my research stay in La Paz. I recall with pleasure numerous occasions we spent together, and will always be thankful for the enthusiastic support they have given me. I also want to offer special thanks to Marek and Susana Ajke, Werner and Eva Guttentag, and Graciela "Leli" Kudelka—a friend of mine since childhood—for the hospitality and immense help they extended to me during my research visits to Bolivia. Professor Herbert S. Klein, whose knowledge of Bolivian history and politics is vast, helped to orient and familiarize me with the Bolivian research scene and to put me in touch with Bolivian intellectuals. And I am grateful to Josefa Luzio Antezana, Clara López Beltrán, and Laura Escobari for facilitating my journey into the daunting holdings of the Archivo de La Paz and other Bolivian governmental repositories.

In the United States, I had many opportunities to talk about our family's flight from Austria, and about the refugees' adaptation to Bolivia, with my uncle Julius Wolfinger—a gentle, giving, and insightful man with a spectacular memory for detail and the narrative skills of a poetic storyteller. I wish our conversations could have continued and I had been able to present him with this book, in which his voice is so central; but he died before I could show him even the draft of a portion of it, and I miss him profoundly. I am also especially grateful to Liesl Lipczenko, her late husband, Heini, and to Hanni and Heinz Pinshower for hosting me in their homes in Cleveland and Chicago, and for spending many hours with me detailing their emigration and time in Bolivia. The encouragement and guidance of Liesl and Heini, who were among my parents' closest friends, and whom I used to call "Tante" and "Onkel" as a child in La Paz, has been especially important to me.

Along the way, I have been the happy recipient of a number of fellowships to fund my work on this book. Faculty research and travel grants from Dartmouth College in 1990 and 1991, the directorship of Dartmouth History Department foreign-study program in London, a grant from the Marion and Jasper Whiting Foundation in 1991, travel funds from the Holocaust Education Foundation in 1993, and a Lucius N. Littauer Foundation Grant in 1994, supported research trips in the United States, and to Bolivia, Austria, Germany, England, and Israel.

My research and writing were also enabled by a residency at the National Humanities Center in 1992–93 (where I was the Lucius N. Littauer Fellow), by a fellowship from the John Simon Guggenheim Memorial Foundation in 1994–95, and by a fellowship/residency from the Rockefeller Foundation at the Bellagio Study Center in October–November 1995.

I have made intensive use of memoirs, documents, and visual materials located at the Leo Baeck Institute, the American Jewish Joint Distribution Committee and YIVO archives in New York, the Wiener Library in London, the Dokumentationsarchiv des Österreichischen in Vienna, and at the Institute of Latin American Studies at the Hebrew University in Jerusalem. The librarians and archivists at these repositories and research centers were most helpful in my searches. I am also especially appreciative of the assistance I received from Jean Houston in the library at the National Humanities Center, from Eric Nooter, Director of Archives and Records of the American Jewish Joint Distribution Committee, and from Patricia Carter, the interlibrary loan specialist in Baker Library, Dartmouth College. They and the other reference librarians in these institutions were indefatigable in tracking down many obscure books and articles for me. One could not hope for a more dedicated or more professional support staff. Many thanks also to Jim Levine, Uli Knoepflmacher, and Kent Mullikin for their encouragement and invaluable assistance, and to Gail Vernazza for her practical help with my manuscript.

Over the past few years, portions and drafts of this work have been read by many colleagues, friends, and persons directly or indirectly connected to the "Bolivia experience," and I have benefited from their comments, critiques, and specialized knowledge. Susanne Zantop, Todd Endelman, Judith Laikin Elkin, Geoffrey Hartman, Gisela Brinker-Gabler, Sander Gilman, Milton Shain, Angelika Bammer, Khachig Tölöyan, Egon Schwarz, Jane Coppock, Nancy Miller, Irene Kacandes, Susan Suleiman, Jeff Lesser, Syd Nathans, and Lotte and Carl Hirsch were especially kind. I also profited immensely from the questions, discussions, and congenial intellectual interactions in our seminar group on "Autobiography and Subjectivity in Scholarly Writing" at the National Humanities Center in 1992–93, and in the 1996 Humanities Institute on "Cultural Memory and the Present" at Dartmouth College. For their patience, guidance, insightfulness, goodwill, and close readings I am especially grateful to my Humanities Center colleagues Temma Kaplan,

Steve Caton, Kate Bartlett, Susan Porter-Benson, and Alex Zwerdling; and to fellow Humanities Institute members Ernst van Alphen, Carol Bardenstein, Jane Bellamy, Susan Brison, Ann Burlein, Katharine Conley, Bruce Duncan, Christina Dupláa, Lessie Jo Frazier, Gerd Gemünden, Irene Kacandes, Mary Kelley, Henri Lustiger-Thaler, Tamara Northern, Larry Polansky, Marita Sturken, and Melissa Zeiger. To Jonathan Crewe, who co-directed this Humanities Institute with me, and to Mieke Bal, our Senior Fellow, I extend a special *abrazo fuerte*. I have learned much from their critical sophistication, clarity of thinking, and theoretical range.

Earlier versions of some of the material in this book were published previously: part of Chapters 2 and 3 as "An Emigration to the Edge of the Holocaust," in *Ideas* 1, no. 2 (March 1993) and "Andean Waltz" in Geoffrey Hartman, ed., *Holocaust Remembrance: The Shapes of Memory* (Oxford: Blackwell, 1994); part of Chapter 3 as "Invisible Baggage in a Refuge from Nazism," in *Diaspora* 2, no. 3 (Winter 1993); part of Chapters 3, 5, and 6 as "Andean Two-Step: The Encounter between Bolivians and Central European Jewish Refugees," in Todd Endelman, ed., *Comparing Jewish Societies* (Ann Arbor: University of Michigan Press, 1997); part of Chapter 5 as "Persistent Memory: Central European Refugees in an Andean Land," in *Poetics Today* 17, no. 4 (Winter 1996).

Elisabeth Sifton, unparalleled editor, seems always to have understood my goals in this project and to have been sympathetic to my special relationship and approach to it. Her editorial suggestions have been superb; her lucid sense of language and of cadence inspiring. I am immensely grateful to her. I also wish to thank her assistant, April Lamm, for her helpfulness and good humor.

Marianne Hirsch, presence, best friend, muse, incisive critic, partner, and encouraging soul mate: all too many pieces and drafts of this book have passed before her eyes. Her intelligence, critical acumen, imagination, and enthusiastic belief in its possibilities have invigorated and influenced every stage of its creation. *Muchísimas gracias, amor.*

And many thanks also to our children, Alex, Oliver, and Gabriel, for their strong support, patience, good humor, and their readiness to discover old and new worlds so meaningful to their parents. Gabriel, especially, has also been a willing and acute listener to out-loud draft readings of chapter sections of this book, and his sharp sense of good prose, his smiles of approval, and his keen interest in the past have been extremely rewarding and important to me. Indeed, acts of transmission such as these have been fundamental and motivating forces in my writing *Hotel Bolivia*. In wishing to convey the history and memory of displacement, survival, and renewal from the generation of the early- and mid-twentieth century to a generation that will extend well into the twenty-first, I dedicate this book to our children, and to my nieces and nephew—the children of my siblings, Elly Shapiro, Tony Spitzer, and Carl Spitzer, and grandchildren of our refugee parents, Eugene and Rose. This is a story that is now theirs to pass on.

HOTEL BOLIVIA

DESPERATE

DEPARTURE

Mine are superficial roots, along the railroad tracks across Europe, through the paths of emigration and deportation. But I neither emigrated nor was deported. The world that was destroyed was not mine. I never knew it. But I am, so many of us are, the orphans of that world. Our roots are "diasporic." They do not go underground. They are not attached to any particular land or soil. Nor do they lie . . . at the bottom of a well in Jerusalem. Rather they creep up along the many roads of dispersion . . . Such roads are endless.

—Henri Raczymow,
"Memory Shot Through with Holes"

RECHNITZ

It is summer 1978, and I am about to make my first visit to Austria. My intention is to spend two months researching materials on Stefan Zweig and the Zweig and Brettauer families for a book I am writing, but before I undertake this work I set out for ten days of European sight-seeing with Manon, my eight-year-old son, Alex, and my mother, Rose. Starting in Paris in a leased Renault, we drive through parts of France, Germany, and Switzerland, and then cross northern Italy and Yugoslavia in order to enter Austria from the southeast, through Burgenland. My mother is quite insistent on this approach, determined that I preface my introduction to "her Vienna" by first stopping to see the town of Rechnitz, where my father was born and where my parental family had lived for well over a century before being expelled by the Nazis not long after the Anschluss—during the Burgenland Entjudung (expulsion of Jews) in April 1938.

We arrive in Rechnitz in the late afternoon, and take rooms at what appears to be the only inn in the town, the Gasthaus Cserer—a large whitewashed building with red-tiled roof dominating one corner of the main square—and, hungry from our travels, decide to enter the dining room and order a meal. Rechnitz is a small rural town of some 3,500 inhabitants, not a must-see tourist attraction, and our appearance in the room is noticed by the local men and women gathered near the bar, drinking wine or beer in postwork social relaxation. I am feeling somewhat inhibited and apprehensive in this setting—not only by my sense that we are being looked at and assessed within our immediate surroundings, but by our very presence in Rechnitz. Although I have yet to discover details about my family's expulsion from this place, I was aware that Jews had made up nearly a quarter of Rechnitz's population in the mid-nineteenth century, and that some 170 Jews still lived in the town in the last years of the 1930s before local Nazis forced them to leave and officially certified Rechnitz to be "judenfrei" (free of Jews). Years earlier I had also learned that my paternal grandfather and grandmother had owned a small house and a piece of land on Herrengasse, near the town's center, and that property, neglected after the war, could legally still be claimed by a member of our family.

To be sure, although we registered for our rooms at the Cserer by providing our passports and names, it is unlikely that any of the locals would know who we are when we enter the dining room. But even though we speak English to one another, and would appear to be nothing more than off-the-beaten-track tourists from America, the thought flashes through my mind that these staring people (whom I have no reason to distrust other than that they seem to live in Rechnitz) may somehow sense our real identity and misconstrue our intention. I fall prey to the fear that they may take us to be potential claimants on a house and land that had been taken from my grandparents; that indeed, as one of the basest of anti-Semitic stereotypes maintains, our external physical appearance marked and revealed us. They know that we are Jews who have come to take a meal and to spend a night in an inn and in a town that, not so very long ago, celebrated having "cleansed" itself of our kind.

And just at the very moment when these fearful ideas take shape in my mind, my mother, animated and in a loud voice, using Austrian dialect that I had not heard her employ for years, speaks to an older woman who had approached our table and introduced herself as the inn's proprietor.

"Grüss Gott. I wonder if you could give us some information? Do you remember the Spitzer family? Leopold Spitzer? Lina Spitzer? Jenö Spitzer? We would like to see the place where they used to live. And we also want to get in touch with Herr Lotzi Radl. Can you tell me how I can contact him?"

For a second (or am I imagining this?) the blood runs from the old woman's face. She pales and seems visibly shaken. It is only later that I learn that the Gasthaus Cserer used to be the Gasthaus Spiegler before the war. My grandmother Lina had been widowed from a Spiegler (and had two Spiegler children) before her remarriage to my grandfather Leopold.

"Spitzer? May I ask, how do you know Spitzer? And Lotzi? Are you from around here?" Her innkeeper's smile is absent.

"*I am Rosie Spitzer,*" *my mother answers without hesitation, and in an emphatic tone. (Is she being naïve, or goadingly confrontational?)* "*I was married to Jenö Spitzer for twenty-eight years. He died in 1967. Lotzi Radl and Jenö were in the same school class here, and they were close companions. I met him when we visited Rechnitz after we were married. I would like to see him again if he is still around.*"

Then, almost as an afterthought: "*This is my son Leo. And his wife, Manon. And my grandson, Alex.*"

"*I'll telephone Lotzi and let him know you are here.*" *The innkeeper responds directly to my mother, after a brief glance and nod in our direction.* "*I'm sure he'll take you to the Spitzer property. It is in ruins, you know. And maybe he'll show you around—give you a tour of our town.*"

She then changes the topic abruptly, takes out a pad, and asks if we are ready to order our food. Earlier, in the car, I thought about Eier-nockerl mit grünem Salat *(gnocchi with eggs and green salad), a local dish that my father especially liked, and I had anticipated its delicious taste. Now, I seem to have lost my appetite. But Alex, unable to understand German, and not yet aware of the history and tension surrounding the conversation that has just taken place, is resolute about his favorite meal.*

"*I want Wiener schnitzel and fried potatoes,*" *he declares.* "*No salad, please. And a Coca-Cola.*"

I spend a restless night, repeatedly awake, trying to imagine what happened in this town almost exactly forty years ago—thinking about the townspeople, and my grandparents, and the bitterness they must have felt to be turned upon and cast out by neighbors among whom they had grown up and lived their entire life. I am beset by frightful phantoms, and uneasy about my visit to their haunt. But after rising early in this anxious state, I enter the dining room for breakfast and am surprised to see that a smiling, friendly-looking man in his early sixties is already there conversing with Rose.

"*This is Lotzi Radl,*" *my mother tells me in German.* "*He was your father's best friend here in Rechnitz until Jenö went to technical school in Vienna. Lotzi, this is Leo—Poldi—our oldest son.*"

The stranger embraces me enthusiastically and comments that although I don't seem to resemble Jenö very much physically, my smile reminds him of my father. And he is eager, he tells us, to show us a little of Rechnitz before we continue on to Vienna later that day, that he wants us to have a real sense of the place where my father and my grandparents had come from.

And true to his intention, Lotzi Radl gives us a tour.

We begin by walking to a house a short distance from the inn, where he takes us to pay a courtesy call on Frau Theresia Blau Rechnitzer. She is widowed, lives alone, and is quite old, Lotzi informs us. But we might be interested in meeting her because she would be able to tell us something about our family and Jewish life in the town before 1938. After all, he adds, she is the last Jew in Rechnitz.

The visit, however, is a brief one. Frau Rechnitzer lives in a small, gloomy second-floor apartment, darkened by window shutters that close out the morning sun, and we are invited into a room illuminated only by a small electric floor lamp. She seems quite glad to see us—Lotzi had already informed her of our presence in town—and she is especially attentive to Alex, plying him with candies and chocolate bonbons. She tells us a bit about herself: that her mother and brother, Leo Blau, returned to Rechnitz after the war in order to reopen their dry goods store, and that they were the first of a handful of Jews to do so; that her brother had been a refugee in Shanghai during the war; and that she and her mother had lived in Israel for a time. On the way to Israel, during her passage through Yugoslavia, she had met and married a man named Rechnitzer—an Austrian who, in spite of his name, was not from Rechnitz, she explains. She, too, had then returned to her native town after she was widowed, and took over the store in the 1950s, when her mother and brother died. But her recollection of the 1930s had faded a good deal, she apologized—and she had no photos from that era. She had played the violin to accompany the Rechnitz church choir back then, and she again accompanied the choir in the 1950s and 1960s. Yet she really didn't have clear memories about the Nazi period and the expulsion. And while she remembered my grandfather as a buyer and seller of pelts and as an occasional Fiaker Kutscher (horse-drawn-cab driver), she unfortunately could tell us little else that we didn't already know.

Lotzi and the four of us return to our Renault, and together we drive through the Judengasse to the Herrengasse and the site of my grandparents' house. We stop there briefly, but only traces of a foundation and decaying wall are visible from the street, and I am suddenly reluctant to get out of the car, walk into the ruin, and make physical contact with these remains. "Not much to see here," I say, "not much left." Lotzi agrees. He and my father and other town boys sometimes played soccer in the street here, he tells us: most Jews lived on the Herrengasse or Judengasse, but their children all attended either the Rechnitz Catholic or Protestant primary school with non-Jews. Close friendships were

The Herrengasse, Rechnitz, Burgenland, Austria c. 1930. Grandmother Lina Spitzer (in white apron) stands between my father and Frau Radl, a neighbor, near the entrance of the Spitzer house. The others *(left to right)* are Frieda, Rosi, and Ferry Kohn (children of my father's stepsister, Gisi)

forged in these circumstances, he assures us. He and Jenö were not unique in that respect. In my head, however, a different image springs to mind. I recall my father's story of post-Anschluss days in Rechnitz when Jewish men were forced to sweep the streets—my grandfather Leopold among them. And as I look at the debris of the house and at the Herrengasse, I wonder if this is the place where they made him do it. And my impulse to flee this spot—to get away from its haunting shadows—becomes indomitable.

But Lotzi insists on guiding us to one last sight of "Jewish Rechnitz" before we leave. He directs me to drive to the outskirts of the town, to a heavily wooded spot edging the highway. "Look at that stone wall through those trees," he tells us. And I stop the car, and we stare out the window. "That was a gate to the Jewish cemetery," Lotzi says, "the place you went to where the bodies were laid out and washed before burial."

We get out of the Renault and start walking toward the stone wall. We climb through an opening and find ourselves in a forest. We walk by thickets of bushes and gnarled trees—through an undergrowth of bumpy surfaces and leafy mounds where discarded trash, old beer cans, charred twigs, and burned-out charcoal fires attest to cookouts and visits by fun-seeking picnickers. It is only when we bend down closer to the ground and look again at the swollen under-

growth that we see that hundreds of overturned gravestones are embedded within it: German and Hebrew writing is engraved on these stones, some of it ancient and virtually illegible, and others, more recent, still carrying names and dates with the loving inscriptions by the living to memorialize the dead. Tears begin to roll down my face, and as I walk and weep through this vast field of desecration—my mother close by and Alex holding my hand—I nearly trip on a felled gravestone by my feet. It is cracked in two. Visibly engraved on it, in intact capital letters, is the name "SPITZER." It is during this shuddering moment of discovery that I realize I have truly entered Austria, that I have come back to the land of my ancestors. But I also know, I have in no way come home.

In 1988, on the occasion of the fiftieth anniversary of the Anschluss and Kristallnacht, Austrian authorities, in cooperation with renascent Jewish community organizations, cleaned up neglected and desecrated Jewish cemeteries and, wherever possible, reset and repositioned overturned gravestones. The Jewish cemetery in Rechnitz benefited from this cleansing as well. In 1990, however, during the night of November 9, unknown vandals knocked down sixty gravestones and painted them with swastikas and slogans.[1]

TWO PHOTOGRAPHS

Among the very few possessions my parents were permitted to take with them when they emigrated as refugees from Austria to Bolivia in June 1939 was a box camera and two family photo albums. Soon after their arrival in La Paz, they somehow acquired two additional albums—one in which my father pasted snapshots taken during their ocean crossing as well as photos of family and friends in the early years of the emigration, and a second, largely devoted to pictures of me as a baby and young child, alone, or surrounded by seemingly doting relatives and acquaintances.

Although my parents may not have thought of it in this way at the time, their safeguarding the old picture albums and creation of new ones in Bolivia expressed both resistance and hope on their part. In preserving the European albums, they maintained a tangible connection with—and a kind of pictorial control over—the world they had been raised in and were now excluded from. They retained ownership of a visual memory of life, place, and cultural engagement that subverted the alienation the Nazis had tried to force on them. At the same time, the old and new albums testified to my parents' faith in the future. They showed familial experience over time—they were family documents intended for viewing in the *present* as well as in the *future*, not only by those alive at the time but also by those yet to come.

On the very last page of my parents' Austrian photo album they had pasted two seemingly unrelated photographs. The first, taken by my father, perhaps with the Rolleiflex he had to sell before he emigrated, is a time exposure of nine stages of a lunar eclipse—full moon fading into shadow and darkness. The other shows a pretty woman, young, dark-haired, wearing a patterned white dress, dark belt, stockings, open-toed medium-heel shoes, a flower pinned beneath her left collar. She is sitting on a park bench, a slight smile on her face. Her left arm is draped over the top of the backrest of the bench, relaxed, her hand extended down-ward. It rests as though stroking the painted-on sign which reads NUR FÜR ARIER—FOR ARYANS ONLY. The back of the photo is inscribed *"Denkt oft und gerne an eure Lizi"* (Think often and gladly about your Lizi) and dated "30.VIII.38"—August 30, 1938, almost six and a half months after the

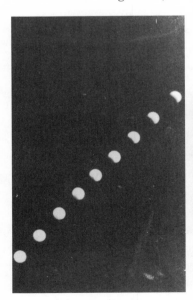

A lunar eclipse in
post-*Anschluss* Vienna

Lizi Rosenfeldt

Anschluss. The woman in the picture is Lizi Rosenfeldt, a Jewish neighbor of my maternal grandparents in the Schreigasse apartment house in Vienna's Second District, where they lived, and a close friend of my mother. She eventually managed to leave Austria and, after the war, she emigrated to London.

I don't really know why my parents placed these photos where they did in the album, or exactly what these pictures meant to them. I remember when I was a young boy, my father once talked to me about the lunar photo with technical pride, explaining how he had set up his camera on a tripod, and the method he used for the time sequence he captured on film. I'm quite sure I was interested, but I don't recall being particularly fascinated by this photo or by Lizi Rosenfeldt's. When I look at these pictures now, however—informed with a knowledge of events hardly imaginable at the time—they have become remarkable revealing icons for me. Obviously, I now think, the photos wouldn't have been placed on the album's last page in juxtaposition if my parents hadn't intended them to be ironic commentaries on the period. The darkening moon, the eclipse of light: what better way to represent and convey the advance of forces extinguishing the Central European era of emancipation and cultural effervescence in which Jews had been so prominent? And Jewish Lizi on the forbidden park bench, brazenly subverting a prohibition the Nazis had imposed: what a magnificent encapsulation of the confrontation of racist exclusion and Jewish resistance! How clever of my parents to display the essence of the times in such an understated but powerful manner.

Yet I also wonder, how did anyone manage to take Lizi's photo? To get away with it? Exactly where in Vienna, in which public space, was the photo snapped? On what day of the week? How did Lizi and the photographer feel? Were they frightened? Exhilarated? Empowered? As a child of persons who fled Vienna only months later, my desire is to search beyond the boundaries of this photo, beyond the moment when it was taken and the moment it quotes, into the subjective realm of emotion. *I want to know what it was like—I want to know what it felt like.* After all, weren't the photographs of Lizi and the eclipse emblematic of unfolding terror—of persecution and horror unleashed? Weren't their defining signatures, despite their playfulness and wit, intimidation, oppression, exclusion, extinction?

TERROR UNCHAINED: 1938

> *Das is dieses Jahr,*
> *von dem man reden wird.*
> *Das ist dieses Jahr,*
> *von dem man schweigen wird*
>
> This is the year
> that will be spoken about.
> This is the year,
> of which nothing will be said.
> —*Bertolt Brecht*

On March 11, 1938, almost five years to the day after the establishment of the National Socialist regime in Germany, Austrian chancellor Kurt von Schuschnigg resigned, and the German *Anschluss* of Austria began. Immediately after Schuschnigg ended his final radio address with the words "God protect Austria," and even before the closing notes of the national anthem had faded from the airwaves, thousands of men and women streamed into the streets of Vienna and the provincial cities and towns to proclaim and welcome the new era. *The New York Times* correspondent G.E.R. Gedye wrote about the scene he witnessed:

> As I crossed the Graben to my office, the Brown flood was sweeping through the streets. It was an indescribable witches' sabbath—storm-troopers, lots of them barely out of the schoolroom, with cartridge-belts and carbines, the only other evidence of authority being Swastika brassards, were marching side by side with police turncoats, men and women shrieking or crying hysterically the name of their leader, embracing the police and dragging them along in the swirling stream of humanity, motor-lorries filled with storm-troopers clutching their long-concealed weapons, hooting furiously, trying to make themselves heard above the din, men and women leaping, shouting and dancing in the light of smoking torches which soon began to make their appearance, the air filled with a pandemonium of sound in which intermingled screams of "Down with the Jews! *Heil Hitler! Heil Hitler! Sieg Heil!* Perish the Jews! . . ." "To-day we have all Germany, to-morrow we have the world."[2]

Gedye's and other accounts of that night, and of events in the days immediately following it, leave no doubt that the mob's celebratory surge of triumph carried through into fury and released vengefulness against Communists, Socialists, members of the Austrian nationalist Vaterländische Front, against all perceived political enemies of *Anschluss* and the ascendancy of the Nazis. But the primary victims of the unleashed fanatical aggression were the Jewish citizens of Austria—almost 225,000 of them, of whom 185,000 lived in Vienna. They alone were collectively targeted for persecution.

The popular victimization of Jews took many forms. In Vienna and provincial towns like Graz and Linz, invasions, searches, appropriation, and outright plundering and looting of Jewish homes, businesses, and institutions began almost at once after the Nazi triumph and continued unchecked for many weeks. The perpetrators—squads of swastika-bearing Austrian storm troopers as well as unofficial gangs of private citizens, so-called *Rollkommandos*—bullied or forced their way into private apartments and "requisitioned" money, jewels, furs, furniture, and other valuables. On some occasions, as victims and observers declared at the time, the commandeering of private property was carried out with "cynical courtesy"; on others, it was done with the utmost brutality, including the wanton wrecking of furniture, shooting up of mirrors, and smashing of paintings.[3] "I am sixty-nine years, eighteen years a widow, a resident of Vienna for forty-eight years, a German citizen, Jewish," Rosa Eisinger wrote Gauleiter Josef Bürckel, relating one such incident and seeking restitution of her property:

> On March 17, 1938, a number of gentlemen in uniform appeared in my apartment and—despite the fact that I am an old woman who has never been involved in politics—carried out a search. When they concluded, they confiscated property valued as follows, for which they gave me a receipt: S700 loose cash, S500 sweepstakes tickets, and KC400 in bills.
> Again, on March 19, more gentlemen in civilian clothing appeared again and again and searched my apartment, at the conclusion of which the greater part of my furnishings, pictures, etc. were destroyed, and various letters and ledgers were taken away from me.[4]

Rosa Eisinger was only one among tens of thousands of Jews whose homes were invaded, robbed, and vandalized, and whose property was taken. Jewish shops were pillaged in Vienna night and day, not only in the Jewish districts but in the city's main business areas as well. The largest and finest department stores were attacked and looted, but so were small, modest grocery stores, candy stores, flower shops, craft shops, restaurants, and cafés. The looters encountered virtually no opposition or hindrance from the official guardians of civil order, the police, who, on the contrary, frequently facilitated their pillaging or joined in to share in

the loot, and arrested Jews who filed complaints or denounced their vic-
timizers.[5] On the Taborstrasse in Vienna's Second District, a few days
after the Nazi triumph, Gedye witnessed "a long string of lorries" outside
a big Jewish-owned clothing store, "into which storm-troopers were
pitching all kinds of millinery goods as they took them from the shop.
Police stood by to see they were not interfered with in the work of plunder and moved on the curious."[6] The Vienna correspondent of the New
York–based Jewish Telegraphic Agency confirmed Gedye's account of this
sacking—identifying the locale as the large Schiffmann discount department store—and related that looting on that street had been ongoing
continuously for three days. On March 17, two days after Hitler spoke in
Vienna to a victory rally of some 200,000 people in the Heldenplatz, that
journalist filed the following report:

> A quick survey of the city . . . reveals the thoroughness with which Storm
> Troopers and S.S. men, the Nazi Black Guards, had accomplished the work of
> terrorizing the Jewish community.
>   Overnight Jewish shops have been forced to put identification signs in their
> windows, inscribed "Jewish Enterprise," or "Non-Aryan Enterprise." Some of
> the larger shops and cafés have been forced to display . . . "Aryans do not buy
> from Jews."
>   A large number of Jewish establishments have been completely closed down
> . . . One of the Margaretenstrasse shops was closed after the proprietor had
> tried to wash the word "Jude," scrawled in red paint, from the window. His
> attempt was met with a brick thrown through the window and the robbery of
> the shop . . .
>   During last night and preceding nights, gangs of men appeared at the homes
> of several Jews after midnight, forced them to go out into the street with only
> their overcoats thrown over their night clothes and ordered them to open their
> shops. The gangs then helped themselves to merchandise and scribbled
> receipts for what they had taken on pieces of wrapping paper.[7]

From the very outset, the Viennese street mobs—of adults, young people, teenagers, even children from every class background—seemed to
find pleasure and amusement in publicly humiliating Jews. Initially this
humiliation was carried out in so-called *Reibpartien* or *Reibaktionen*
("scrub parties") in which Jewish men and women, young and old, were
indiscriminately dragged from homes, offices, and shops and forced to go
down on hands and knees to scrub pavements and walls to remove the
painted-on traces of anti-*Anschluss* political propaganda that the defeated

and now defunct Schuschnigg government had placed there. Their clean-ing implements consisted of pails of paint remover, water, soap, and brushes. On occasion, to make the scrubbers' work even more difficult and to enhance the onlookers' entertainment, the tormentors substituted toothbrushes for cleaning brushes. "*Wie verwandelt a Jud in Araber?*" ("How does a Jew turn into an Arab?") was a favorite street joke, in Vien-nese dialect, at the time—a guffaw based on the premise that *ein Reiber* (a scrubber) and *Araber* were pronounced in virtually the same way.[8]

Photographs taken during these days—some for use as propaganda by the Nazis in their newspapers—as well as contemporary written accounts, provide powerful images of these "scrub parties." Gedye's description of one he witnessed is among the most vivid and moving:

> The first "cleaning squad" I saw was at the Praterstern [in the Jewish quarter]. It was employed to wash off the stenciled portrait of Schuschnigg from the ped-iment of a statue. Through the delighted crowds, storm-troopers dragged an aged Jewish man and his wife. With tears rolling silently down her cheeks, looking straight ahead and through her tormentors, the woman held her old husband's arm, and I could see him trying to pat her hand. "Work for the Jews at last, work for the Jews!" the mob howled. "We thank our Führer for finding work for the Jews."[9]

Alternatively, Jews with paint buckets and brushes were compelled to mark Jewish-owned stores with signs reading "Jew" or with the Star of David—always, it seems, to the general merriment or, at least, with the acquiescence of the crowd that accompanied them.[10]

Instances in which any Austrian publicly objected to these actions are rare in the contemporary records.[11] "Either deficient civil courage, cow-ardice, or tacit agreement with the anti-Semitic excesses," the historian Elisabeth Klamper observed, "led many Viennese who were not Nazis to become passive accomplices of the regime—to look away, perhaps, when their Jewish fellow citizens were being mistreated, but not to raise any protest against it."[12]

And when the "scrub parties" were no longer "necessary"—after all the public traces of Schuschnigg propaganda and the Austrian nationalist Dollfuss Cross were brushed away and gone—Jewish men and women of all social ranks and ages, as well as young girls and boys, continued to be rounded up and pressed into degrading labor: forced to wash cars, clean streets, sweep parks and public spaces, and, after the arrival of the SS regiments, to clean and wash barrack latrines as well.[13] In one incident, Jews caught in the Seitenstaettengasse synagogue by an armed *kommando* were forced to strap on their wrists the sacred tefillin, their prayer bands containing the Ten Commandments, and made to scrub the floors and clean out lavatory bowls. In a number of other synagogues roaming mobs extracted Torah scrolls from their arks and set them on fire or threw them into the Danube canal. Incidents occurred in which teenage Nazi enthusiasts ganged up on old, Orthodox Jewish men and shaved off their beards in public. The seventy-six-year-old Chief Rabbi of Vienna (*Oberrabiner*), Dr. Taglicht, was surrounded by a crowd of youths upon leaving his synagogue and compelled to stand and hold up an anti-Jewish boycott sign, first in front of a Jewish store on the Praterstrasse and then by the entrance of the Jewish-owned Café Continental. He was allowed to leave only after a younger Jew volunteered to take his place.[14]

Degraded not only publicly but painfully, Jews were coerced into performing open-air physical "exercises" for the enjoyment of onlookers: knee bends, stretches, jumping jacks. The fun, apparently, was not only in watching the "exercisers" stumble or struggle but in seeing them collapse and drop from exhaustion. On April 25, some sixty terrorized elderly Jewish men were compelled to march in goose-step style, back and forth across one of the Danube canal bridges carrying broomsticks on their shoulders as if these were rifles. In Graz, scores of Jews were forced from their homes into the street at night and ordered to shout: *"Wir sind Saujuden!"* ("We are Jewish swine!") and *"Heil den Nazis, die Österreich vom Judenjoch befreit haben!"* ("Hail the Nazis, who have liberated Austria from its Jewish yoke!"). Physical violence in the streets—slapping, punching, kicking, beating, spitting on Jews—was rampant.[15]

The frequency and intensity of these so-called spontaneous anti-Semitic "street actions" diminished somewhat in the course of the summer of 1938, but the nastiness never faded out altogether. On the eve of Yom Kippur, the holiest of the Jewish High Holidays, which that year fell on October 4, it reemerged with renewed intensity. That evening, and on the Day of Atonement itself, storm troopers and Viennese Nazi Party stalwarts invaded Jewish homes, seizing cash, furniture, and personal possessions. Their motivation, according to the contemporary documentation, seems to have come from a feeling that they had been short-changed in the allocation of rewards for service: that they had not received the jobs, apartments, or "new ownership" titles to businesses from which Jews had been removed in the first months of the *Anschluss,* and which, they believed, should have come to the "Old Fighters" as recognition of loyal support.[16] Their actions—executed either individually, or through intimidation and appropriation of money and personal property, or through *Rollkommando* raids leading to the plundering of stores—continued throughout October and into early November. Indeed, heralded as they often were by bricks thrown through windows or storefront showcases, and punctuated as they were by attempts to burn down synagogues and the destruction of Torah scrolls in bonfires and in the Danube, these events were a prelude to *Kristallnacht*—distinguishable from the horror yet to come only by their relatively more spontaneous and less centrally directed character.

In effect, the renewal of widespread looting, intimidation, and theft was a response to what had indeed been a quite successful attempt by top Nazi Party officials and strategists to regain control over the potentially great economic benefits stemming from the appropriation of Jewish assets. To be sure, in the days right after the *Anschluss,* the public degradation of Jews, the violent excesses against their persons, properties, and institutions, and the plunder of Jewish homes and businesses did satisfy the immediate needs of Nazi Party leaders. In the short run, these excesses were psychologically and politically useful to them. They permitted the venting of mass popular resentments that had been building up in the years since the end of World War I and that, especially during the Great Depression, might otherwise have served to fuel a radical, perhaps left-leaning, revolution.[17] More practically, the plundered goods, "confiscated" personal possessions, and appropriated moneys and jewels initially served as "immediate gratification" for many rank-and-file Austrian Nazi Party members and sympathizers, as reparation for their perceived past material deprivation and social frustration.[18] They were thus a payoff with a number of positive returns for the "new order"—instrumental in satisfying some of the crowd's immediate wants, releasing its frustrations in hatred against a long-resented, envied, and vulnerable target, while at the same time implicating its individual perpetrators in activities that would necessarily bind them as accomplices supporting the future well-being of the new Nazi regime.

But while this "terror from below" served a number of useful and necessary purposes for Nazi authorities and policy makers, key high-level officials despaired of the massive economic losses to the state resulting from the mob's uncontrolled and indiscriminate acquisition of Jewish properties. Hermann Göring, who had been appointed by Hitler in 1936 as plenipotentiary to implement a Four-Year Plan designed to reinvigorate the Reich's economy and speed up its rearmament program, was one of these. A year before the *Anschluss* he had declared that the removal of Jews from Germany's economic life (*Entjudung der deutschen Wirtschaft*) and the expropriation of Jewish property and assets would serve as a basis for financing the expansion of the economy and the rapid growth of the armaments industry.[19] When he spoke to a massive crowd in Vienna in the Northwest Station Hall, near the Jewish quarter of Leopoldstadt, on March 26, 1938, two weeks after the *Anschluss*, he admonished that Austria "was in danger of becoming a Jewish state" and that "Jews were in control of trade, finance, art, everything." He promised to alter this, emphasizing, "We don't like Jews and they don't like us . . . The Jews must get out." At the same time, however, Göring also stressed that all Jewish businesses were to be "taken over legally as part of the Four-Year Plan" and that "Aryanization" would be implemented systematically, *directed from the top* and *effected by the state*. This was a clear signal that "wild" looting and unauthorized "private" confiscation of Jewish properties— which appropriated assets for individual enrichment that should rightfully come to the state for its planned economic, military, and political purposes—would no longer be given free rein or tolerated. In the estimation of government authorities, several million reichsmarks had already disappeared into private pockets in the few days since the *Anschluss*, and this drainage of capital resources had to be plugged.[20]

Gauleiter Josef Bürckel, Hitler's designated commissar for the unification of Austria with the German Reich and the top Nazi Party official in Vienna, provided the high-level administrative follow-up to Göring's declaration. In April he published orders forbidding "illegal" searches of Jewish homes and "unauthorized" seizure of personal property, warning offenders of heavy fines and swift punishment for any discovered transgressions, and limiting search and appropriation activities only to "legally constituted agents of the police and security branches" acting under orders.[21] The siphonage of Jewish possessions into private hands, while never totally eliminated, was thus curtailed.

The summer-long hiatus in unauthorized appropriations, looting, and *Rollkommando* theft of Jewish-owned personal properties was certainly not, however, a respite from persecution altogether, especially not from what became known as "terror from above." Official, "legal" activities against the Jewish population were relentless in their continuity, harsh in their execution, and increasingly coordinated between high-level Nazi authorities in Germany and Austria. Indeed, it is important to view and understand these official activities against Jews within the framework of their intended purpose—as "logical" components of what by then had become the predominant policy concerning the "Jewish problem." They supported a campaign by National Socialist Party and government authorities that had been gathering momentum in Germany for some years: to displace Jews from active economic and social life and replace them with "Aryans," to seize their assets and material property, and, by physical and psychological intimidation, *to force Jews into the abandonment of German lands through emigration.*

"Authorized" terror, perpetrated by officials and embedded in law, took many forms. In Vienna and in the provinces, arrests of Jews, including prominent and not so prominent financiers, business people, and intellectuals, as well as of Jewish and non-Jewish Communists, Socialists, and opponents of the new regime, began almost immediately after Chancellor Schuschnigg's resignation. On March 13, 150 Jewish businessmen and bankers were arrested in Vienna by Nazi storm troopers acting as auxiliary police.[22] In the days following, Dr. Desider Friedmann, president of the Israelitische Kultusgemeinde (Jewish Community Organization); Dr. Josef Löwenherz, its executive director; and a host of other prominent Jewish leaders including Dr. Jacob Ehrlich, the only Jewish member of the dissolved Vienna town council, were arrested by the Gestapo and held at the Rossauer Laende police station. The community leaders were made responsible for an alleged 800,000-schilling contribution that the Israelitische Kultusgemeinde was accused of having made to support Chancellor Schuschnigg's aborted anti-*Anschluss* referendum, and they were to be detained "as collateral" until they agreed to make an equal "donation" to the National Socialist Party.[23]

These arrests were only the initial swell of an immense tide to come. Thousands of persons—certainly not all, but in large percentage, Jews—were arrested in March and early April and held for questioning. Members of the diplomatic corps estimated that between 30,000 and 40,000 people were rounded up for interrogation in the single week after Hitler's triumphant entrance into Vienna and his momentous greeting by its cheering crowds.[24] The majority of these detainees were later released, but some of them only after divesting themselves of personal properties to "Aryan" recipients, and providing evidence of their intended emigration. Others continued to be held, and were eventually transported to concentration camps. On April 1 the first shipment of 151 prisoners, 60 of whom were Jews, was sent from Vienna to the Dachau concentration camp outside Munich, in the *Altreich* (Germany proper). This group included ex-officials and sympathizers of the Schuschnigg regime, Marxists, monarchists, Freemasons, as well as top leaders of Jewish community organizations, Jewish owners of large businesses, and Jewish directors of financial institutions. Early in May the Gestapo arrested another 2,000 Viennese Jews—this time in a largely random roundup of people whom the arrest order simply referred to as "unpleasant [or disagreeable] Jews" (*unliebsamm Juden*). On May 23, May 30, and June 2 many of these detainees, as well as others seized in late May, were transported to Dachau. In June, 7,000 more Jews were arrested and detained. Indeed, because roundups, interrogations, arrests, and deportations were so central to the official Nazi campaign of harassment and terror against Jews and "other enemies," and because the number of detainees in the Reich had grown so large, the construction of a new hard-labor concentration camp in Austria was initiated almost at once in the days following the *Anschluss*. By August 8 the first prisoners were sent to the newly opened KZ Mauthausen—condemned to break and haul rocks from a deep-pit stone quarry in a camp on the outskirts of a picturesque village in the Wachau region of the Danube. Within a very short time, KZ Mauthausen became one of the most dreaded concentration camps in the Reich.[25]

Arrest, detention, and deportation—in threat as well as in actuality—became the ever-present shadow looming as enforcer over an array of decrees, enactments, orders, and laws by which the Nazis officially curtailed the citizenship rights of Jews and excluded them from all spheres of economic, social, and cultural activity in the Reich. In Austria, this legislated process of dispossession and removal, which in Germany had been spread out over a quite a few years, was accelerated and telescoped into a few weeks in order to bring the newly integrated "*Östmark*" into legal step with the "*Altreich*." On March 15, only days after the *Anschluss*, the Nazi-installed acting successor to Schuschnigg, attorney Arthur Seyss-Inquart, issued a decree stripping all Jews of the right to vote. On the same day, in another decree, he ordered all Jews employed by civil-service governmental agencies, including the police and military, to be suspended from work—a suspension that, within weeks, was transformed into permanent dismissal or forcible retirement.[26]

Much has been written about Jewish emancipation and acculturation in the German-speaking regions of Central Europe—about the century-long legal process of social and political integration beginning in the 1780s, which enabled Jews to "move out" of the subordinated confines and segregated communities of the German states and Hapsburg Empire and to "move up" in and identify with a social order based on the cultural values and standards set by the bourgeois, the most energetic and economically powerful group within the dominant society. Extensive commentary also exists about the eagerness of so many Jews to undertake this assimilationist journey and about the thoroughness of their identification with German bourgeois culture and their love of the German language.[27] In external behavior, outward appearance, artistic and material tastes, and mastery of German, German or Austrian Jews came to be marked as no different from other citizens—except by the invisible marks of descent and faith. Socially and symbolically, some *Yekkes* (as these acculturated German-speakers were called by their Yiddish-speaking Eastern European co-religionists) reinforced the distance they had traveled from their pre-emancipation origins. They positioned themselves at a remove from those they came to consider as the Jewish hoi polloi: those "lesser assimilated," as well as the many poor, less educated, and less sophisticated Jewish immigrants who had flocked to German and Austrian urban centers from *shtetls* and settlements in Eastern Europe. And yet, even though "during the years known as the German-Jewish symbiosis, Jews believed that one could remain a Jew and be a good German at the same time," as Peter Gay has put it, it was clear that Jewish emancipation and acculturation failed to eliminate the ominous undercurrents of anti-Jewish bigotry or to prevent the development and growth of racial anti-Semitism. Indeed, as many have argued, Nazi efforts throughout the 1920s and, especially, the 1930s, were to turn back the emancipatory clock and to nullify the massive integration and involvement of Jews within the German *kulturkreis*. To do that, they had to "re-*mark*" Jews once again—to reestablish their inherent *biological/racial* difference and inferiority, and to convince the masses that these characteristics were insurmountable and unchangeable.[28]

For the legal definition of who would be included in the category "Jew,"

Nazi government and bureaucratic officials relied on the Nuremberg Laws of 1935—the Reich Citizen Law (*Reichsbürgergesetz*) and the Law for the Protection of German Blood and German Honor (*Gesetz zum Schutze des deutschen Blutes und der deutschen Ehre*). These laws, together with their implementation orders, defined Jews according to various criteria of ancestral descent, as members of an inferior *racial* group distinct from Germans. They prohibited marriages and forbade out-of-wedlock sexual relations between Jews and persons of "German or related blood." Most important, they furnished the legal foundation for anti-Semitic discrimination and exclusion, serving as the "racial" basis for the political and civic disenfranchisement of all persons categorized as "not of German blood." Although they were not formally incorporated into statute in Austria until May 1938, in effect they functioned immediately after the *Anschluss* as guidelines for the implementation of anti-Jewish measures.[29]

In very short order, laws were enacted throughout the Reich mandating all females who fell within the definition of "Jew" to add the middle name "Sara" to their existing names, and all males the middle name "Israel," and to carry special identification cards designating them as Jews. To avoid a penalty, all Jews fifteen years of age and above were required to have these cards on their person at all times in public, and to show them on demand when asked to identify themselves. Their passports were also stamped with a large red letter *J*, to make them distinct from those carried by the Reich's "Germanic" citizens.[30] Jews were thus officially stigmatized as different not only within the Reich but in foreign countries as well. More ominously, both the stereotypical "Sara/Israel" identification and the *J*-mark were harbingers of a process intended to strip them of their individuality. Turning distinct "persons" into an undifferentiated, faceless "mass" was an imperative move in the Nazi agenda seeking the humiliation, diminution, and removal of Jews. A considerable distance certainly still lay between this process of symbolic "othering" and the physical erasure that would be implemented in the Final Solution, and the course in that direction was, in 1938, by no means yet definitively set. But a portentous step toward it had been taken.

A deluge of discriminatory legal measures and exclusionary orders fell on Jews throughout the Reich in the spring, summer, and early fall of 1938. Thousands of Jews were ousted from their occupations, driven from their positions, and forced into unemployment and the loss of their means of subsistence. Austrian authorities led the way by forbidding Jewish jour-

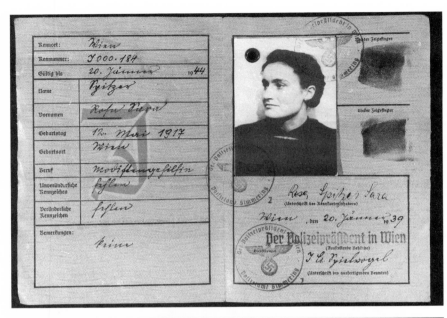

Rosa *Sara* Spitzer and Eugen *Israel* Spitzer: *Deutsches Reich* identity cards with the J-mark imprinted on them were issued to Austrian Jews after the *Anschluss*

nalists, actors, and musicians from practicing their professions, replacing them with Nazi Party loyalists or sympathizers whenever feasible, and by appointing other Party functionaries to take up the directorships of theaters and cabarets that Jews were forced to vacate. Jewish lawyers were barred from courts and, eventually, from practicing in any capacity except as advisers to "Aryan" attorneys, and only in legal matters specifically relating to Jews. Jewish notaries public and patent attorneys lost their licenses. Jewish physicians and nurses were eliminated from all government medical services and, eventually, from practicing in any hospital, clinic, or homes for the aged, except in the ones specifically set aside for Jews. On September 30, 1938, Jewish doctors lost their practicing licenses altogether, and they were demoted to the special category of "Jewish medical practitioners" (*jüdische Krankenbehandler*). The licenses of Jewish dentists, pharmacists—even veterinarians—were revoked as well. Jewish patients and elderly Jews were excluded from all except segregated Jewish health and elderly-care institutions. Jewish pupils were removed from all public elementary and middle schools to special all-Jewish schools, and all Jewish teachers in public schools were ordered to go on indefinite leave. By decree from the Ministry of Education, all Jewish faculty members at Austrian universities and higher technical schools were summarily dismissed, the registration of new Jewish students was canceled, and a *numerus clausus*, severely limiting the number of Jewish students in attendance at institutions of higher learning, was established.[31]

Beginning in the summer of 1938, Jews in Vienna were prohibited from using city sports or playing fields or attending sports events as spectators. They were forbidden to wear any of the traditional Austrian Alpine clothing: lederhosen, dirndl, Alpine kneesocks, or Styrian hats. And, by police order, they were banned from most public parks and gardens, restricted from sitting on any bench marked "For Aryans Only," and barred from visiting or using outdoor pools and bathing facilities.[32] The only recreational space left for Jews after these interdictions, Franz Werfel caustically observed at the time in a poem, *"Der gute Ort zu Wien,"* were the park grounds in the Jewish section of the Central Cemetery:

> Volksgarden, City and City Hall Park,
> Their spring was never so intense.
> Forbidden to the Jews of Vienna,
> whose only greenery grows by the dead.[33]

"WHY DID YOU WAIT SO LONG TO LEAVE?"

On a number of occasions when we spoke about the past, I remember asking my parents and relatives a question that I recently again raised in conversations with Austrian- and German-born Jewish refugees who emigrated to Bolivia. "Why," I inquired, "did you wait so long to leave?" My parents and paternal grandparents left Austria in June 1939, only months before the outbreak of the war, only months before the possibility of emigration was totally shut down. My question was asked from a vantage point in time and space distant from the events, of course, and informed with knowledge of subsequent events that they had not then possessed. With my parents, I realize, I must sometimes have articulated my query about the "lateness" of their departure in a somber tone containing an ironic innuendo—a veiled reference to my own connection to their emigration and to the truth that I am alive only *because they still got out when they did.* Had they missed their chance to leave, they might have been among those thousands who were eventually deported from Austria and killed. But posed more generally, the question also invited them to give me more historical context and comparative material, as well as personal recollection of perception, desire, and possibility. Quite apart from wanting to know about the very real problems and practical issues involved in refugee departure and emigration (how to get out, where to go, how to get there, how to gain entrance), I was asking how my parents and others who left their homelands viewed their situations in Germany or Austria after the Nazis came to power—how their perceptions of their life chances changed, until emigration was the only viable alternative.

In my parents' case, my question was certainly naïve. The central issue for them, and no doubt for every other refugee from Nazi persecution, was not *when* but *how* to get out. When I first began to ask the question, I am sure that I didn't take into account a fundamental difference between Austria and Germany—the fact that Hitler and the Nazis had gained power in Germany in 1933, five years before the *Anschluss,* and that, despite the development of an indigenous version of fascism and a worrisome growth of popular support for National Socialism, comparatively few specifically anti-Jewish measures and certainly no racial laws were enacted in Austria before 1938. On the other hand, the utter failure of an attempted Socialist workers' rising in Vienna in 1934, and the subsequent dissolution of the Social Democratic Party and suppression of all of its institutions throughout Austria, did profoundly affect many Jews. Almost

80 percent of Austria's Jewish population of 225,000 in the mid-1930s was, after all, concentrated in Vienna. The capital had predominantly been a Socialist city, and many Viennese Jews were closely tied not only politically but also economically to the city's Socialist institutions and public services. Numerous Jews who were Social Democratic Party members or Socialist sympathizers lost their jobs when the Party-identified organizations for whom they worked were dissolved or purged. Teachers in the public schools and trade schools were fired; doctors affiliated with the Socialist public health service and health insurance were discharged; lawyers engaged by Social Democratic service organizations found themselves unemployed. Eleven of the thirty arrested leaders of the banned Republikanischer Schutzbund, the Social Democratic militia, were Jews.[34]

But, although anti-Semitic enemies of the Social Democrats pointed to the Party's top-level Jewish leadership, its large Jewish membership and support, and its failure to transform Austria's severe economic woes as a way to stir up anti-Jewish passions and to lure workers and the lower-middle classes to a Nazi alternative, the retributive actions taken in the wake of the crushed Vienna uprising were primarily directed against Socialists, not Jews. During the disturbances and in their aftermath, the Jewish districts of Vienna were not threatened and remained quiet, and Jews *as Jews* were not harmed.[35]

Nevertheless, one could argue that despite these relatively benign indications, Jews in Austria should have discerned more ominous storm clouds on the horizon. After all, the National Socialists had also tried to stage a revolution in Austria in July 1934 in order to take over the government, and one of their fanatic activists had killed the Austrian Chancellor, Engelbert Dollfuss. Even though they failed this time, it was more than probable that Hitler would continue his attempts to incorporate the land of his birth into the expanded German Reich he hoped to construct. He had articulated this desire on many occasions, and developments in neighboring Germany were certainly not a secret to any Austrian Jew interested in the surrounding world. Press coverage was extensive. Radio news, film newsreels, and eyewitness accounts were readily available and graphically informative about Nazi actions against Jews in Germany. Long before 1938, in coffeehouses or at social gatherings with colleagues and friends, Austrian Jews could every day encounter German immigrants, or persons returning from a visit to Germany, who would relate frightening stories about arrests and concentration camps, boycotts of

Jewish businesses, and anti-Semitic discriminatory measures and violence.[36]

In Austria itself, the new corporative constitution adopted in May 1934 stressed the "Christian-German" character of the state. It did guarantee equality of rights to citizens of all denominations, yet it also permitted the establishment of discriminatory quotas against Jews in schools, hospitals, industry, banking, and the civil service. More portentously, Nazi anti-Semitic propaganda and agitation made major inroads among the disillusioned and disgruntled in society—not only attracting middle- and lower-middle-class sympathizers and supporters, but also appealing to young people and to workers whose "natural" affiliations had previously been with the banned Socialist or other Marxist Parties. By 1936, two years after Chancellor Dollfuss's assassination, Austria's illegal Nazi organization had gathered significant popular support throughout the country and had deeply penetrated all classes of society. It presented itself as oppositional to the failed economic and social policies of the ruling government, as pro-*Anschluss* with Germany, as a "workers' party," and, consistently, as vehemently anti-Semitic.[37]

And yet, despite the highly menacing currents that were apparent and intensifying before 1938, the question "to leave or not to leave?" remained a daunting one for numerous Jews as well as for other potentially threatened Austrians. Reflecting back on those times, the Austrian-born writer Hans Maier (who, after the war and his incarceration in Auschwitz, renamed himself Jean Améry) offers a poignant insight into the confusion of perceptions about the present and future among Jews of his generation—about the interpretation of signals, the false optimism, the attraction of cultural roots, the allure of familiar natural surroundings, the seduction of the known and the loved. He asks of himself in the third person:

How could a young man . . . have been smarter? He waits with the rest . . . He is neither able nor willing to leave—in part because he lacks the money to do so, in part because he doesn't want to: a resolve influenced by a subjectively real but objectively foolish notion that he belongs in this place—that only here is he capable of writing his poetry and his novels. Wandering with a friend through the woods of the Raxgebiet on a warm summer's eve, he glances over to the peaks of the Semmering mountain chain immortalized by Peter Altenberg and, feeling sentimental, puts his arm on his companion's shoulder and says: "We, no one can take us from here" . . . "I, no one can take me from here" . . . And suddenly, in broadest dialect, he begins to sing an old song: "*Erst wenn's aus wird sein, mit aner*

Musi und an Wein . . ." ["only when the end is here, with a bit of music and wine
. . ."] . . . It's a good song: only when the end is here. Is it over already? He knows
it is. Yet he remains nonetheless—until he is hunted, like a rabbit.[38]

In Germany more than in Austria, the immediate consequences of the
Nazi accession to power in 1933 did perhaps make it easier for some Jews
to decide the question "to leave or not to leave." The physical violence
carried out against "enemies of the regime," the boycott against Jewish
businesses, and the measures initiated by Hitler's government to remove
and exclude Jews from the economic and cultural life of the nation led to
the departure of some 37,000 Jews from Germany in the first year of Nazi
rule—about 7 percent of the estimated 525,000 Jews in the country at the
time. Included in this number were political opponents of the Nazis who
fled because their lives were endangered, or because they feared impris-
onment in concentration camps, as well as many individuals who had lost
their employment and sought livelihood outside the German Reich.

By the fall of 1935, before the promulgation of the Nuremberg Laws, a
total of more than 80,000 individuals had left Germany to seek asylum
elsewhere. The vast majority of these emigrants initially found temporary
refuge in neighboring European countries—primarily in France, but also
in the Netherlands, Czechoslovakia, England, Belgium, Switzerland,
Denmark and other Scandinavian lands, and even Austria. Of the more
than 40,000 who did not manage to gain permanent asylum in these
places, the largest number—approximately 25,000—went to Palestine.
About 10,500 went to the United States, and the remainder to some
thirty overseas countries, including a few to Bolivia.[39]

It is significant, however, that after the initial panic flight in 1933, Jewish emigration from Germany dropped off considerably in 1934 and in the
nine-month period preceding the Nuremberg Laws. "From 400–500 a day
in April–July 1933," reported Mark Wischnitzer, who until 1937 served as
secretary of the Hilfsverein der Deutschen Juden (the organization
charged with helping Jews to emigrate), "the number of individuals seeking emigration aid from Jewish agencies fell to 100–200 in the fall of 1933
and even to 10–20 early in 1934. The impression prevailed in the Jewish
agencies that the problem would be merely one of small-scale emigration,
carefully planned and prepared, but that the vast majority of the Jews
would remain in Germany and readjust themselves to the new conditions."[40] Indeed, many persons who had left in the first wave of emigration

returned to Germany after finding themselves unable to earn a living in the countries of refuge, or after concluding that the worst had passed and that continued existence in the land of their birth was again possible. "My father, whose leanings were Left, and who had lost his job soon after Hitler gained power," recalled one of the people who went to Bolivia, "left Frankfurt at the end of 1933 and went to Paris to look for work. He was terrified about what might happen with the Nazis in charge. My mother and I were supposed to follow. But he roamed around unsettled, couldn't find a way to make a living, heard that things had calmed down a little back at home, and he returned. We didn't finally leave until late in 1938."[41]

The slowness of economic recovery in Europe and overseas from the Depression was certainly a major obstacle—and a deterrent—for anyone who did contemplate settling elsewhere in the early 1930s. The fact that these asylum-seekers were in large part middle-class business and professional people further impeded their acceptance elsewhere. While some countries were willing to permit permanent residence to skilled industrial workers, agriculturalists, and certain types of craftspersons, they barred professional and business people who would be moving into direct competition with their own citizens.[42]

But apart from these externally determined limitations, there were internal conditions—and assessment of them in light of existing options and possibilities—that influenced decisions about emigration. As Herbert A. Strauss has indicated: "The factors that made Nazi policies towards Jews polymorphous also created a confused reality, and led to confused perceptions among almost all parties to the deed, including the victims."[43] Choosing not to emigrate, to stay in Germany—a decision made by the vast majority of German Jews in the first years of Nazi rule—or returning to Germany after an exploratory sojourn abroad was not a blind or irrational response at a time when it appeared to many that the government had retreated from its initial economic attack against Jews and that, despite continuing anti-Semitic propaganda and harassment, the situation had stabilized and even become relatively tolerable. The president of the Hilfsverein der Deutschen Juden declared at its annual meeting in May 1934 that German Jews desired "to stay in their homeland . . . whose future was their own"—a sentiment his successor reiterated at the meeting a year later. Despite a resurgence of street violence against Jews throughout Germany, and a new wave of anti-Semitic propaganda in the spring and early summer of 1935, persons directly involved in Jewish social and emigration work generally continued to advise questioners not to seek emigration unless economic necessity demanded it, or as a way to ensure the continuing education of children who could no longer be educated in Germany. During these first years of Hitler's rule, some of the Jews who later emigrated even maintained a degree of optimism about the future: a hope that the Nazi regime would not survive long, that a democratic government would return in short order, and that the anti-Semitic madness would dissipate and, once again, fade away.[44]

The number of Jews applying for emigration began to increase again, however, after the passage in September 1935 of the Nuremberg Laws and of the implementation orders stripping Jews of their German citizenship rights, excluding them from all public service employment and from artistic and cultural participation, and curbing many of their social freedoms and professional possibilities. As reported by Mark Wischnitzer: "Again the offices of the Hilfsverein became crowded. The central office in Berlin again began to advise more than 200 persons every day. The traveling subsidies granted by the Hilfsverein to emigrants rose from 123,000 marks in the first eight months of 1935 to 208,800 in the last trimester of the year."[45] It was in the two years following the passage of these laws, moreover, that Nazi policies aiming at the economic exclusion of Jews and acquisition of their assets combined with an increasingly focused effort to realize *Entjudung* through massive and accelerated Jewish emigration. The German Reich, Nazi policy makers now seemed to agree, should become *judenrein*—its population cleansed of Jews—and to accomplish this end, pressures to induce Jews to depart were intensified and expanded.[46]

Indeed, after the Nuremberg Laws, it took no talented visionary among German Jews to perceive the restricted chances they faced in the future. As Jewish economic activities were progressively curtailed, and Jews were eliminated from participation in commerce, banking, brokerage, transportation, and even from clerical work in department and chain stores, more and more Jews found themselves unemployed, seeking jobs with little hope of finding any. Many who had not considered emigration before began to line up at embassies, consulates, travel agencies, and the Hilfsverein anxiously seeking a potential haven, eager to find a way out. And yet, even though responsible Jewish leaders were now reconciled to the reality that Jews had to leave Nazi Germany, they still assumed that emigration would proceed in a rational manner: that Jews could and would clear out of Germany over a period of about ten years, at the rate of some twenty thousand to twenty-five thousand per year—a rate that could be supported financially by the various international emigrant-aid societies and that would not be unacceptable to recipient countries throughout the world.[47]

Unfortunately, the assumption of these leaders was flawed, deriving as it did from an underassessment of the number of Jews still remaining in Germany and a misreading both of the time still available to move them elsewhere and of the Nazis' willingness to allow the *Entjudung* to proceed so slowly. In effect, twenty-five thousand German Jews did manage to emigrate in 1936, but that number declined to twenty-three thousand in 1937 due to new international circumstances. British-ruled Palestine, which in the initial phase of emigration had admitted well over one-third of the total number of German-Jewish refugees, was by 1936 much more restrictive, partly because of resurgent Palestinian Arab unrest about the growing number of immigrant Jews.[48] European countries, the main targets for legal emigration between 1933 and 1935, tightened admission and employment requirements for prospective immigrants so that, by 1936, they had reduced their admission percentage from approximately three-quarters to one-quarter of the total number of German-Jewish refugees.[49] North and South America, South Africa, and Australia now assumed greater importance as potential emigration sites. But, in spite of improved economic circumstances in some of these countries, few significantly relaxed their restrictive immigration measures. On the contrary, some began to exclude new immigrants altogether.[50]

By early 1938, five years after Hitler's accession to the Chancellorship, approximately 140,000 Jews had left Germany—including about 10,000 who settled elsewhere illegally; i.e., the population of Jews declined by more than 25 percent from the approximately 525,000 in Germany on January 1, 1933. However, some 385,000 Jews *still remained* in Germany—to which the *Anschluss* added at least another 225,000. On March 12, 1938, in other words, the greater German Reich contained some 610,000 Jews, approximately 85,000 *more than when the emigration first began five years earlier, in 1933.*[51]

The "forced emigration" tactics of Nazi authorities have to be understood in light of this demographic reality. By the logic of their own aims, in early 1938 *Entjudung*, which had become the chief objective of National Socialist Jewish policy, *needed to be intensified and accelerated,* induced through continuous and increasingly severe economic and physical persecution. But it also needed to be managed more effectively, its operations rationalized and centralized.

The annexation of Austria presented the Nazi leadership with an opportunity to demonstrate their strengthened resolve concerning the elimination of the "Jewish problem" and to put a new, managed system of forced emigration into practice for the first time. Only days after the *Anschluss*, Adolf Eichmann, the rising young "Jewish expert" in the Security Service branch of the SS, was charged with organizing an "efficient and accelerated" emigration of Austrian Jews. In Vienna, he immediately made clear the three basic principles on which the system would operate: emigration was not a choice for Jews but compulsory; Jewish agencies involved with any aspect of emigration would have to operate through a centralized organization under supervision of the Security Police; emigrating Jews would be stripped of all their assets except the minimum amount of money required to enter the countries receiving them.[52] In a mansion that had formerly belonged to the Rothschilds, Eichmann's Central Office for Jewish Emigration managed all aspects of the process, and through it all persons seeking the requisite documentation to leave Austria had to pass.

By November 1938, Eichmann's coercive and bureaucratic systematization of Jewish emigration in Vienna came to be viewed with such great favor by high Nazi officials in Germany that his Austrian model served as the basis for the establishment there of an emigration center grounded on similar principles, procedures, and institutional arrangements. The appeal of this apparatus for many Nazis during this period, one witness at Eichmann's trial in Israel later testified with sardonic humor, was that it resembled "a flour mill tied in with a bakery. You put a Jew in at one end . . . [and] he comes out at the other with no money, no rights, only a passport saying: You must leave the country within two weeks; otherwise you will go to a concentration camp."[53]

GETTING OUT

A photograph taken by an anonymous photographer—undated but certainly from the period of panic emigration between 1938 and 1939—shows hundreds of people lined up in a tight grouping by the entrance of the Police Commissariat in the Margarethen section of Vienna. It appears to be a late spring or summer day: the men are wearing jackets and ties, women are in light-colored dresses, and no overcoats are in sight. Many in the crowd are carrying briefcases or packets of papers. People at the head of the line are presenting what may be their identification cards to uniformed policemen and the suited civilian guarding the entrance. One man, out of the queue, is talking—or perhaps arguing—with a policeman, and both he and the officer are pointing and looking at each other with some intensity. The simple snapshot cannot indicate how long these persons have been standing in line, but impatience can be read in many of the faces—a concentrated glare at the front and the doorway of the police station, unsmiling seriousness of purpose. These people are waiting their turn to obtain one among many official certificates required for their exit papers. Their goal is to emigrate—to get out.

Certainly, in the aftermath of the *Anschluss* of Austria and the November 1938 *Kristallnacht* pogroms throughout Greater Germany, the previously equivocal, or ambivalent, attitudes of Jews and other "racial" and

Lining up for emigration documents, Margarethen Police Station, Vienna (Courtesy Dokumentationsarchiv des Österreichischen Wiederstandes)

political "undesirables" toward emigration were transformed into a desperate search for a way to leave. Day after day, starting long before dawn, hours before offices opened their doors to the public, thousands of people lined up outside central emigration agencies, police stations, aid societies, consulates, and embassies seeking the necessary documents, clearances, and economic support to exit Austria and Germany and find asylum elsewhere.

> My father and mother awoke while it was still dark, and by six in the morning they were already standing in line, waiting for the offices to open in which they had to acquire a document or a clearance certificate. But even with such an early start they had exhausting waits before they were finally admitted, because others were already there, ahead of them. Some persons were paid to stand in line for others. It was one way to earn a little money during those days when Jews had no other options.[54]

The rationalization of bureaucratic procedures obliged everyone seeking emigration to satisfy many exit requirements according to a preset sequence and within the time limit set by a stamped expiration date. If paper or permit number two was not acquired before number one had expired, it was necessary to begin anew. Documents, signatures, transactions sealed with the proper stamps: the formalities seemed endless. After one acquired clearances affirming that one owed no past taxes—local, government, utility, sales, or even dog taxes—one needed a form testifying to one's "nonobjectionable" character and lack of a criminal record. For this, visits to a district police station and to various municipal offices—prime sites of lengthy lines, long delays, and potential harassment—were necessary. Given the vehemence of the measures employed to force Jews and other "objectionable inhabitants" to leave Germany and Austria, certification of payment of the *Reichsfluchtsteuer*, a tax levied for "*fleeing*" the Reich, was perhaps the most ironic commentary on the perversity of it all.[55]

But for the final acquisition of an official exit permit, one needed a valid entry visa to a foreign land: that key stamp and official signature on a passport which, in the late 1930s, had become the most difficult endorsement of all to obtain. Exit visas, transit visas—indeed the ultimate validity and utility of *all* acquired emigration certificates and documents—hinged on the procurement of an *entry visa*.

All the frustrations and obstacles that refugees faced in acquiring the necessary exit documents were superseded by the difficulties they encountered in trying to gain residence elsewhere. "How" to get out was invariably accompanied and complicated by the question "where to go?" With country after country restricting admission of new immigrants or excluding them altogether, the victims of Nazi exclusion searched more and more frantically for places that would allow them in and give them a chance of asylum. To obtain a valid entry visa, somewhere, anywhere, became an obsession. At one point, perhaps, the United States, Great Britain, Palestine, Argentina, or Brazil—the better known nations outside of the now virtually "closed to immigration" lands of Europe—might have been their preferential "countries of choice." But since they now virtually had *no choice*, they were ready to go anywhere. To find a haven from the madness was what mattered.

In Jewish communities throughout the German-speaking lands, special rescue campaigns were initiated or intensified, and the organization of the safe emigration of children and teenagers to Western countries, especially to England, became a priority.[56] In many instances, unscrupulous travel agents and consular officials took advantage of the panicked desperation of the would-be emigrants, managing to amass sizable personal profits from the receipt of illegal "supplemental fees," bribes, and the black-market sales of documents and visas. Applicants were sometimes cheated altogether in these transactions: their promised "travel papers" and admission documents never materializing even after payments had been made; or they discovered, belatedly and painfully, that their visas were worthless, not acceptable by immigration authorities at ports of entry, and that they had undertaken "journeys to nowhere."

Within the population of the "undesirable and unwanted," rumors of potential havens were rife. Paraguay was accepting all applicants! New Zealand sought immigrants! Mexico was a transit possibility, as was the Dominican Republic: possible backdoor avenues for later entrance to the United States. Word spread: travel agents, consular officials, embassy officials were selling visas "under the table" for admission and residence in Uruguay . . . in Bolivia . . . in Cuba . . . in Brazil! Time and again, masses of persons thronged the British and the United States consulates seeking visa approvals and financial help. At one point, when it was rumored in Vienna that visas were available for Jewish youths seeking emigration to Australia, more than six thousand applied to the imperial agency for Australian affairs at the British Consulate—only to learn that visas would be granted "on a most selective basis," restricted to persons trained in "useful occupations" able to produce 200 pounds in cash "landing money" or 50 pounds in cash and a guarantee from an Australian resident covering their welfare. The few who qualified were also informed that no quick admission would be possible—the waiting period for visas was at least four months.[57] Some days after *Kristallnacht*, word gained ground that the United States, having apparently liberalized its immigration policy, was prepared to admit and cover the costs of passage for some twenty thousand immigrants; charity funds were supposedly also available at the United States consulate. So widespread was this belief that the consular authorities had to address applicants in groups, repeatedly explaining that these rumors had no foundation and that people seeking visas had to be prepared to furnish all necessary documents, affidavits, and passage money.[58] The additional fact that instead of liberalization, immigration to the United States would actually be impeded *beyond* these requirements by *even greater restrictions* on the annual quota was not a component of this official clarification.*[59]

Visas! We began to live visas day and night. When we were awake, we were obsessed by visas. We talked about them all the time. Exit visas. Transit visas. Entrance visas. Where could we go? During the day we tried to get the proper documents, approvals, stamps. At night, in bed, we tossed about and dreamed about long lines, officials, visas. Visas.[60]

ELLA

"Ella preceded your grandparents and me to Switzerland," Uncle Julius, my mother's brother, reminded me. "We all tried to flee there not long after March '38, when all hell broke out in Austria. Our parents and I couldn't get across

*Of the thousands who stormed the U.S. consulate in Vienna after the *Anschluss*, only a few hundred had the remotest chance of actual emigration to the United States, since the annual quota still stood at 1,413, proportionately smaller than the German quota of 27,370. Ironically, only through the de facto recognition of the *Anschluss* and Austria's incorporation into "Greater Germany" did Austrians qualify for admission to the United States under the German quota figure. Still, only in 1939 was the actual German-Austrian quota fulfilled, and 27,370 admitted; in 1938, only 17,870 were admitted. After the outbreak of the war, the number declined to 26,080 in 1940; 13,050 in 1941; 4,760 in 1942; and 1,290 in 1943.

the border then. Ella did make it. She was the first in the family to reach Switzerland successfully. But then she decided to go to Bolivia. And it is thanks to her that we survived."

I remember little about my mother's sister Ella. What I know about her is a shadow memory, a memory once removed. I was three and a half years old when she died in La Paz. She was twenty-three. My father and two uncles were in Oruro when they received the news, installing plumbing and electrical wiring in the new city slaughterhouse being constructed there, and my mother and grandparents were in Cochabamba with me, during my recovery following a difficult tonsillectomy and a serious bout with rheumatic fever. Omama Bertha and Opapa Nathan were never told the truth about the cause of their youngest daughter's death, although they must certainly have been familiar with the circumstances surrounding it. "Death from blood poisoning following a typhus infection": that was the "official" explanation they were given, I later learned—one that they seemingly acknowledged in public but never, at least in my presence, brought up within the family. Death from a "broken heart," I once overheard my mother tell someone when I was still a boy, an intriguing account that stayed with me because it conveyed such profound sadness and paralyzing despair. "It was rumored that she found herself pregnant, an unmarried divorcée," I was told a few years ago by two people who claimed to have known her well. "She died after a botched abortion." "Ella committed suicide. She killed herself with sleeping pills. That's the real story," my paternal grandmother Lina confided to me during our sea voyage from Colón to Baltimore—this was when the two of us traveled together without additional family on our emigration from Bolivia to the United States. "Omama Bertha and Opapa Nathan don't know the truth about this, and they should never be told," Lina cautioned me at the time. "But Ella killed herself because she was so unhappy in Bolivia. Bertha would never forgive herself and would die if she found out."

Although I was indelibly impressed by my grandmother's revelation and the responsibility she placed on me—I was ten years old at the time—not to divulge "the secret" to my maternal grandparents, the intensity of her words, and the mystery surrounding the very notion of death by suicide, left Ella's story incomplete and unresolved in my mind. Indeed, for years, Ella was a phantomlike presence in our family midst, never spoken about in gatherings while my maternal grandparents were still alive, and avoided in public family conversations and recollections even after their deaths. "Your father, one time, wanted to tell me things about my sister," my uncle Julius said to me, "but I told him, I don't want to know. I wanted to remember her the way she was in Vienna: lively, good-humored, very good-looking—a wonderful person."[61] And yet Ella was memorialized within the family with an annual yahrzeit candle lit by my grandmother on the eve of the anniversary of her death, and by the fact that my sister, Elly, born in La Paz in April 1944 (almost exactly a year after Ella died), was named after her. Ella's photograph, in a frame, was always prominently displayed on my grandmother's and mother's dressers, and the picture image of her pretty face, animated by large, deeply set black eyes, a fine nose, full-lipped mouth, lustrous, wavy dark hair, became firmly imprinted on my consciousness, a familiar icon of my younger years. In some intangible yet profound fashion—through the sound of her name, in thought, remembrance, and in the unspoken emotions she engendered in those who had known and survived her—Ella remained with us.

In seeking clarification of the circumstances of Ella's death, some insight into her character and state of mind at the time, some better sense of that event within the broader context of her life history, two sentences spoken by my uncle Julius have repeatedly echoed in my mind: "But then she decided to go to Bolivia. And it is thanks to her that we survived." Much that was not said—by him, and by others—I now realize, is embedded in these words. Ella did play the central enabling role in our family's South American emigration and survival: it was she who made it possible for my maternal grandparents to leave Europe and find haven in Bolivia; it was she who helped ease the acquisition of Bolivian visas for my uncle Julius, my cousin Ferry, and for my parents and paternal grandparents. But the role she played was neither a simple nor unfettered one; it was informed and influenced by ideological expectations and cultural conventions that were broadly accepted among the Central European refugees who were her contemporaries. In part, these expectations and conventions were familial in character; in part they were tied to gender. And it is in the connections among all these factors that some clearer understanding of her Bolivian refuge and final years must be found.

Relatively few concrete traces from Ella's life still exist. My mother saved two of her letters, a poem, and over twenty loose pages, densely filled with writing, from a journal she kept in Bolivia a little more than a year before she died. Mother also had more than a score of photographs of her younger sister, both unmounted and pasted into our family albums, depicting moments in Austria, in Switzerland, on board ship crossing to South America, and in Bolivia. And she preserved the telegram my father sent to my grandmother Lina in Cochabamba informing her of Ella's death, as well as a few photos of Ella's grave in the Jewish Cemetery in La Paz.

These few traces, in conjunction with the sometimes hesitant recollections of people who had known her, suggest Ella as a complex young woman—fun-loving, smart, impulsive, sensual, and romantic, but also prone to darker moods, to disconsolate melancholy and to feelings of insurmountable powerlessness. That Ella had an excellent sense of humor, marked by a slightly biting yet self-inclusive edge, is conveyed in one of these surviving traces: in a poem she wrote in 1937 in Vienna when, as a seventeen-year-old, she worked as an apprentice at a small dressmaking firm, "Flora Weiss & Co." "Unser Los" ("Our Fate") bemoans what must certainly have been an extremely exploitative and disagreeable situation for her, marked by long hours, the pettiness and downright stinginess of her bosses, and by tasks that went well beyond apprentice dressmaking to include kitchen work and cleaning the employers' living quarters. Still, the tone is light and spirited throughout; she pokes fun without much rancor. She is accusatory yet hopeful—affirming that "this too will end"—and her moral is ingenuously didactic, simple, and quite direct:

> *And this advice we still impart*
> *Don't let your children toil so hard.*
> *This on our honor we do mentor:*
> *An apprenticeship, never enter.*
>
> Wir wollen euch noch sagen,
> Lasst eure Kinder nicht so plagen,
> das raten wir euch auf Ehre,
> geht in keine Lehre.[62]

But although wit such as this, and other instances of lightheartedness and cleverness, are clear in Ella's surviving writings and in the representations made of her by others, her sense of entrapment, of life's unfairness, of despair, and loss of control, emerge as well.

She and a female friend had left Vienna in late summer or early fall of 1938 and had crossed the Austrian border illegally in Vorarlberg, between the Austrian town of Hohenems and the Swiss village of Diepoldsau, a route that Ella's Viennese beau, Peter C., had already successfully managed before her, and that Julius, and then my maternal grandparents, Bertha and Nathan, would also use some months later. Swiss authorities had seriously clamped down on the massive influx of illegal refugees following the Anschluss, and they stiffened their laws and regulations shortly before Kristallnacht, in time to head off the panicked flight that ensued during the months just before and after the outbreak

Ella in Vienna (1938)

Ella and her charges in Switzerland

Ella in La Paz with my mother
in the background (1940)

of war in Europe.* Even before these restrictions were enacted, Switzerland had limited the length of stay of refugees within its borders, admitting most of them only for a short sojourn if they held valid passports and had or were in process of attaining a visa to another destination. Most of these temporary refugees were placed under police scrutiny, interned in makeshift camps or assigned to obligatory housing, and put to work in specially instituted labor details. But Swiss canton police also pushed illegal refugees back over the frontier, denying them admission altogether, and expelled many others whose papers were out of order or who were accused of transgressing local laws—potential "irregularities" to which Ella, as well as Julius, Bertha, and Nathan were certainly all highly vulnerable.[63]

Soon, however, Ella managed to make contact with persons at the Swiss-Jewish Union for Refugee Aid (Verband Schweizerischer Jüdischer Flüchtlingshilfen), an umbrella organization headquartered in Zurich that gave refugees financial assistance and help in attaining temporary housing, vocational training, and permission to work. Through this organization she was placed in the Zurich home of a well-to-do Swiss family with two young daughters, as a caretaker for the girls. The arrangement was an extremely agreeable and emotionally satisfying one for her. Lively, engaging, warm, with a fine sense of humor and the ability to joke and entertain, Ella became an immediate favorite with the daughters, and apparently enchanted the parents so greatly that they offered to adopt her legally as a way to help ensure her permanent stay in Switzerland. During this period in Zurich, moreover, she met a young Swiss man with whom she fell deeply in love—a man who courted her and delighted her greatly, and whom she considered marrying.[64] She was really quite happy, she wrote her oldest sister back in Vienna, pleased to be among nice people, grateful for the relief

---

*At the Evian Conference of July 1938 Dr. Heinrich Rothmund, head of the Swiss Federal Police, had complained about the massive influx of refugees from Austria (some three to four thousand) after the *Anschluss*. As the historian Leni Yahil has written, "In reaction, the Swiss government required an entry visa for bearers of Austrian passports. The subject was first mooted between the Swiss and German governments in April 1938. In August 1938 the Swiss authorities went a step further by threatening to rescind the right of free entry to bearers of German passports as well; eventually Rothmund hinted to the German consul in Bern that Switzerland would drop its visa requirement 'if there were a distinct mark on the passports borne by Jews.' When Rothmund arrived in Berlin towards the end of September 1938, an agreement to that effect was signed within a few days. On October 5 all passports held by Jews were declared invalid and had to be returned; the new ones issued in their place bore a red J. Thus, in addition to the special identity card that Jews had to carry within Germany, they were now stigmatized in all foreign countries as well."

from the personal anxieties and fears that had darkened her previous months.[65]

She was, however, far from being free of worry. Her sixteen-year-old brother, Julius, had also fled to Switzerland via the Hohenems route. Although he was apparently not in immediate danger of expulsion (a local policeman and his wife had felt sympathy for him and found him temporary lodging and work), his chances for long-term asylum were uncertain. Additionally, after failing in their first attempt to enter Switzerland illegally, not long after Ella's flight, her parents had managed to cross the border successfully on their second try, only to be apprehended a few hours later. They had not been returned immediately to Austria but had been temporarily placed in a refugee reception camp near St. Gallen. Through the refugee grapevine, Julius recalled, they learned there of the possibility of acquiring immigration visas to Bolivia from the Bolivian consul in Zurich. But their internment restricted their mobility, and seemed to allow them few options but to rely on the goodwill and the visa-acquisition efforts of agents of refugee organizations. Since they had little assurance that they would indeed manage to get the Bolivian permits in short order, they believed themselves to be in distinct danger of being sent back across the border.[66]

Details of what occurred at this point are missing from the narrative. It is clear from Julius's recollection that he managed to get word to Ella in Zurich about the precarious position that he and, especially, their parents were in. Ella would then certainly have tried to gain help from her Swiss employers—help to extend their stay in Switzerland, and to ensure that they would not be expelled before acquiring immigration visas to South America. She may indeed, on her own, have made direct contact with Bertha and Nathan in the reception camp soon after their internment, and have personally witnessed their expressions of apprehension and distress. As the only member of the family in Switzerland with access to people able to assist her parents' quest for refuge, she must have felt an immense obligation, perhaps some desperation, to act on their behalf.

At any rate, a potential "solution"—in the form of a marriage offer— reached Ella at this time. The proposal did not come from her young man in Zurich or from anyone else in Switzerland, but from Peter C., with whom she had been involved for nearly a year in Vienna before his departure. Peter, a handsome, self-described "chance-taker," who "survived by wits, fast-talking, and chutzpah," and by befriending powerful protectors for whom he provided a variety of services, had managed to strike up an acquaintance with a wealthy Swiss woman in Zurich and, with her help, had acquired a visa and the requisite funding for emigration to Bolivia.[67] Before leaving Switzerland in November 1938, however, he spoke with Ella and learned about her parents' Swiss internment and the insecurity of their situation. Although he and Ella had had little contact in Switzerland, and she had met and begun a relationship with another man, he continued to regard her, he later recalled, as "his first great love." Soon after arriving in La Paz, therefore, he managed to borrow money from an employer, and to find a way to "purchase" four additional immigrant visas [llamadas] for "relatives left behind." One of these visas he reserved for his mother, who had stayed in Vienna; the remaining three he offered Ella and her parents. But the offer, seemingly so generous, carried a very central condition: the visas for Nathan and Bertha could be used only if Ella used hers as well. She would have to emigrate with her parents, leave Switzerland behind her, and join him in Bolivia as his wife.[68]

Acceptance of Peter's proposal held major personal consequences for Ella. It meant the abrupt interruption of her new friendships, the abandonment of the possibility of Swiss residence, and the likely forfeiture of everything that a new life in Switzerland seemed to promise her. But the proposal also included the possibility of safe refuge for her parents. As such, her love for them, her sense of obligation and responsibility for their safety and survival, had to be weighed against the moments of personal happiness she had experienced since her arrival in Zurich, and against the potential for the additional well-being she might enjoy in Switzerland in the years to come. How intense her internal debate may have been once the proposal reached her, and how difficult it was for her to come to a decision, we shall of course never be able to discover. What we do know, however, is this: Ella agreed to Peter's demand. She made the choice of the dutiful daughter:

"But then she decided to go to Bolivia. And it is thanks to her that we survived."

Given the conflicting accounts as well as the silences surrounding the circumstances of Ella's young death, given the likelihood that she died by suicide, I realize that my employment of the phrase "dutiful daughter" may be read as an ironic, if not sarcastic, commentary on her personal sacrifice. But this is not at all my intent. Rather, I mean to identify and underscore the character of Ella's response and to flag its connection to a widespread phenomenon within the Central European refugee experience of which she was a part—its connection, indeed, to the general experience of displacement. "In times of external uncertainty," the cultural critic Angelika Bammer has written, "when the world outside appears a threatening and alien place, the family can seem the bedrock of constancy and security that one must hold on to at all costs." It provides "the sense of coherence that holds the individual in place."[69] Ella's response—to rescue her parents, to stay with them, to provide a safe base in emigration that her younger brother and other relatives might also join—was typical of the general effort made by individuals torn from the moorings of home and kin to piece together, reconnect, and reconstitute a "family" forcibly broken apart in the panic of induced dispersion. For her, as for so many others among her contemporaries, "bringing the family together again," "rescuing those left behind," "repairing the torn," was an elemental necessity, both a dutiful responsibility and a fundamental expectation born of a decent upbringing. The fact that Bolivia was perceived not only as haven for individual refugees but as potential site for familial reconnection and restoration was a major component of its appeal, a repeated theme within refugee recollection. And yet, as Ella's story also indicates, familial survival was at times purchased at great cost: in her case, with the currency of personal happiness and the coin of self-denial.

Shortly after Ella and my grandparents came to La Paz, she married Peter C. in a small wedding officiated, as he jokingly recalled, "not by a rabbi, but by a mohel."[70] My parents and my paternal grandmother, Lina, arrived there some months afterward, from Vienna via Genoa—aided in their visa acquisition, according to Peter, by the fact that he and Ella were already in Bolivia and able to "oil" the Bolivian bureaucratic machinery by means of personal lobbying and small bribes. Julius joined them at the very end of 1939, and my father's nephew, Ferry Kohn—the last person in the family able to find refuge in Bolivia before the virtual shutdown of immigration by the war—came in February 1940. A few, from what had been a quite close-knit family group in Austria, emigrated elsewhere: Regi, the oldest of my mother's three siblings, her husband, Ernst, and infant son, George, to Trinidad; Kathe Spiegler, my father's half-sister, to England; Sigi Schneider, my mother's cousin, on a children's transport to Palestine.

Those in the family who did find asylum in Bolivia pulled close together during the initial years of the immigration, trying to endure the sharp emotional shocks of displacement and to overcome the difficult economic and physical trials of resettlement, by pooling resources and assisting one another materially and psychologically. Mutual responsibility and mutual help were their operative modalities. Within the familial collective, the ones able to find work contributed to the sustenance of the others. Eighteen-year-old Julius routinely gave a portion of his earnings from his job as a waiter in the Café Viena and the Automobil Club to his parents; my maternal grandmother, Bertha, an excellent cook and baker, hired herself out as a private "chef" to supplement the family income; my father worked as a plumber and electrician on various new con-

struction projects; and my grandfather, employed on an on-again, off-again basis as a house painter, did likewise. Members of the family also shared meals, information, even physical space with each other. My parents, grandparents, and, for some months, Julius, lived together: initially on the Pasaje Villegas, in a single large room divided by a curtain; later, in three smaller rooms in the Calle Beni; later still, in an apartment in Miraflores.[71]

The familial togetherness had its negative consequences—monetary worries, anxieties about health, apprehensions about the war and its course, generational differences, concerns about relatives in Europe and elsewhere, frayed nerves, harsh words, accusations of meddling, hurt feelings. All these were intensified by the pressures of crowded quarters, an alien environment, and the initially difficult conditions of everyday existence. My mother, at the age of twenty, with a small baby, was certainly tested by having to live with her own parents and her mother-in-law in such close quarters—bothered both by lack of privacy and by the real or imagined scrutiny and criticism leveled at her inexperienced infant-care and homemaking efforts. She resented that aspect of "togetherness" long after she had left South America. Julius, young, spirited, curious about his new surroundings and prepared to let himself go—ready to separate himself psychologically and emotionally from the controlling reins of parental authority and the critical gaze of parental oversight—found the burden of familial demands during these early immigrant years stifling.[72]

But it was Ella, so central to our familial refuge and continuity in Bolivia, who was most profoundly and tragically affected. It was she who ultimately found it impossible to accommodate the contradictions between the heightened demands of familial existence in an alien environment, a genuine sense of familial duty, and her own personal desires for independence, adventure, and self-development. These contradictory pulls gave rise to instability and apparent directionlessness within her that she was able neither to overcome nor to escape. Within a year of the wedding, when she was barely twenty, her marriage to Peter came to an end. The precise reasons for its rapid demise will, of course, never be known, but one can imagine that the very pressures Peter had used to get her to come to Bolivia and make her "his," and the very sense of familial duty and responsibility that had impelled her to abandon Switzerland and leave a suitor behind, had engendered resentment and regret, profound unhappiness and despondency. She seems to have found herself at loose ends. She was a twice-displaced stranger in a new land, an attractive young woman within a small refugee community in which divorce was stigmatized and unattached divorcées distrusted and preyed upon. She sought solace in a brief, intense, and dead-ended relationship with a man separated from his wife.[73] She engaged in flirtations and in two or three short affairs. She tried to start a small leather-goods store, only to realize after a few months that she lacked the capital to keep it going. She wrote letters to her older sister Regi—first in Trinidad, then in the United States—imploring that she help her leave Bolivia and that she rescue her.[74] Increasingly, as her life spun out of control, seemingly going nowhere, she looked to the family in Bolivia for stability, grounding, and support. Paradoxi-cally, that very effort also seemed to restrict and bond her within the confines of parental oversight and familial expectations that could be met only through pro-found—ultimately unbearable—psychic cost.

"AND YET WE WERE THE LUCKY ONES . . ."

"And yet we were the lucky ones," my mother said to me once, when we spoke about the emigration and about Ella. "We did make it out. Some in the family were not so fortunate." She was talking about my father's half-sister, Gisi, her husband, Leopold Kohn, and their three daughters, Frieda, Rosi, and Hilde. They had stayed in Vienna until the end of 1941, living in ever-increasing squalor and desperation until they were transported to Riga—where Leopold, Gisi, and the youngest daughter, Rosi, were killed at once, and Hilde and Frieda selected for forced labor. Only Frieda survived the war. Late in 1939, when some chance to flee Austria had still existed, Kohn had let his son, Ferry, make his own way out of Vienna—to Switzerland and then to Bolivia—but had stubbornly forbidden his wife and daughters to leave without him. He had a brother near Budapest, and it was safe in Hungary, he had maintained. He expected to be able to join his brother "any day."[75]

My mother was also speaking about her aunt Ida and Ida's son, Dolfi, who had been unable to get visas in time and who had to stay in Vienna: Ida until she died from the bone cancer from which she had been suffering for many months, and Dolfi until he was sent off in a transport to Poland—and to his death—in late fall of 1941. She and the other family members in Bolivia had continued to be in touch with the two by mail, and to receive increasingly imploring letters from Dolfi (addressed to my father at "Poste restante, La Paz, Bolivien," closely typed to the very margins of the translucent-thin paper) until October 1941, one month before the deportations of Vienna's remaining Jews began again in massive numbers.[76] Handicapped by a serious limp that had

impeded his receipt of the "Good Health" certificate that was usually a neces-
sary prerequisite for an entry visa to any asylum land, Dolfi had nonetheless
kept up some hope that the family would someday be together again. Even in his
last letter, he reiterated his wish for a soon-to-be family reunion, but also sig-
naled despondency about the seriously deteriorating conditions of life for the
Jews left in Vienna. "When you write next time," he noted in his censored com-
munication, "then please cover the envelope with numerous Bolivian stamps of
small denomination, properly franked. I urgently need these for my collection."
In reality, he must have hoped to barter or sell the stamps to collectors in
exchange for food.[77]

These "less fortunate" relatives stayed in the consciousness of my parents
and others in the family in Bolivia throughout the war years, and long after-
ward. They were among the many Jews in Austria and Germany "who didn't
make it out in time"—thousands among the millions of Jews in Europe who
became victims of the Final Solution. The horrors accompanying the Nazis' rise
to ascendancy in the years after 1932, the desperation in finding visas to coun-
tries that would accept Jewish refugees, the shocks of displacement, and the tri-
als in starting life again, anew—all these were in some sense compared and
measured against the fate of the many "less fortunate" who were left behind.
For some, like Ella, this measurement and comparison ultimately could not out-
weigh the immediacy of the trauma they themselves had endured, or the
immense difficulties of the adjustment they were forced to make. For others, the
sense of counting themselves among "the lucky" emerged as a dynamic, even
inspiring, justification to continue living, to endure and, most important per-
haps, to remember and bear witness for their children and the generations to
come.

2

THE
CROSSING

*As a very young child, I am told that my paternal grandfather, Leopold, died
on the ship when he and my grandmother and my parents were on the way from
Austria to Bolivia. I am shown photos of the ship, the Italian passenger liner
Virgilio, and am impressed by its bright white color, its large funnel spewing
smoke, and its two masts. I am also shown pictures of my parents and other
passengers. My mother has a big belly in the photographs, and my parents
explain jokingly that I am "in there"—a stowaway on the voyage. I eventually
learn that the Virgilio, in this July 1939 voyage, is transporting hundreds of
refugees from Nazi Germany, Austria, Czechoslovakia, and the civil war in
Spain to South America. I am also told that the Virgilio's captain wanted to
bury my grandfather at sea, which would have been a violation of Orthodox
Jewish law mandating the interment of a body in the ground. My grandmother
and father objected—less, I find out, from any religious reservation on their
part than from some elemental unwillingness to have his final resting place be
an unmarked spot in the ocean. Only after a more persuasive fellow passenger
interceded on their behalf did the captain change his mind, agreeing to convey
the corpse to the ship's next port of call, the Venezuelan harbor of La Guaira.
There, my grandfather's body was taken from the ship, dressed in a shroud, and
buried in earth in the Jewish cemetery in Caracas.*

*When I am born in La Paz some months later I am named Leopoldo, after
my grandfather, given his Hebrew name, Gershon, and nicknamed Poldi: the
same diminutive that had been his during his lifetime. While I am still a young*

The *Virgilio*,
June–July 1939

Rose, pregnant, en route to South
America, July 1939

child, my parents tell me that they gave me my grandfather's names to honor the
departed and to maintain a continuity between the past and the present. Only
many years later, in hindsight, do I realize in how many different ways they
made their effort to maintain continuities—to perpetuate something of the lost
in the new—during their years in Bolivia. Indeed, I realize that this effort was
a central characteristic of the Jewish refugee experience in that Andean land.

THE ALBUM

The album containing the photos of "the crossing," as my family and many others of the refugees referred to their month-long sea voyage from Central Europe to South America, has long been an object of fascination for me. German or Austrian in origin, it was acquired by my parents in Bolivia shortly after their arrival—a well-crafted small, rectangular binder volume with textured gray and tan cloth-wrapped covers, dark brown photo-pages, and fine-quality translucent tissue separators imprinted with spiderweb designs. Held together by a braided cord with tassel ends, the album must certainly have been quite elegant and appealing when it was new, and it still looks modern and feels good to the touch despite its age and wear, continuing to invite examination and perusal. Like a beautifully bound book, its aesthetic qualities have drawn me back to it again and again over the years, but the real power of its attraction has always come from the eight pages of photographs of "the crossing" at the beginning, photos that helped to satisfy some of my early curiosity about my parents' *Virgilio* sea journey and their move to Bolivia, photos that I also associated with the death of grandfather Leopold:

A page from the album of the crossing

the grandfather for whom I was named but whom I had never met.

Unlike other albums of my parents', this one does not include my father's or mother's written subheadings to describe the contents of photos or to identify persons portrayed. It contains photographs identified by my parents for me as the port of Marseilles, the *Virgilio's* first stop after its departure from Genoa, where most of the Austrian and German refugees had started their sea journey. Only the indistinct outline of a man wearing a flat-topped, stiff-visored cap typical of French police suggests the identity of this harbor. It also includes a group of fascinating pictures of heavy bomb- and shell-damaged buildings and equipment in Barcelona, where the ship stopped next to pick up émigrés in the aftermath of the Spanish Civil War. It then displays a series of photographs taken in Cristóbal, on the Caribbean side of the Panama Canal, where passengers were permitted to disembark for a short period of sight-seeing. My mother, smiling, dressed in what appears to be loose-fitting, lightweight pedal-pushers, is in one of these photos, posing in a park. She is standing with some fellow passengers—a comely couple in their early twenties and a young boy—and with my grandmother Lina, who wears a tannish dress with a white-bordered collar, dark stockings and shoes, and who is shown carrying a large black purse and squinting into the bright sun located somewhere above and behind the photographer. Two other photos, of the five in the album recalling this particular stopover, show young Afro-Panamanian girls in white dresses—their inclusion perhaps indicative of how unusual an encounter with children of African descent must have been in my parents' lives up to that moment. Photographs of locks of the Panama Canal, of the port of Buenaventura in Colombia (which again focus on black subjects), as well as of numerous persons posing on the deck of the *Virgilio*, make up the remainder of pictures from this voyage. Most of the latter are of fellow Central European refugees and their children (although one is of an elegantly dressed Asian man with his young son)—posed photos rather than snapshots, generally showing ship's passengers on deck, with smiles on their faces and in a seemingly relaxed frame of mind. Some of these pictures include either my mother or grandmother (or both) in the pose; a number of them do not.

It never occurred to me while my parents were still alive, however, to ask them to explain or clarify what I eventually came to view as puzzling omissions and curious incongruities in this album. There are no pictures of Genoa itself, for instance, or of their departure from that city, or of var-

Barcelona harbor
from the *Virgilio*,
June 1939

Rose, Lina, and fellow
passengers during a
stopover in Cristóbal, not
long after Leopold's death

An album photo of Afro-Caribbean girls in
Panama

ious other ports of call normally visited by passenger ships belonging to the fleet of the Italia Line.¹ Was this because there were restrictions on photography in Genoa and other "sensitive" harbors during the tense months preceding the outbreak of war? Italy, after all, had invaded and occupied Albania only two months earlier, and a close political and military alliance with Germany had been forged in May 1939. Or were the omissions inadvertent, due to my parents' personal worries and distractions? Or do they perhaps reflect conscious selection by them, in both choice of subject and arrangement of images? Why are there no photos of Arica, Chile's northernmost port, where my parents, grandmother, and most of the others disembarked to travel overland, by train, to Bolivia? And no photos of the train journey? Had they run out of film by the time they reached Chile? Or was it conservation on their part, a decision to employ the box camera judiciously so as not to use up all their film, a scarce and, for them no doubt, expensive resource? Why, moreover, is there no photograph of grandfather Leopold in this album? He died as the *Virgilio* was approaching the Caribbean, somewhere at high sea between Trinidad and La Guaira, almost three weeks after they had left Italy. Had he been ill this entire time, lying in his berth or in the ship's infirmary, in no condition or mood to be photographed? He was seventy-three years old when he died. But in photos in another family album, taken of him and my grandmother in Vienna not very long before their emigration to South America, he can be seen smiling, dressed in a three-piece suit, and he seems to reflect the demeanor of an urbane elderly gentleman. He does not look ill, certainly not like a person long-suffering from a debilitating or incurable disease, near death. In this album of "the crossing," he is an invisible presence for me, a mysterious phantasm that begs for explanation.

If I did not know about my grandfather's death on the *Virgilio*, or about the escalating Nazi intimidation and persecution that was the background for the emigration of my family and the other Central European refugees on this voyage, my "reading" of the photos in this album might lead me to conclusions about their historical and psychological content that would be very different from what they actually express. A "naïve" viewer, encountering the album and its pictures without any background information, might be curious about the bombed-harbor photos and the pictures showing the canal locks and machinery. He or she might also puzzle about the identity of the people in the *Virgilio* photographs, and, while probably able to conclude from their dress and surroundings on the ship that they were not first-class passengers on a luxury voyage, would not necessarily discern that they were on a refugee voyage of displacement and escape—on a flight from oppression.

For a long time now, however, I have qualified as neither an innocent nor a naïve examiner of these photographs. I have looked at the album on numerous occasions over the years in the presence of persons depicted within it. Since early childhood, I have also listened to emigration accounts that have certainly helped me to put some of its contents in context and to clarify many of its representations. And I have always been privileged as a viewer in an even more special sense: I could view the family photos in our album of "the crossing" with an "affiliative look"; I could understand these images as an insider, as a member of the family; and I could adapt them into what I came to consider our familial narrative.[2]

It was perhaps *because* I had this special relation to many of the photographs in this album that the incongruities between *what I came to see* as the outward appearances of my parents and grandmother and *my expectations of what I should have been seeing* took on enormous importance for me. Knowing that my family, within a short time, had undergone a series

Leopold and Lina in Vienna in 1939

My father, posing on the deck of
the *Virgilio*

of traumatic experiences—the loss of homeland and familiar surroundings, the death of my grandfather, the threat of his burial at sea—I scru-
tinized the photos, searching my father's, mother's, and grandmother's
faces, their dress, their postures, their apparent involvement and interaction with one another and with their fellow passengers. I was determined
to gain a deeper insight into their feelings and state of mind at the time.
Yet what I saw I found bewildering.

I had expected their "look" to indicate the intense grief and sorrow of
their mourning, which my grandmother and father must surely have felt
after his death. While my family's circumstances on shipboard no doubt mit-
igated many of the observances that Jewish practice required of a deceased
man's wife and son, I had at least wanted to find some visual expression,
even if only symbolic, of lamentation on their part.[3] But no physical indications of their status as mourners—no sorrowful stances or hurtful looks, no
black clothing or armbands—were apparent to me. Indeed, given the background and circumstances in which the photographs were taken, the very
matter-of-factness and casualness of many of them were not only puzzling
but jarring. How was I to read my grandmother's and parents' facial expressions and body language—their smiles, and their seemingly relaxed attitude
and bearing—in the photos taken on the ship and in Cristóbal only a few
days after my grandfather's death and burial? How could I understand this
apparent incongruity between the visible and the historical?

It is, of course, possible that Leopold had already been so seriously ill when he boarded the ship, or in such great pain, that my family viewed his death as a release from extreme suffering. This perception would perhaps have allowed them to console one another more readily, to cheer up more quickly, and to present a relatively placid and unstrained external image of themselves. Their loss and bereavement, moreover, might also have been counterbalanced by the more general sense of personal relief that they undoubtedly shared with many of their fellow refugees on the *Virgilio*, and with others who had managed to flee from Nazi persecution. On their journey toward a potential new haven, after maneuvering through all the prejudicial and bureaucratic obstacles to get visas and tickets, they could, after all, take some comfort, breathe more freely, engage in life with some hope of renewal. As Arthur Propp, another refugee, remarked in his journal not long after he embarked on a ship taking him to Arica: "All is forgotten—Nazis as well as forced departure. This is the beginning of becoming human again." ("*Und alles ist vergessen . . . Nazis und Austreibung. Es is der Beginn der Wiedermenschwerdung.*")[4]

But while such feelings of relief and of the exhilarating possibility of "becoming human again" may indeed explain the seemingly untroubled facial expressions and outward appearances captured in these photos of the refugee voyage, the incompleteness of such speculations became shockingly clear to me when I decided to restore the album by detaching a number of the pictures from their pages in order to clean and refasten them with newer bonding. On the *back of each photograph*, in my father's handwriting, I found a brief explication of the photo's content and setting. The identity of fellow passengers whose names I had forgotten or never known was thus suddenly revealed: Mr. and Mrs. Rubenstein, with whom my parents seem to have become good friends on the voyage, and who appear in a number of pictures; Mr. and Mrs. Reiss, with their young son, Peterle; the Kesslers and their teenage daughter with braided blond hair; Miss Jedinger, leaning on a railing, standing with my pregnant mother and my grandmother; the dapper José Miro, who had fought in the 27th Division of the Karl Marx Brigade in the Spanish Civil War; Mr. Lau Hong and his son, two Malay Chinese emigrants sailing to Callao. I could then also confirm or correct the location of all the sights and ports depicted in the album (some of which I had misidentified over the years), as well as of the third-class deck areas that served as shipboard social spaces for the immigrants during the voyage. Most dramatically of all, however, my father's commentaries exposed the very intense feelings of grief and sadness that he associated with his voyage on the *Virgilio* and that the photos themselves certainly do not make apparent. They revealed his profound sorrow about the death of his father and the pain of his forced rupture from the world in which he had been raised and reached adulthood. "Our bad-luck ship *Virgilio*," he wrote on the back of one picture, "that accursed transport where our unforgettable father died." "Flying Dutchman aboard a ship of sadness," he declared on another. "Fore deck of the confounded *Virgilio*," he inscribed on a third, "far from homeland [*Heimat*], somewhere at sea."[5]

I thus inadvertently discovered the obverse, hidden side of the photographs' smiling faces and relaxed demeanors—desolate and unhappy representations of self and voyage that, if nothing else, supported my initial expectations about the nature of appropriate responses to the traumatic events my family had experienced. My father's handwritten inscriptions and comments were profoundly touching lamentations of mourning for parent and origin, and they were unambiguously explicit. On a more general level, my discovery of these notations also brought home to me how very complex the character—and how knotted the meanings—of the refugee experience encapsulated in the words "the crossing" really had been for its participants.

"WE HAD ALL BECOME REFUGEES . . ."

> I always thought the term they used for us was wrong:
> Emigrants.
> After all, it refers to willing travelers. But we
> Did not travel of our own free will
> Choosing another country. And did not travel
> To a country to settle there, possibly forever.
> Instead we fled. We are the driven out, the banished.
> And the country that took us in is not a home but an exile.
> —Bertold Brecht[6]

An emigrant's voyage aboard a tempest-tossed ship making its way slowly to a new world has been compared to the stormy and agitated period of adolescence, the long voyage from childhood into adulthood. The emigrants on board, having left behind the world they know, move toward a world of which they do not yet have a realistic picture. Far from the shore, they live in an unreal state shared only with their shipboard companions . . . Much time will elapse, even after they have touched terra firma, before they feel that the ground beneath them is truly firm. The "seasickness" of their trip does not easily vanish on land.

—L. and R. Grinberg[7]

My uncle Julius Wolfinger remembered his "crossing"—not on the *Virgilio*, but on the Italia flagship *Augustus*, in December 1939, a few months later.[8]

There were Jewish emigrants in first and second class, people who must have stashed some money to pay for the tickets. There were more than a thousand of us: Austrians, and Germans, and Czech refugees, and there were some who had come out of Dachau and Buchenwald. I really felt then that even though we came from different places and from different backgrounds, we had one big thing in common on the ship. We really were in the same boat! We had all become homeless.

People played games, cards, chess. Lots of conversation. Stories about how everybody got out. Arguments sometimes. Boredom sometimes. We younger ones flirted and entertained ourselves. We laughed, but there was also sadness and tension in the air. It came from leaving Europe and the relatives who stayed behind. I couldn't help thinking: what was going to happen?

I was seventeen years old when I emigrated to South America. I clearly remember one day standing by the railings of the ship looking out at nothing but the ocean. I felt a little homesick, I think, and lonely, and also a little unsure about what I was going to find in Bolivia. What was it going to be like? How would I make out there? But I was young, and also felt this was an adventure. I started talking to a man and woman standing near me who were also going to Bolivia, and who also began to tell me their stories and to talk about their worries and mixed-up feelings. And at some point, when we were talking about this, one of us said: "Maybe this is what it feels like to be a refugee." And we had a good laugh.[9]

In the 1990s, in which the word "refugee" appears every day in news accounts and is the reality of existence for millions of people in Africa, Central America, the Middle East, Southeast Asia, and Europe, it may seem surprising that Julius Wolfinger and his shipboard companions in 1939 struggled to define and *name* what they were experiencing and feeling during their passage from a world of persecution to a world as yet unreal. Possibly, of course, he misremembered the *exact* words spoken on the *Augustus* a half century earlier, and inadvertently substituted a term of more recent vintage for one in use at the time he left Europe. The designation "refugee," or *Flüchtling,* was not commonly used as a self-identifying label for Central European emigrants in the late 1930s, and an awareness of a collective and shared common experience of "refugeehood" (as opposed to a shared sense of persecution) does not seem to have been widely developed among them as yet either.* "Emigrants," *Auswanderer* or *Emigranten,* was their term, and the one by which they were grouped together, defined, and generally known by others at the time.

But, exactly remembered or not, it was precisely a "refugee identity," a sense of "refugeehood," that "the crossing" seems to have catalyzed and helped to construct among the emigrants, an identity and awareness of condition that were reflected psychologically and manifested socially in many ways in ensuing months and years. The emigrants' long ocean journey in the close company of others who were also dispossessed and excluded, and their collective experience of a passage "in-between," between continents and between existences, brought to the surface the complex constellation of emotions and responses that Julius recalled so vividly and that he so aptly and concisely identified in the phrase, "This is what it feels like to be a refugee."

In thinking about Julius's narrative in relation to the many other personal recollections about "the crossing" I have heard or read, my belated discovery of my father's comments concealed on the underside of photos in our family album taught me a lesson. It led me to realize that the complicated, seemingly contradictory feelings and emotions that the album revealed when I expanded my inquiry from visible, externally apparent, images to include hidden and nonvisible messages, were emblematic of the collective responses of Central European emigrants during this era; that, indeed, the "refugee identity" and general sense of "refugeehood" that emerged on the emigrant voyages were Janus-like themselves, ambivalent, and defined in responses that were not always visibly or ver-

---

*In English the term "refugee," referring to "one who, owing to religious persecution or political troubles, seeks refuge in a foreign country," was first applied to French Huguenots who came to England after the Revocation of the Edict of Nantes in 1658. It came to be applied to displaced people in general—to people driven from home by war or the fear of attack or persecution—and was used descriptively by British officials and writers in the Boer War, World War I, and in the course of the late 1930s and World War II.

bally expressed, or immediately perceptible. In my uncle Julius's narrative, in my father's notes, and in the accounts of other émigrés, "what it feels like to be a refugee" seems to have emerged and gained definition in relation to two poles: to that of the known Europe, to an origin and homeland that was culturally familiar, forcibly abandoned, left behind, seemingly lost; and to a new land of refuge—alien, unknown, other. Relief and thankfulness such as that expressed by Arthur Propp for having gotten out alive, if not intact, were felt by the very same people who were also suffering the intense pain of separation from relatives and friends, the traumatic loss of home and possessions, and who had had to break connections with place, social, and cultural milieus, lifework and professions. Emigrants on "the crossing" now found themselves in a liminal space: occasionally disoriented, nervous, lonely, yet also in the midst of an incipient new community of people who were "in the same boat." Memories of past times, and feelings both joyful and hurtful, whirled about simultaneously, engendering moments of nostalgia and yearning but also instances of lightheartedness and gladness: tears as well as smiles.

Thus the exhilaration they could feel on occasion—brought on by the possibilities and challenges of renewal, by the pleasures of imagining a new, perhaps better life in another land—had a counterpart in anxiety about the future and in fears of the unknown. The place to which they were emigrating was vague and unformed in their minds. It was offering them respite, a potential haven, a different—hopefully friendlier—social and political environment, yet they were uneasy about its "strangeness" and about their own life-chances within it. *"What was it going to be like? How would I make out there?"* Julius had wondered about Bolivia, quickly reassuring himself on the *Augustus* that things would work out well, that he was young and having "an adventure." Within the multifaceted "refugee identity," hopefulness and optimism frequently alternated with disquietude.

The refugee identity had yet another, perhaps central, characteristic. In broad psychological terms, this feature expressed that very intense emotion revealed in my father's notations on the backside of our album's photographs: his sorrow concerning my grandfather's death and his mournful lament about his own forced separation from people and places to which he had a lifelong connection. Mourning like his, I realized, was deeply embedded within the refugee identity *in general*—a dynamic feeling of pain, suffering, and loss that surfaced occasionally, submerged again, changed in intensity over time, but affected *all* refugees personally and profoundly for years to come. Indeed, the universality of this grief, not only for these refugees but for all emigrants and exiles, has been described by the psychoanalysts León and Rebeca Grinberg on the basis of extensive clinical work with voluntary and involuntary immigrant groups. Metaphorically and psychologically, "the one who leaves dies," they write, "and so does the one who stays behind. The feelings of mourning with which each side responds to the separation may be compared to those one has at the death of a loved one. The unconscious association between leaving and dying [is] extremely intense."[10]

It is important to stress that the complex emotions and expressions that characterized and defined "refugeehood" and the "refugee identity" were embedded within lives and human interactions that appeared on the surface to be routine and normal. Refugees conversed, argued, gossiped, laughed, played games, read, flirted, listened to music, sang songs, took photos, touched, and considered each other and their surroundings. They continued, in other words, to pass many of the hours of the days and nights of their lives in ordinary activities, activities that were not obviously marked by the traumatic experience of displacement and flight. And these ordinary engagements were usually their salve for survival; their distraction in the present, the immediate, and the normal would eventually enable many of them to work through and come to terms with the vicissitudes, losses, and pain of the refugee experience.

EXITS, PORTS, AND CROSSINGS IN BETWEEN

With the exception of the events at La Guaira for the land burial of my grandfather, the voyage of the *Virgilio* that took my parents and grandmother to Arica seems to have been routine, not atypical of many other refugee voyages to South America during the period of "panic emigration" between the *Anschluss* in March 1938 and the outbreak of war in September 1939.

At 11,718 gross tons, the *Virgilio* (which had been built in 1927) could attain a top speed of 14 knots and was designed to carry 110 passengers in first class, 200 in second, and 400 in third, plus a crew of approximately 240 mariners. It was slightly larger than its sister ship *Orazio* but much smaller than the huge flagship of the Italia Line, the *Augustus* (32,650 gross tons), which in third class alone had a capacity for more than 1,000 passengers.[11] Like all the Latin American passenger ships in the Italia fleet, its normal service took it from Genoa to Valparaiso, Chile, and back to Genoa in an approximately ten-week round-trip, with scheduled in-between stops on the outward journey in Marseilles, Barcelona, Las Palmas, Trinidad, La Guaira, the Panama Canal, Baranquilla, Callao, Arica, and Antofogasta. Although perhaps as many as 10 percent of the refugees who reached Bolivia during this period entered the country after an initial transit landing in Brazil, Argentina, or in another South American country, most arrived after first disembarking in Chile's most northerly city, Arica. Arica became the predominant site associated with "the crossing"—the "landing place" at which the next phase in the refugee journey began. The city itself, built at the foot of the Morro headlands and fringed by sand dunes in a desert area that rarely receives rainfall, was in part selected by the Chilean authorities as the port of disembarkation for the refugees because of its isolation. Neither Santiago nor any other of Chile's potentially more attractive central cities were reachable by land from Arica. Other than by sea, the only way to get from this port was by a train that, twice a week, climbed thousands of feet from the coast up the Andes highlands to La Paz.

In its June 1939 voyage to South America, when my family was aboard, the *Virgilio* was filled beyond its designated capacity with European refugees, mainly Jewish. Cabins originally intended for two persons now slept as many as six; third-class dormitory rooms, separate for male and female passengers, slept fifty to eighty persons in tiered bunks—almost twice the number they had been designed to contain. "The steamer was overcrowded and the trip was no enjoyment, though we did not feel seasick," one of the third-class refugees on this voyage complained in a letter to the Joint Distribution Committee in New York. "The Italian crew was not very friendly or kind to us, and the low quality and unfamiliar Italian food did not add pleasure to the journey." "I remember the crew as very nice," recalled another passenger, however, "but our quarters were stuffy and the third-class dining hall had a strong fish smell, so we didn't stay there or in our cabins very much. We spent most of the day time outside, above deck."[12]

The open and covered decks of the ship, where many of the photos in our family album were taken, were indeed the logical places to escape from the overcrowded sleeping quarters and pungent odors of the third-class food hall. This was no doubt true during this period of heavy refugee traffic on every ship carrying emigrants across the oceans. During the summer months especially—as these ships sailed into the hotter air and sunnier climate of the Caribbean, through the Panama Canal, and down the Pacific coast of South America—the decks became the sites of refreshment and breezy repose: airier, potentially cooler, less confining spaces than interior lounges or cabins. On the month-long voyages, they were the most popular areas for group social activity and interaction, where passengers exchanged stories, passed information along to one another, considered the past, speculated about the future, and developed shipboard camaraderie.

"We traveled steerage and were not permitted to forget that fact for a moment," recalled Egon Schwarz who, at the age of seventeen in late February 1939, sailed from Europe with his parents from the French Atlantic port of La Rochelle aboard the British Pacific Steam Navigation Company's SS *Orduña*.[13]

> The food was nearly inedible; the dormitories and cabins were hidden deep in the bowels of the ship and, because we sailed through tropical waters, saturated by humid heat. The service personnel confronted us with unmitigated contempt. Allegedly, the captain said that he felt pity for the countries in which the off load of his ship disembarked . . .
>
> At every moment one was reminded that this "crow" was no ordinary passenger ship but a transport of displaced and vanquished people. Our ship was densely populated not only by fugitives from every corner of Greater Germany, but also by Spaniards and Latin Americans who had fought on the side of the Republic and who now, after their defeat in the Spanish Civil War, were either returning home or searching for a land of refuge where their language would be understood. Never again have I encountered a more fascinating hodgepodge of humanity thrown together as on that voyage: people who had been in concentration camps, whose stores had been boycotted by the SA, whose pianos had been thrown out of the window into the street on Kristallnacht, and those who, with inadequate means and at the cost of unimaginable casualties and privations, had put up resistance against Francisco Franco. Here one could encounter unbelievably quick-talking, cigarette-smoking Chileans, chess-playing Cubans (every one of them a small Capablanca), and well-educated Jewish seamen from Cologne and Frankfurt; here were North German doctors and university professors who spoke in cultivated intellectual prose, and Bavarian country boys with their broad dialect who, God knows how, had come into conflict with the Nazis; business people from the Tauentzienstrasse; East European Jews from Galician shtetls; impoverished Austrian aristocrats who still tried to cling desperately

to a little bit of distinction and luxury; and folk from widely dispersed places who had become intimately acquainted with barns and flophouses, with the Parisian underworld, with unclean jails and the pitiless immigration police of every nation. And every one of them was able to narrate not only one but many novels. This ship would be my first university for many years to come, and by no means my worst one.[14]

The primary embarkation ports in Europe for the many refugees seeking haven in the Americas and elsewhere changed during the 1930s, and especially in the months after the start of the war until mid-1942. Exit ports with access to sea lanes were intensely affected both by internal political developments within their own countries and by the international political and military situation. As was the case with lands into which refugees tried to gain admission, fewer and fewer places from which to leave Europe remained open or accessible to them.[15]

Before the *Anschluss* emigrants from Germany itself generally had departed from Bremerhaven or Hamburg. In order for Nazi Germany and its "recognized citizens" to maximize their profits from the emigration, these deportees were "encouraged" to book tickets and make their baggage shipping arrangements through German-owned agencies and to travel on German ships or airplanes. But many German-speaking emigrants, among them people who had not succeeded in finding permanent refuge in neighboring European countries, left from ports outside of Germany, including Amsterdam, Rotterdam, Antwerp, Marseilles, La Rochelle, and Southampton. After the *Anschluss* and especially after the *Kristallnacht* pogroms in November 1938, departures from all these places continued and intensified, but Austrian refugees (leaving from Vienna or from temporary asylum in Prague) usually made their way through Hungary or Yugoslavia to the Italian ports of Trieste and Genoa, or to the French port of Marseilles. Precise passenger statistics from this period no longer exist, but most oral and documentary evidence suggests that ships of the Italia Line and the Lloyd Triestino transported a majority of these Central European refugees to the west coast of South America—i.e., to Arica—during the peak months of the "panic emigration" between 1938 and 1939.

During the frantic initial months of the panic after the *Anschluss* and *Kristallnacht*, numerous incidents involving "false" or "invalid" visas occurred—of high-priced, yet ultimately worthless, documents being provided to frantic asylum-seekers by unscrupulous consuls, shipping-

Revised 1/30/39

PANIC MIGRATION

REMARKS

NAME OF BOAT	NO. OF REFUGEES	DATE & PLACE OF DEPARTURE	ORIGINAL DESTINATION	DATE & PLACE OF ARRIVAL	REMARKS
	18	Austria		Haiti	Report received 9/7/38. Supposedly valid passports and visas. Ordered deported. Thru intervention, secured temporary stay. 2 went to Cuba. Remainder still there with no definite plans, except general desire to migrate to other country.
SS. Orinoco	300	Germany	Mexico	Havana Oct.Nov. '38	Officials refused to allow them to land, in spite of guarantees of maintenance, etc. Had to go back to Havana Oct. 18,1938, where granted temporary stay (intervention of Joint Relief Committee) plus exp. of $1500. (Hias)
SS. Iberia	43		Mexico	Havana Sept.14, '38	Attempted entry at Vera Cruz in vain. Temporary stay in Havana Nov. 14,'38, with guarantees of maintenance $60. per head ($2500).
SS. Copiapa	110		C. & S. American ports	New York Dec.Jan.'38/'39	Stopped in New York enroute to C. & S. America. Papers in order but no money. Some received additional transportation expenses and incidentals, better care on board, etc.
SS. Imperial	143		S. America	Venezuela Feb. 1939	Investigated in Baltimore 1/10/39. Papers of 37 refugees headed for Peru, declared invalid. Upon arrival declared valid thru intervention. Finally permitted to land at Mollendo for 60 days. Penniless.
SS. Caribia	63		Trinidad	Caracas, Venezuela 3/2/39	Refused 2/39 Trinidad. Attempts to secure permission to land in several C. & S. American countries in vain. Finally secured permission thru intervention of Venezuela for temporary stay. Granted permanent stay.
SS. Koenigstein	170	Germany	Barbados	Venezuela 3/29/39	Refused admission to Barbados 2/20/39. Attempts to secure permission to land in several C. & S. American countries in vain. Finally secured permission thru intervention for temporary stay. Granted permanent stay.

- 2 -

NAME OF BOAT	NO. OF REFUGEES	DATE & PLACE OF DEPARTURE	ORIGINAL DESTINATION	DATE & PLACE OF ARRIVAL	REMARKS
	42	Germany	Costa Rica	Costa Rica Dec. 1938	Temporary visas. Many others since then. 100 altogether. Maintenance guarantees by American agencies. Under threat of expulsion.
SS. Monte Rosa	10		Uruguay	Dec. 1938	
SS. Istria	12		Mexico	12/4/38	Refused admission to Mexico. Admitted to Cuba on a guarantee of N.C.C.
SS. Orazio	20		Lima	12/6/38	Penniless
SS. Cottica	30		Trinidad	1/18/39	Admission arranged thru intervention. However, no provision made for others due on "SS. Pericles, De la Salle, Stuyvesant, Amazon (on high seas)
SS. General Martin	25	2/3/39 Boulogne	Uruguay	3/12/39	Refused admission Argentina, Chile, Bolivia. Boat to stop at Rio on 3/15/39 on way back to Europe. Expected in France April 1.
SS. Oceania	10	2/14/39 Boulogne	Uruguay	3/12/39	Refused admission Argentina, Chile, Bolivia
SS. Virgilio	150	Genoa -2/17/39	Bolivia		Majority illegals
SS. Cap Norte	21	Boulogne 2/17/39	Uruguay	3/12/39	Refused admission Argentina, Chile, Bolivia. Boat to stop at Rio on 3/29/39. Thru intervention transit through Uruguay to Chile 3/28/39
SS. Cap Arcona	40	Boulogne 2/21/39	Uruguay	3/12/39	Refused admission Argentina, Chile, Bolivia. Boat to stop at Rio 3/15/39. Admitted 3/29/39 Boulogne, France, on way back to Hamburg.
SS. General Artigas	10	Boulogne 2/24/39	Uruguay	3/12/39	Refused admission. Boat to stop at Rio on 3/15/39. Thru intervention, transit thru Uruguay to Chile 3/28/39
SS. Aconcagua	150		Bolivia Chile & Ecuador		Baltimore 2/28/39. No landing money. No other information.
SS. Montepasquale					No detailed information
SS. Arturias			Uruguay	3/12/39	

- 3 -

Photocopy of document on "Panic Migration" accompanying a March 9, 1939, report, "Bound for Nowhere," prepared for the JDC in New York by Cecilia Razovsky, executive director of the National Coordinating Committee for Aid to Refugees and Emigrants Coming from Germany. The chart indicates the many instances when refugees, possessing allegedly invalid documents, were refused admission at ports of entry company brokers, and Gestapo agents. Upon reaching their destinations, refugees bearing these false visas were often not permitted to land. They were left literally afloat at sea, "bound for nowhere," as Cecilia Razovsky described their plight at the time.[16] The best known of these incidents involved the Hamburg-America Line luxury ship *St. Louis*, whose 936 passengers discovered in Havana that their Cuban visas were invalid. After long and largely fruitless efforts by the American Joint Distribution Committee to resolve their situation and gain permission for their dis-embarkation in Cuba, the United States, or in other Latin American countries, the ship and all but a handful of its passengers returned to Europe, where perhaps as many as two-thirds of their number became victims of the Holocaust.[17] Other smaller-scale but similar instances of invalid documentation and impeded disembarkation at ports of entry had happier endings—in large part through the intervention and efforts by societies such as the Hebrew Immigrant Aid Society and the National Coordinating Committee for Aid to Refugees and Emigrants Coming from Germany. These incidents were consequently less well publicized and less well known, yet they were undoubtedly also agonizing ordeals for the many people who had to endure the fright and humiliation they engendered.

During most of the first year of the war, Italian ports remained open for exiting refugees, and Italian ships, sailing mainly from Genoa, continued to transport thousands of Jewish and non-Jewish refugees from Central Europe to South America. But this ceased by the end of 1940, after Fascist Italy officially ended its "neutrality" and joined the Axis militarily. Marseilles had also remained an important Mediterranean port from "unoccupied" Vichy, even after the German victory over France, but after mid-1940, as transport via the customary route was curtailed, refugees sailed from Marseilles to Algiers or Oran in North Africa, then continued by train to Casablanca for reembarkation on ships traveling to the east coast of South America, or to South Africa, or occasionally to North America. Then Marseilles, too, was closed to all passenger traffic in November 1942, as an act of retaliation by the Germans for the Allied invasion of North Africa.[18]

With so few "traditional" seaward departure options available, many people threatened by the Nazi onslaught sought to flee Europe through the few remaining open "neutral" harbors, or by overland travel, through Central Asia, to seemingly safer, if harder to reach, Asiatic havens and ports of emigration. Until the German invasion of the Soviet Union in June 1941, the land exit route over Siberia to Shanghai (where no entry visa was required), or via Shanghai and various intermediate stopovers to South America, was the primary eastern gateway used by thousands of refugees.[19] Between the summer of 1939 and November 1942, Spain and "neutral" Portugal became ever more important "departure" countries, with Barcelona, Cádiz, Seville, and, especially, Lisbon the places from which emigrants left. After the fall of France in June 1940 and the severe restrictions on refugee transit and emigration through Spain imposed by the Franco regime, Lisbon remained the last hope for the thousands of Central Europeans who had initially fled to Paris and other French cities and who were now stranded and being rounded up for internment camps in the "unoccupied" regions of France.[20] In June 1940, hundreds of refugees in the Portuguese capital awaited transport overseas. Reaching Lisbon, however, quickly became an incredibly problematic undertaking. To do so by legal means required transit visas for both Spain and Portugal, visas that could be acquired only if the entrance visa to the asylum country, plus travel tickets and landing fees, were already in hand. Delay in the receipt of transit visas frequently resulted in the expiration of primary visas. In March 1941, 423 refugees without valid visas were sent back by Portugal to France. Soon, exit from the port of Lisbon also became largely impossible.[21] For much of the duration of the war, refugee crossings by sea from the European mainland virtually ceased.

THE ORAZIO TRAGEDY

On Friday, January 19, 1940, the *Virgilio*'s sister ship *Orazio* left its home port, Genoa, en route to Valparaiso, Chile. The vessel had made this journey numerous times and had already transported thousands of refugees to South America. But this sailing would be the *Orazio*'s final voyage. The ship had a capacity for 710 passengers but because of the outbreak of the war in September 1939 and the severe restrictions on new immigration by all of the American nations, only 442 passengers were on board—the majority in steerage, destined for Bolivia. There were also 231 crew members on the *Orazio* on this voyage.

Adolf Kronberger, one of the survivors of what would be known as the

"*Orazio* tragedy," recalled the events in March 1940, shortly after his arrival in La Paz:

> I was a third-class passenger quartered in a "camerone," or dormitory, crowded together with some thirty others. When we left, it was on an uncomfortable, gray winter morning, with the bone-piercing Genoa wind accompanying us out of the port. But the sun came out, and we sailed close to the shoreline along the Riviera. We could see all the most beautiful land spots in the bright sunshine—places like San Remo, Ventimiglia, and later Monte Carlo and Nice. Our spirits began to improve noticeably—and understandably, since most of the passengers were emigrants from Germany who, after many years, were again able to breathe in an air of freedom. Besides, they believed they had attained the goal for which they had worked months and years—their emigration.[22]

Even before Italy officially declared war on Britain and France, Italian mariners in the Mediterranean were alerted to the potential dangers their ships faced at sea—not from mines or submarines as yet, but from French naval patrols halting and searching neutral or potentially "unfriendly" vessels for the possible presence of enemy agents. A number of the passengers on this voyage of the *Orazio* had heard rumors before leaving Germany and Austria that the French often boarded Italian ships to search for suspicious passengers, and that detainees were then not permitted to proceed on their journey but, instead, were interned in France and treated as prisoners of war.[23]

Such a dreaded interdiction did in fact occur to the *Orazio* off the French coast on the evening of January 20: the vessel was stopped at sea and boarded by officers and sailors from a French warship. Many emigrants became terrified when this occurred, and the earlier sunny mood of departure was overshadowed by a general fearfulness. But a number of the refugees, confident that the red J the Germans had placed on their passports would identify them as Jews—as victims of persecution and not potential threatening enemies—remained calm. Eventually, after a three-hour-long intensive scrutiny of the identity papers of all passengers and crew members, and the direct questioning of some fifty emigrants by French naval officials, seven men and two women were removed from the ship and the journey was permitted to continue.[24]

But the relief, even joyfulness, felt by the many who had been spared and allowed to remain on board was soon dispelled by the very noticeable onset of a powerful wind and rough sea: in these stormy conditions the ship began to be tossed about like "a play ball," according to Kronberger, and the possibility of finding sleep in the steerage dormitories became nearly impossible.

Suddenly, in the early-morning hours of Sunday, January 21, when the ship was about thirty-eight miles south of Toulon, a powerful explosion occurred in the engine room. It was later revealed that five Italian mariners were immediately killed in this blast and that it had ignited a fire that began to spread, slowly yet uncontrollably, to other parts of the ship. Perhaps because of the vehemence of the storm and their distance from the explosion, however, none of the third-class passengers in the steerage dormitories seem to have heard or felt anything at the time. They were not aware that anything unusual had occurred. No alarm went off, and the ship's officers and crew issued no warning or instructions to the hundreds of unsuspecting passengers. Kronberger remembers,

Around 3 a.m., one of our dormitory companions tried to leave our room but could not open the door until, finally, some powerful fellow actually broke the lock for him. But we didn't think much about this incident at the time. A few minutes later, however, a woman came into our dormitory looking for her husband and, in great excitement, told him something was happening on the ship because she had seen crew members wearing life jackets rushing about . . . Soon other wives also came, urging their husbands to dress and check out what was going on up top, outside, on deck.

Suddenly, all the lights went out and we found ourselves in complete darkness. The excitement increased, and we heard voices of men and women searching for each other and for their children. Some shouted that there was a fire; others yelled that no one should panic, that the problem was only a power outage. But everyone tried to make their way, stumbling over suitcases and baggage, in order to get out and reach open air. Only a few managed to get fully dressed. Outside the cabins, the narrow corridors were totally clogged with people. Children were screaming. Women were crying, and no one knew as yet what had happened. Some people speculated that we had struck a mine; others, that fire had broken out; still others, the optimists, tried to calm everyone down by maintaining that it was nothing more than a power outage. But no one could go out on deck because the doors were shut and we were locked in . . .

And then, after about half an hour, a door to the deck was pulled open and the order Avanti! was shouted into the cabin corridors . . . Those of us who emerged on deck from this section of the ship will never be able to put out of our minds that first sight that greeted us in the open. The ship's command-bridge and the first-class section connected to it were enveloped in a sea of flames. The bridge was burning like an ignited fuse along its entire width, spewing a tower of fire rising some thirty meters high . . .

It was still nighttime, but the sky was brightly lit by the high flames, which were

being whipped up more and more strongly by the storm's howling winds. Around us was the tumultuous ocean on which our burning hulk was being tossed back and forth like a nutshell. And in front of the ship, tightly packed together and illuminated in reddish brown by scarlet flashes from the flames, stood a shivering mass of people: children, women, men, and the elderly huddled in a luminous blend, everyone speechless, paralyzed by the shock that none of us could yet grasp. Our eyes were drawn to the flames and we all stared in the direction from which death would certainly soon be coming . . . And so we all stood, each one of us preparing spiritually to take our ultimate farewell from our loved ones . . . Prayers—in many languages, and to the gods of every religion—were said.

Distress signals were sent out from the *Orazio*'s radio room almost immediately after the engine-room explosion and the start of the fire, and were repeated numerous times in the ensuing hours. It was not, however, until two o'clock on Sunday afternoon, some nine or ten hours after the S.O.S. had initially been broadcast, that a French hydroplane appeared in the sky, circled the burning ship a few times, and flew off once again. The first rescue ship on the scene appeared around 4 p.m.—ironically the very same French warship that had halted the *Orazio* the day before, and that had been so feared by the emigrants. In short order, it was joined by three Italian ships of the Lloyd Triestino fleet: the *Conte Biancamano, Colombo,* and *Edera.* The delay was in large part no doubt caused by the terrible weather and rough seas. But given that the *Orazio* was as yet relatively close to shore, uncertainty about the cause of its explosion may also have contributed to the rescuers' slow response, some hesitation on their part to sail quickly and fully exposed into an area of the Mediterranean where another ship, hours earlier, might have hit a submerged mine or come under submarine attack. The fact that so many hours after the initial distress signal was broadcast only Italian ships and a French naval vessel appeared to aid in the rescue operations, lends further support to this conjecture.

By the time the first lifeboats from the rescue ships reached the blazing vessel at 6 p.m., the *Orazio*'s main mast had collapsed and fallen into the sea, and it was clear to Captain Carli, who commanded the French naval ship, that the passenger liner was beginning to flood and would soon sink. Its bridge and first-class quarters were by now largely consumed by the flames, and most of the wooden planking of the decking had burned away. Only glowing embers and a smoking ash, muddied by rain and sea spray, remained as a residue where the decks had lain. Like ribs and bones of a giant skeleton on whom skin and flesh had not entirely decomposed, the metal girders and structural beams of the ship were now largely exposed beneath the ashes and smoldering wood. The exhausted, cold, thoroughly drenched and terrified survivors of the ordeal—many of them suffering cuts and burns, their lungs raw from smoke inhalation and their eyes swollen nearly shut—were forced to find footing, and to balance themselves, on these slippery and dangerous supporting structures. Squeezed together on these precarious perches, they held on to one another, and to what remained of their hopefulness, as best they could.

Slowly and cautiously, however, their rescuers reached them, and the difficult rescue operation was initiated: children first, then women, lastly men were instructed to climb down the side of the burning ship on extended rope ladders into the waiting lifeboats below. If they were physically incapable of this, the survivors were lowered by cables and makeshift hammocks. But, no matter by what means, the evacuation was dangerous and problematic for nearly everyone. A number of people, weakened by the ordeal aboard the fiery ship, slipped and fell from the rope ladders and had to be fished from the stormy ocean. Others suffered more burns on their hands, knees, and faces when they accidentally touched the flame-heated metal sides of the ship on their way down. Children cried as they were separated from their parents; husbands and wives feared losing each other and their families. But finally, around 1 a.m., the last of the survivors left the hulk, and the rescue was complete. A few hours later, with the bodies of the victims of the engine-room explosion and fire still entombed within its burned-out, flooded passages, the *Orazio* sank to the bottom of the sea.

According to the Italian authorities who provided the final accounting some weeks later, 114 people lost their lives in this disaster: a handful at sea during the rescue or in the aftermath, the overwhelming majority on the ship. Hundreds more suffered burns, wounds, and fractured limbs—in some cases, severe injuries that left them physically debilitated and emotionally traumatized for years to come. Practically everyone who had been aboard, moreover, lost all their clothing except what he or she was wearing at the time of rescue, as well as luggage and money, losses that were particularly devastating since all the refugees needed cash funds to "show" immigration authorities when landing in Chile and entering Bolivia, and who now had no material possessions to help ease their move and resettlement into their South American asylum.

News about the sinking of the *Orazio* reached the refugee community in Bolivia very quickly. By Friday, January 26, the German-language immigrant weekly newspaper *Rundschau vom Illimani* published a lengthy front-page account headlined "*Das Drama der 'Orazio'* " ("The Drama of the '*Orazio*' ") in which details about the explosion, fire, rescue efforts, and general condition and care of survivors were pieced together for readers in La Paz and Cochabamba from a variety of international news sources. This article made reference to German propaganda charges blaming the sinking and tragic loss of life on French sabotage, on a clandestine fire that French mariners allegedly set when they had interdicted and boarded the *Orazio* the day before the explosion. But it also dismissed these accusations as blatant and vulgar Nazi inventions, stressing the centrality of the French ship in the rescue operations, as well as the official thanks that Italy had extended to the French for their assistance.[25]

Questions about who was to blame, and about the true cause of the explosion and fire were nonetheless raised by the immigrants at the time, and they reemerged in refugee recollections many years afterward. Despite official Italian and French reports identifying the origin of the fire as the accidental consequence of spilled fusel oil in the engine room that led to a boiler explosion, many immigrants remained convinced that either sabotage or a submarine attack had been the cause.[26] But, regardless of their lingering queries and suspicions, the primary concern of the refugees in Bolivia was for the victims and survivors of the disaster. A number of them had been expecting relatives and friends who had sailed on this *Orazio* crossing, and they quickly tried to ascertain their fate: if they were dead or alive, where they were now located, the nature of their injuries, when they would be released, and when they would be brought to Bolivia. Indeed, in a rally coordinated by Ernst Schumacher, publisher of the *Rundschau vom Illimani*, individual refugees, as well as recently established refugee clubs and organizations, pulled quickly together to support and facilitate the continued immigration of the survivors, now recovering in hospitals or held up in temporary lodgings in southern France and Italy. They collected used and new clothing, bedding, furniture, and donated a variety of services in anticipation of the arrival of the immigrants in La Paz. Members of the Juedische Jugendbund, the Jewish Youth Organization, went from house to house gathering money for the survivors, often from people who themselves had very little cash to contribute. The Círculo Israelita and the Macabi sports and social clubs sponsored benefit entertainments to raise funds. Multifoto, a new refugee-owned photographic establishment, offered to make passport photos and to photo-copy documents for the survivors free of charge after their arrival. And the owners of a newly created inn at the hot springs of Urmiri, a few hours from La Paz, contributed four five-day "recuperative" holidays at their valley establishment for particularly stricken *Orazio* victims.[27]

Both the news that all of the Bolivia-bound *Orazio* survivors would be gathered for departure once again from Genoa on the *Augustus,* and their actual arrival in La Paz on March 19, 1940, became occasions for great rejoicing and celebration. A benefit garden feast was organized at the Finca Elma in Miraflores, sponsored by the Jüdische Gemeinde, or Jewish Community Organization, and by the Macabi sports club; it was the largest collective gathering of the refugees in La Paz since the mass emi-gration to Bolivia had begun some two years earlier. Those who came had a chance to enjoy Austro-German food and drink a variety of beverages, to dance to live band music, and to be entertained with Jiu-Jitsu and gym-nastic exhibitions by Macabi members, comedy skits and readings by amateur and ex-professional performers, and a choir from the Jugenbund singing German youth songs and *wanderlieder* (hiking songs). The entrance fees, plus a percentage of the day's take on drinks and food, and the earnings from a "great American auction," to which stores and indi-vidual donors had contributed various articles, were pooled in a fund for distribution to the *Orazio* immigrants.[28] A poem written by Richard Moss-mann captured the spirit of the communal feeling at this event. Its con-cluding stanzas welcomed the survivors, but they were clearly intended to rouse and rally the refugees already in Bolivia as well.

> Forget, if you are able, the yesterdays
> And think about the morrow, the time to come.
> You fathers—mothers—brothers—sisters
> Rise. Rise, and for a new battle be freshly prepared.
>
> Defend human rights and human love.
> May freedom live, may hate be silenced.
> And may it be that luck remains on our side forever—
> "Full steam ahead."
>
> Welcome to La Paz[29]

For long after, the *"Orazio* tragedy" remained engraved on the con-sciousness of refugees who had not directly experienced it. It was recalled time and again during the years of the emigration, and afterward, by people who eventually left Bolivia to emigrate once again—to the United States, to Europe, to Israel. Some of my own early childhood imaginings about "the crossing" were about the sinking *Orazio*—initiated perhaps because my parents spoke of this event with such solemnity as a "might have been"—it happened to a sister ship of the *Virgilio*, on which they had sailed, after all—or because I had been told that my uncle Ferry had been scheduled to be on that voyage and had fortunately transferred to another ship, or because I had actually met some of its survivors or encountered people who had arrived on an earlier *Orazio* sailing. The album with the photos of my parents' crossing also has in it a photograph of my family at that big benefit gathering at the Finca Elma. Even though I did not know the details about the disaster until much later, the name *Orazio* and a mental picture of a sinking, burning ship, of drowning victims in turbulent sea waters, have been in my consciousness for as long as I can remember.

That this particular incident took on such importance among the refugees in Bolivia might seem somewhat surprising, given that the majority of passengers on the doomed ship managed to survive and that many other events had a much more direct and personally traumatic impact on the refugees' lives. But in a very profound sense, for many immigrants in Bolivia the "*Orazio* tragedy" became an emblem of their collective experience—an icon of the entire ordeal of emigration, acknowledging both destruction and renewal. The sinking ship was in microcosm the European world they all had been forced to abandon; the plight of its victims encapsulated the horrible human and material losses that all of them suffered in the painful process of rejection. Yet survival was also an aspect of the *Orazio* story, a central component of the drama that raised it from despair to hopefulness.

3

INVISIBLE

BAGGAGE

INHERITED RELICS

After my mother died in New York in 1988, I became the keeper of memorabilia that she and my father had brought to the United States from our nearly twelve years spent in what she used to call "our time in Bolivia." Among the items I inherited is a framed, hand-colored, artist-signed lithograph of Vienna's St. Stephen's Cathedral and Stephansplatz in dusky late afternoon light—an early-twentieth-century print that my father particularly loved and displayed as a central icon on the wall of our family room in La Paz. It seemingly never occurred to my father and mother, and certainly not to me until recently, that there was something incongruous for Jews like us to have the image of a Catholic cathedral occupying a shrinelike space in our home, a position the picture continued to fill even after my family came to the United States and my parents became American citizens. I don't precisely know when they acquired the lithograph—apparently my father had received it in payment for some work he did for another Austrian refugee not very long after arriving in Bolivia—but I remember the picture from very early childhood, its identification with "beautiful old Vienna," my father's estimation of its potential value as a signed artist's proof, and the sense of wonder it inspired in my imagination about a city that I had never seen, in which I had almost been born, and about which my parents, relatives, and their friends spoke so often and with such immense nostalgia.

Sifting through the other items, I also found five of my childhood books. One is in Spanish, in large print on war-time paper now yellowed by age: *Beethoven: El Sacrificio de un Niño* (*Beethoven: A Child's Sacrifice*), an illustrated biography of the young Beethoven who, together with Mozart, Schubert, and Johann Strauss the Younger, had been in my father's small pantheon of composers whose music was "worth hearing" and whose prodigious talents as child pianists I secretly fantasized to have somewhere within me as well, dormant, awaiting only discovery and a piano (which we did not possess). Two other books, an illustrated German children's edition of *Grimm's Fairy Tales* and Frida Schanz's *Schulkindergeschichten*, both printed in Gothic script, were read to me for many months by my grandmother Lina, during late afternoons and evenings in our apartment on the Calle México, moments that I can still recall with tremendous affection and pleasure. These two volumes and the *Beethoven* biography were undoubtedly books I had been given after I had already learned to read. But two others—Wilhelm Busch's *Max und Moritz: Eine Bubengeschichte in sieben Streichen* (*Max and Moritz: A Boys' Tale in Seven Episodes*), published in Santiago de Chile by refugees, using Busch's original illustrations and text, and a European edition of Heinrich Hoffmann's *Der Struwwelpeter* (*Slovenly Peter*)—were, according to my mother, brought to Bolivia as gifts for the newly born me. I associate these two cautionary tales with my youngest formative years: they literally were my first books.

Tattered, mended with tape, fragile with age and use, *Max und Moritz* contains what is probably the earliest existent example of my own handwriting—my nickname, POLDI, printed in capital letters in pencil on the flyleaf. I don't know when I wrote this, but next to my name, in smaller letters, I also tried to write "Y PUPPI" (in a kind of Spanish blended with German) to indicate that the book also belonged to my sister, Elly, born in 1944 and affectionately referred to as "*Puppe*," "Doll." The *Struwwelpeter* is, perhaps, in even worse shape from repeated handling and intensive examination, having emerged after its numerous "readings" detached from its spine-binding, with its title page missing, and with my preliterate, spiderweb-like scribblings in pencil spread over the illustrations on its cover and first page. Its status as a scarred veteran is unmistakable. Like its contemporary survivor, *Max und Moritz*, it practically demands gentle retirement and kind treatment in old age.

Unlike the other books from my early years, both *Max und Moritz* and

Der Struwwelpeter elicit more in my mind than mere nostalgic memories of childhood innocence and familial togetherness. *Max und Moritz's* rhymed "history" of two terribly nasty, mischievous boys (who in the United States inspired the Sunday comic strips "The Katzenjammer Kids" and "The Captain and the Kids"), and the cautionary tales in *Struwwelpeter* also arouse both sad and quite unsettling feelings within me. In part this is so because these two books, more than any other physical items I associate with my father (who died from cancer at the age of fifty in 1967), bring back vivid memories to me of the *sound* of his voice. They were the children's books he liked to read out loud, works that he reserved as *his* to narrate and from which he recited long passages by heart. Looking at them now, I can again hear the peculiar dramatic sing-song way he modified his regular tone of voice and the expressive resonance on those many occasions when he "performed" sections of *Max und Moritz* and *Struwwelpeter* for us.

My aural memory, of course, comes to me in German:

> *Ach, was muss man oft von bösen*
> *Kindern hören oder lesen!!*
> *Wie zum Beispiel hier von diesen,*
> *Welche Max und Moritz hiessen.*

> Ah, how oft we read or hear of
> Boys we almost stand in fear of!
> For example, take these stories
> Of two youths, named Max and Moritz.

and

> *Sieh einmal, hier steht er,*
> *pfui, der Struwwelpeter!*
> *An den Händen beiden*
> *liess er sich nicht schneiden*
> *seine Nägel fast ein Jahr;*
> *kämmen liess er nicht sein Haar.*
> *Pfui, ruft da ein jeder:*
> *Garst'ger Struwwelpeter!*

> Look at once. Here he stands,
> With his dirty hair and hands.
> Pfui, it's Slovenly Peter!

> See! his nails are never cut;
> And the sloven, I declare,
> Not once this year has combed his hair!
> Pfui, they call in meter,
> Disgusting, nasty, Slovenly Peter![1]

The very sound and familiarity of these rhymes in German make me realize that my childhood books, like the framed lithograph of St. Stephen's
Cathedral in our family room in La Paz, helped to expose and connect me
to a Central European world that my parents and other refugees in
Bolivia had fled but not abandoned. Imperceptibly to me at the time,
unconsciously, they contributed in my early childhood to shape an image
of that world for me, a notion of its proscribed conduct and encouraged
behavior, an impression of its places, customs, objects, and people that
resonated, indistinctly but profoundly, with the refugee memories that
surrounded me.

I lived in La Paz, an Andean city almost two and a half miles in altitude, above which Mount Illimani towered in awesome majesty. I was
born in a place of immense natural beauty and cultural richness, whose
native inhabitants had descended from great Inca and pre-Inca Indian
populations, and from their Hispanic conquerors. I was a citizen of

The book cover of Der Struwwelpeter
decorated with Poldi's scribbles

Bolivia. I expressed myself most fluently in Spanish. And yet, even as a young child, word and image seemed to convey and reinforce a feeling in me that I did not truly belong in this place: that my origins lay elsewhere, and that I was not really at home.

On the other hand, I now realize that what had been cultivated and fortified by the books and images of my early childhood also contained a sense of ambivalence toward Europe and its values—a less attractive, less positive, more apprehensive and disturbing quality. Seeing my penciled scribblings covering the picture of Struwwelpeter—markings defacing the unkempt, blond-haired boy who refuses to permit his bushlike hair and witch-length fingernails to be cut and who is displayed for universal shaming (*"Pfui, ruft da ein jeder: Garst'ger Struwwelpeter!"*)—I remember how fascinated and how very frightened I had been by the moral tales in this book. It was, I am now quite certain, because of the horrible penalty that Konrad pays in *"Die Geschichte vom Daumen-Lutscher"* ("The Story of the Thumb-Sucker") and Paulinchen pays in *"Die gar traurige Geschichte mit dem Feuerzeug"* ("The Truly Sad Story with the Lighter"), that I never sucked my thumbs and was fearful about playing with matches. I still shudder and recall my childhood horror when I see the color illustration showing Konrad's thumbs being cut off with long, sharp scissors in punishment for his thumb-sucking transgression (*"klipp und*

From "The Story of the Thumb-Sucker"

klapp," the text alliterates), and I am aghast on seeing him depicted in the final frame: facing the viewer, a tear falling from his right eye, arms extended, both thumbs missing from his hands, and blood dripping from the stumps.

My reaction to *Max und Moritz* was similarly pleasure tempered by trepidation. I loved my father reciting its episodes; I delighted in the sound of the language and in the humor of its rhymes and illustrations. Yet I feared this book as well—frightened by its violence and sadism. Max and Moritz, the two smiling tricksters and practical jokers who torment widows, torture animals, and inflict searing burns and painful distress on unsuspecting victims, are ultimately punished for their cruelty by being ground up into feed and eaten by the miller's ducks. Some lasting positive lesson, I would like to believe, must have been imprinted on me from this gruesome moral tale. Something of enduring value must surely have been conveyed by its morbid humor and mocking tone. But for a long time (as I subsequently found out from my mother), I wanted the *Max und Moritz* kept in my parents' room; I would "read" it only in the presence of an adult.

I certainly make no claim that my childhood grasp of an outside political world beyond the boundaries of family and acquaintance was in any

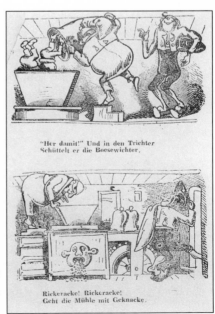

"Her damit!" Und in den Trichter
Schüttelt er die Boesewichter.

Rickeracke! Rickeracke!
Geht die Mühle mit Geknacke.

Feed for Master Miller's ducks: the end of
Max and Moritz

sense extraordinary. Looking at these mementos now, I have no difficulty in understanding my attraction to them at the time, why I found in *Max und Moritz, Der Struwwelpeter*, and my other childhood books such powerful resonances, and imaginary extensions, of the European world from which my parents, relatives, and the other refugees had come. It doesn't really surprise me that they frightened and intimidated me. It is in the nature of cautionary tales and fairy stories to present models of behavior for emulation and avoidance by tweaking, and arousing, some of childhood's fundamental psychological fears. But the *quite extreme* childhood anxiety I associate with my books, my very great dread and apprehension, make me realize that something else may also have been involved: that no "innocent" reading of German children's stories could have taken place within the immigration. How, after all, could it have been possible for recent refugees from Nazi terror to insulate the traumatic aspects of their past experiences in Europe, and their fears about the future, from their children? The people around me, with whom I had the most intimate contact, spoke with one another and in my presence about cruelty and persecution, about the war and relatives left behind, about loss and destruction, about Nazis and Hitler. I was a young boy: certainly I didn't understand much of what they said at the time. But something about the darkness of their tone and the strain in their voices did not escape me. The truly frightening, violent, and sadistic aspects of a world reflected in whispered adult conversation became, for a child of refugees in the early 1940s, a shadow within my imagination. Europe, the culture of Europe, was a lost origin steeped in nostalgia. It was also a fount for my nightmares.

"THE MOON WAS MORE REAL TO US . . ."

Before my parents and other refugees left Europe, Bolivia had been little more than a place on a map of South America for them. They knew virtually nothing about its physical geography or climate and even less about its history, government, and economy. In their eagerness to find a country that would accept them, they had been ready to go anywhere that would permit them to live in safety. "Bolivia—quick, where is it?" Egon Schwarz had asked after receiving his visa from the Paris consulate with the aid of the Hilfsverein. "We would have gone to the moon," the refugee Andres Simon recalled. "Bolivia was a closer possibility, but the moon we saw every night. It was more real to us." "I knew about Bolivia what you know about the North Pole," Renata Schwarz said to me. "Maybe you know more about the North Pole."[2]

If the refugees knew anything at all about the inhabitants of the country to which they were emigrating, it was either extremely limited or stereotypical. My father, like many others, met his first "real" Bolivian national at the consular office—in his case in Munich, where he had gone from Vienna to acquire the four visas that allowed him, my mother, and his parents to leave Austria. Many, perhaps most, refugees had only a remote and impressionistic sense of the cultural and ethnic milieu they were entering. Spanish-speaking, Catholic, Indian: these were terms they vaguely associated with the inhabitants of the country offering them asylum. But they were merely broad descriptions, generic identifiers that hardly prepared the refugees for the immense cultural and social differences they would have to face. Their preconceptions of Bolivia and its people were shaped by information that varied greatly in reliability and perspective. Some of it came from old, half-forgotten world geography and world culture lectures they had heard in school, or from photographs and descriptions in widely circulated German travel books from the 1920s with intriguing titles like *In Darkest Bolivia* (*Im dunkelsten Bolivien*) and *From the Jungle to the Glaciers of the Cordillera* (*Vom Urwald zu den Gletschern der Kordillere*).[3] More up-to-date but not necessarily more trustworthy information came in letters from those who had preceded them to Bolivia or from the second- and third-hand retelling of the contents of such letters. Some information was acquired "post visa," by looking up the entry "Bolivia" in encyclopedias and geographical atlases or from information in the pamphlet *Jüdische Auswanderung nach Südamerika* (*Jewish Emigration to South America*), especially prepared in Berlin for emigrating Jews by the German-Jewish Hilfsverein. In that publication they would have been able to read:

BOLIVIA

Bolivia is one of the poorest, least developed, and for a long time, least stable of the South American lands. The economic importance of the country derives predominantly from its abundance of valuable minerals, particularly tin. As a consequence, possibilities for professional employment are best for technicians, chemists, and others who might be retrainable for mining-related work; they are less opportune for manual workers and farmers.

Up to now, relatively few German-Jewish immigrants have reached the country. Owing to the extremely high altitude at which they are located, the most promising regions of this land can only be tolerated by persons with a very strong heart and healthy lungs . . .

Bolivia is the country with the greatest percentage of pure-blooded Indians in its population. Indians and persons of mixed-racial background live in primitive cultural circumstances.[4]

But images of Bolivia and its inhabitants also derived from widely disseminated, highly romanticized adventure literature—a literature that routinely represented the landscape and people of South America as mysterious, primitive, exotic if not forbidding, and that simplified or blurred the particularity and diversity of both. Werner Guttentag, for example, who emigrated from Germany to Bolivia via Holland in 1939, decided before leaving Europe that he would move to the city of Cochabamba (where he still resides) simply on the basis of its relatively central location on the map of Bolivia—which, he relates, he studied closely only after learning that he and his parents had visas to go there. But, as was true with Heinz Markstein, Egon Taus, Julius Meier, and many other young refugees, his most vivid predeparture image of Bolivia's indigenous populations came from reading *Das Vermächtnis des Inka* (*The Bequest of the Inca*) and *In den Cordilleren*, two of the "South American novels" of the prolific and immensely popular German author of adventure books Karl May. May, best known for his numerous "Wild West" thrillers and for his hero "Old Shatterhand"—a fascinating mélange of Teutonic knight and pulp-novel cowboy hero—did not visit North America until long after his retirement as a novelist and never set foot in South America. Although his colorful and seemingly authentic ethnographic representations of Indian peoples and their life were largely invented—the imaginary creations of a fertile mind—they helped to enliven and strengthen popular Central European stereotypes about the "otherness" of American Indians. "One came away from May's novels," Guttentag observed, "confirmed that the glories of the Indians' past were gone, that civilization had passed them by, and that they fit into one of three categories. They were either wild, backward, or noble." For refugees whose preconceptions of indigenous peoples were influenced by this captivating author, it would undoubtedly have seemed highly ironic at the time to discover that Karl

May's works had also been the favorite reading of the young Adolf Hitler—that, according to the cultural critic Klaus Mann, he had indeed been "Hitler's Literary Mentor."[5]

"SO STRANGE, SO UNBELIEVABLY STRANGE . . ."[6]

Heinz Pinshower:
We absolutely didn't know what was awaiting us. We didn't know about the people or their customs or traditions. We did not expect the altitude to be so oppressive. On the train from Arica to La Paz, people's noses and ears were bleeding. Some were hemorrhaging.

Hanni Pinshower:
The Indios. We never had seen anything like them. Already on the train, at stops, a real novelty: we looked at them; they looked at us.

Renata Schwarz:
What immediately impressed me about La Paz was the smell—a terrible impression. The streets smelled horrible. The Indians urinated and defecated in the streets. The women squatted right down in the street, lifted up their skirts, and did their thing. There were no public sanitary facilities. And they brought their llama herds through the streets. And the llamas spit and left their little traces.

The Indian women wore multiple skirts and colorful mantas. They were sometimes beautifully dressed, richly dressed, with gold and silver pins and gold earrings. But they had no culture. They had no civilization.

Werner Guttentag:
I noticed that I was in a black land. Not that the people were Negroes, but so many men and women were dressed in black or dark clothing. Only some time afterward did I learn that they were still in mourning clothes—mourning their dead, casualties in the disastrous Chaco War that Bolivia had fought with Paraguay.[7]

Egon Schwarz:
Music . . . the noise of a never-before-heard, never-ending melancholy Indian music, whose monotone initially grates on the nerves but which one never again forgets after hearing it played night after night for months on end . . .

[Here] practically nothing is as one knows it, either in society or in nature. The person who applies middle European standards to what is seen and experienced will never understand.[8]

La Paz in the early 1940s, with Mount Illimani in the background (Courtesy Foto Jiménez)

Recalling their initial reactions after their arrival in Bolivia, these and other refugees reflected how little in their Central European cultural background or experience echoed sympathetically or gave familiar references to help ease their integration into their new land. Neither the cities nor the countryside reminded them of anywhere they had been before.

Many who had come to landlocked Bolivia by way of Chile experienced their disembarkation and brief stopover in Arica, and then the two-day train journey, climbing from sea level up the Cordillera Occidental of the Andes to more than 14,500 feet, as one of the most unforgettable passages of their life. It was their first corporeal, truly sensual understanding of their physical remoteness from Europe.

Julius Wolfinger:
It was Christmas 1939 when my ship anchored off the coast and hundreds of us were put on boats and landed in Arica. Arica was dry and hot, and sandy like a place in the desert. It seemed very strange. We were met by a refugee, a man from the Jewish immigrant-aid society who had been sent down from Bolivia to handle our transport. And because there were so many of us, he helped to place us in different hotels and residencias all over town, where we had to wait a couple of days until the arrival of the next train from La Paz. The trains usually ran

only two times a week, but our train was late because of a landslide on the tracks.

Funny. What I remember most about Arica were the bedbugs in my hotel room, bedbugs in my bed biting me. I remember the bedbugs more clearly than what Arica really looked like, or how the people looked . . .

The train was very crowded with refugees and luggage. I didn't have a sleeper so I sat up, mostly in the dining car, looking out the window. I think the train had at least two steam locomotives, maybe one in front and one in back, and soon after we left, the train started climbing up and up, going higher and higher. We climbed for a whole day, and then came to Charaña, the border town between Chile and Bolivia, where the train stopped overnight. I remember it was really cold, and I didn't have warm clothes. Some of us, who didn't have sleepers, got off to look for a hotel. But we couldn't find one, and so we slept in a church.

When we returned to the train again in the morning and started off again, I think everyone got sick. I was sitting in the dining car, feeling weak and sick, but also looking at the scenery, wild, harsh. I saw my first llamas and alpacas in the distance, only I didn't know then what they are called. And I was higher up in altitude than I had ever been before in my life, feeling very sick, having a hard time breathing.

I had my head down on the table, my eyes closed, when suddenly in Viacha, on the altiplano, the train stopped and I heard someone come into the dining car shouting, "Julius! Julius!" I looked up, and there stood my two sisters and my brother-in-law! They had come from La Paz by taxi to meet me and pick me up. We had not seen each other since Vienna, for more than a year and a half.

And then, driving along the altiplano at dusk—it was an amazing sight—I saw the yellow and white twinkling lights of La Paz stretched out below us. We were facing

Avenida 16 de Julio: "El Prado," La Paz, early 1940s (Courtesy Foto Jiménez)

Mount Illimani, which we could still see in the distance. We were above the city descending into it, as into a bowl. It was magnificent.[9]

Spectacular nature had a caustic side as well. For incoming refugees, the rugged, severe physical environment was also their first impediment to adjustment. When they first arrived in La Paz, or anywhere in the Andean highlands, most of them came down with altitude sickness—*soroche*—and suffered shortness of breath, sleeplessness, and aches in the head and body, as happened to Julius. Those with lung or heart problems generally found the altitude unbearable. If they moved to Bolivia's semitropical or tropical lowlands, with their high temperatures and humidity, they faced the danger of illnesses for which the temperate-climate disease environment from which they had emigrated had provided no immunity or tolerance. But aside from the adjustment difficulties and medical dangers, it was the immense *foreignness* of the environment that compounded their feelings of alienation—the refugees' sense of being distinct "outsiders," truly strangers in a strange land. Bolivia's various indigenous people looked different, they dressed differently, their customs, practices, festivals, and foods were unfamiliar, they communicated in languages that none of the immigrants had ever heard before, their psychology and worldview seemed unfathomable.[10]

It is July 1941 in Cochabamba. Dr. Heinrich Stern, born almost sixty years earlier in Nordhausem am Harz, Germany, and a recent refugee arrival in Bolivia, reflects in a note written to himself:

The path was rocky and rough, steep and lonely. Now I sit on a rock and look about me. Thorny shrubbery, thicket, tall cactus, stones and stones. In the distance, two, no three, wretched huts; mountains all around, giant, furrowed mountains. The sun sinks lower; its rays bring a magic glow to the peaks. Loneliness, frightful loneliness, and strangeness. In the far distance two women, wrapped in red ochre shawls, climb uphill. Their appearance increases my sense of loneliness, of abandonment. Indianerlandschaft! Indian landscape! My new homeland! Is this my new homeland?

Dark thoughts waltz through my brain. They torment me, they repeatedly knock and sting against my forehead. They circle about the horizon and want to penetrate the distant mountain wall; and they search and ask, The sky above me, is it not the sky of the old homeland? No, it seems to be—or am I only imagining it—more glaring, more poisonous. Only the clouds cast a smile of friendliness on me, reminders

of other environs. But the land remains hostile. A landscape of the uncivilized—
Indianerlandschaft, *Indian landscape. Gigantic, strange, melancholy and lonely.*[11]

It is not difficult to discern in this text the sensibility of Romantic poetry and its emotional language: influences of Herder, the young Goethe, even of Wordsworth's "spontaneous overflow of powerful feeling."[12] The individual—here, Dr. Stern, sitting on a mountainous hillside at dusk—explores his personal emotions in relation to the landscape and the surrounding forces of nature, while seeking to make a connection and to establish some form of balance between them. Stern, after all, was raised in a cultural milieu in which the literature and music of Romanticism had been vital elements of both formal schooling and popular culture; his generation was steeped in the subjective touchtones, the "language of the heart," of the Romantic arts. But, in Stern's contemplation, the encounter with Bolivian nature is hostile and melancholy. In his new setting, he senses that no Romantic balance of forces between individual body and natural environment can be achieved. He perceives himself to be in an alien world, a world of others, an *Indianerlandschaft.* Nothing in it except the clouds seems familiar.

Indeed, the only other human presence, two Indian women in ochre shawls, accentuate his sense of difference and emphasize the cultural distance of his disconnection. He feels alone, abandoned. And the forbidding landscape itself—that "landscape of the uncivilized," as he calls it, capped by the "glaring . . . poisonous" sky above him—appears to reject him, to heighten his nostalgia, to increase his loneliness and his yearning for the homeland he was forced to relinquish.

"Here I sit in captivity. Nations, continents, an ocean separate me from my homeland. Coolly, I try to take into account that hate, cruelty, and misery now reign there. But the heart overcomes the mind. And the heart suffers."[13]

IMAGES OF DIFFERENCE

As I look through the family photos I inherited from my parents, and at photographs of the same vintage in the homes of other refugees or people connected to the Bolivian refugee experience, the widely shared character of immigrant representations of their early encounters with the land

and people of Bolivia is underscored. As in the oral accounts or written memoirs, images of difference predominate. I begin to wonder about the meanings of these images—their contents, their structures, their effects. I note that in albums especially—where sense of period and place is expressed in principles of selection and arrangement—three types of pictures predominate.[14] The first, of the refugees and their relatives, are of course a visual private record, a way of telling about the past, about aspects of family history: birthdays, celebrations, leisure times, scenes of work, occasions with friends and acquaintances. These images connect generations, link the photographer, subject, and viewer, and seem to provide reassurance of survival, familial solidity, and endurance in the aftermath of persecution and forced departure. But the albums also contain numerous photos of nature: of the immense snow-capped peaks—the *cumbres*—of the Cordillera Real, of the rugged starkness of the altiplano, of the precipitous roads and pathways down from the *cumbres* to the lowlands, of Lake Titicaca, of the junglelike vegetation and lush beauty of the tropical forests. And they all include photographs of indigenous peoples: women carrying babies on their backs, families with llama herds, market women in bowler or stove-top hats, children and old people, women and men dressed in elaborate costumes, sometimes in exquisite masks, playing instruments, dancing, performing in fiestas.

How are we to read these photographic images of difference—these many depictions of the Bolivian landscape and its inhabitants? In what manner were they constructed, visually and culturally? What is their point of view and framework? How do they represent the social and physical spaces in which the immigrants and Bolivians encountered one another and made contact? What can they tell us about the refugees' conception of self and others—about the construction of difference itself?

"The intelligibility of the photograph is no simple thing," Victor Burgin has cautioned us in this regard. "Photographs are texts . . . and the 'photographic text,' like any other, is the site of a complex 'intertextuality,' an overlapping series of previous texts 'taken for granted' at a particular cultural and historical conjuncture."[15] Certainly, when examined at a surface level, those many photographs of Bolivian landscapes and Indians simply attest to the intense fascination with which my parents and other refugees viewed the strange physical and human environment they found themselves in. The photographs are *tourist photos* in this sense, within a long tradition of souvenir representation inspired by picture postcards,

A primal world

Snow-capped peaks of the Cordillera Real

illustrations in travel magazines, stereoscopic views, and landscape art. They were intended to convey to the viewer the image "captured" by the photographer—to "show it off," or to recall it as event, to attest to a "being present," to a "having been there."[16] In Susan Sontag's words, as tourist photos they provide "a way of certifying experience" while actually limiting it "to a search for the photogenic."[17] But, as Burgin has theorized, these photographs do also carry a less visible, yet profoundly ideo-logical, encoding. As I review the albums, I note that the nature photos are in fact divided into categories. One concerns the refugees' actual physical presence in the landscape—it shows them "there," miniaturized if not engulfed by the immense scale and power of their natural sur-roundings. It also documents their physical involvement with nature: their recreational excursions into its terrain, their hikes and climbs, their

Miniaturized within the landscape

Engulfed by their natural surroundings

Indian market women

Dancing in fiestas

explorations of its topography. A second grouping is marked by the virtual absence of the human subject, by a concentrated focus on dramatic, spectacular, extreme nature. In photo after photo, it is a primal world, a landscape of towering, often volcanic mountains and scrub-covered hills, of darkly opulent tropical rain forests, of lakeviews within windswept and expansive plains.

The persistent characteristics of these categories of pictorial representation seem to link them ideologically to earlier European imaginings of the South American continent—to discourses about a "wild and gigantic nature" and an "aesthetics of the sublime" that were disseminated into

German literature and the German popular consciousness through nineteenth-century Romanticism and the epic writings of Alexander von Humboldt. It was Humboldt, after all, as Mary Louise Pratt has argued, who "reinvented South America first and foremost as nature," and who scaled down, if not totally erased, the human within it. It was through his immensely popular and influential works—volumes like his *Views of Nature* (1808) and *Views of the Cordilleras and Monuments of the Indigenous Peoples of America* (1810)—and the superbly crafted engravings of natural

"Vue of Chimborozo and Carguairazo," engraving based on Humboldt's sketch, executed by Wilhelm Gmelin. Alexander von Humboldt, *Vues des Cordillères et monumens des peuples indigenès de l'Amerique*, 2 vols. (Paris: F. Schoell, 1810)

"The Quindío Pass in the Colombian Andes," Christian Duttenhofer engraving based on Humboldt's sketch, executed by Josef Koch

phenomena within them that South America was reduced, in Pratt's words, "to pure nature and the iconic triad of mountain, plain, and jungle." Through Humboldt and the Romantics, the "image of [South America as] primal nature . . . became codified in the European imagination as the new ideology of the 'new continent.' "[18]

Despite the refugees' lack of specific knowledge about Bolivia and its peoples before their departure from Europe, therefore, it would seem that their impressions and representations of the Bolivian physical environment and its inhabitants were *translations*, rather than *quotations*, from the world they now lived in. They were translations based on notions of nature and culture, and on ways of seeing and explaining, which, like invisible baggage, they had brought with them to South America. Apparently, the "old geography books" and the "old school lectures" that many of them recall having informed them in a "general way" about their New World destination shaped their perceptions more profoundly than they may have realized. And at still another level, "wild nature"—"captured" in photos, reduced in size, sorted, situated, pasted into family albums, and given permanence—became "wild nature, domesticated." With photographic images they supported an illusion of control.

Another ideological encoding, however, a different discourse, seems to be at work in the photos of the refugees in their excursions into the landscape. The new immigrants—young men and women like my father and mother, Heinz Jordan, Lotte Weisz, Heinz Pinshower, Alex Deutsch, Ella Wolfinger, and many others—are relaxed, gathered in small groups, wading through rivers, climbing rocks, viewing waterfalls, sailing Lake Titicaca, challenging glaciers and mountain summits. They are dressed in makeshift hiking clothes—long-sleeved shirts, sweaters, jackets, long or short pants, heavy shoes—and some of them carry rucksacks or rope, or grasp walking sticks. Sometimes the men wear felt hats, occasionally Tyrolean ones. A rugged and healthy engagement with the outdoors is represented in these photos, and the images project youth, vigor, physical fitness, discipline, a sense of camaraderie, and personal fulfillment.

Were it not for the fact that the people are all recent refugees, the photographs would be nothing more than souvenir snapshots—recollections of fun outings into the variated environments of nature. But shared history and the European youth movement background of so many of the younger refugees seem present, too. It was, after all, a central tenet of the Zionist organizations Ha-Shomer ha-Za'ir and Macabi, to which many of

Vigorous excursions into nature (*left and below*)

these young people had belonged in Germany or Austria, to advocate physical exercise, sports, muscular development, bodily discipline, and physical engagement with nature as a means of Jewish renewal.[19] Are they, in these physical excursions into the rugged landscape, performing according to a notion of personal and social rehabilitation in vogue in

European Jewish (especially Zionist Socialist) youth circles? Are they thinking of themselves as examples of a superior "New Hebrew" physical type—strong, fit, self-confident—Jews invalidating the negative image of the effete, weak, stooped *Yid* reviled by anti-Semites? And, paradoxically, is there perhaps also a trace of the physicality idealized by the German and Austrian youth organizations like the Wandervogel, from which Jews had been recently, and systematically, excluded? The tune and words of a song from my childhood creep into my mind:

> *Das Wandern ist des Müllers Lust, das Wandern,*
> *das Wandern ist des Müllers Lust, das Wandern.*
> *Das muss ein schlechter Müller sein,*
> *dem niemals fiel das Wandern ein, das Wandern,*
> *das Wandern, das Wandern, das Wandern.*

> Hiking is the miller's pleasure, hiking,
> hiking is the miller's pleasure, hiking . . .

This is the opening song of Franz Schubert's *Die Schöne Müllerin*, the song most closely identified with Wandervogel excursions in Europe. My parents and their friends often hummed and sang it during our Sunday ramblings in Bolivia.[20]

The refugees' photographic representations of the physical environment, and of their own engagement with nature, reveal some of the ideological encoding that structured their relationship to the land where they found themselves. But their conceptions of the native "other," and of themselves in relation to that "other," emerge most sharply in their photographs of indigenous people. Whether these photos depict Indians in everyday circumstances—working, caring for children, interacting in small groups, or alone—or costumed and masked at festival occasions, they all have a particular quality. Like the photographs of nature, they seem timeless, with a de-historicized constancy of existence beyond the vicissitudes of the era when they were taken. The people in these images, however, are not de-historicized in the grand sense of a mythic nature or geological time objects but as though they were in an ethnographic deep-freeze, removed and disconnected from a historical past or any claims on a political present. Their diverse cultural backgrounds and the differences among them—whether they are Aymara or Quechua, rural or urban, *cholos* or *campesinos*—are subordinated to a composite notion of "Indianness," a stereotype of racial uniformity in which traces of Karl May's imaginary Winnetou and of numerous representations of America's "Indians" in European popular culture can surely be detected.[21]

The pictures would certainly suggest that encounters with indigenous people occasionally brought legitimate pleasures to refugees like my mother and father: the aesthetics of the occasion, its novelty, color, or adventure may have stimulated their taking and keeping these "Indian" photographs.[22] At the same time, it was a consistent characteristic of these encounters that the photographers—European, white, generally bourgeois, and most probably male—were spectators, people looking, observers in possession of the power to record. Rarely in these photos are refugees visible in the same frame with indigenous people. No relationship between the two is depicted, no mutuality of observation. The "Indians" have been photographed as exotics, for the striking character of their difference, and the inequality of the encounter can be seen in their lack of reciprocity to the camera's gaze. They are the ones being observed;

A day trip to Lake Titicaca with friends and family in 1945

"Indians" in refugee albums

their images are the objects being collected. The refugees, out of the frame, behind the camera, gazing at the "other," enhance their own identity in the perceived contrast, shore up their sense of "civilized" self, and perhaps confirm a vision for themselves that many of them may have begun to question during their trauma of displacement—a vision of European cultural modernity and progress.

EL LÁPIZ DE SANDEN

Curiously, only one professional artist is associated with the refugee immigration to Bolivia: the prolific lithographer and printmaker Walter Sanden. My parents accumulated many examples of Sanden's print art—monochromes produced on brittle wartime paper during the early years of the immigration, as well as more elaborate multicolor lithographs he made later. Although the quality of his output was inconsistent, both my parents believed that this man had truly captured the aesthetic essence of the Bolivian environment: its landscape, architectural diversity, blend of Spanish Catholic and indigenous religiosity, and the lifeways of its Indian inhabitants. Indeed, they found such pleasure in his bold depictions of the Andean world that they brought the prints with them when they reemigrated to the United States and framed a number of them for display.

Looking through these works, which have now passed down to me, I, too, am struck by the evocative quality of Sanden's artistic representations. Characterized by an uncomplicated compositional style, sparse detail, distinct outlines and strokes, and his use of bright orange, yellow, and ochre—colors associated with indigenous *mantas* and skirts—his lithographs seem to capture the range of Bolivia's "typical" scenery. Among them I find a picture of straw-thatched adobe Indian huts with Mount Illimani in the background; various Indian market scenes; the Virgin Mary being paraded by dancing and instrument-playing Aymara; a load-burdened Indian man near a Christian cross on La Cumbre on the altiplano near La Paz; an Indian woman with a child and some animals on Lake Titicaca in a mangerlike reed boat. Sanden's conscious intention, it seems to me, is to overlay his indigenous motifs with Christian imagery and to intensify the sentiment about his indigenous subjects through their posture and attitude. My predominant response *is to their emotionality*, to their feeling and affect, much more than to their art or their ability to remind me of actual places or events. But, unlike my parents, I respond like a person manipulated, quite negatively. Sanden's drawings and prints, even more obviously than the photographs of landscapes and Indians in the family albums and collections, have been mediated by a consciousness grounded in a Central European sensibility enraptured by the exoticism and immense "otherness" of the Bolivian environment. Synoptic in perspective, Sanden's lithographs draw on the lyrical Romantic tradition one hears in Dr. Stern's hillside soliloquy, on the Humboldtian triadic view of nature reflected in the landscape photos, and on the

Four lithographs from *Bolivia Pintoresca: 16 Litografías Originales en Colores* by Walter Sanden, La Paz: Sanden private edition, n.d. [early 1940s?]

timeless, de-historicized, notions of Indian life imagined in European popular culture. I look at these works and see but another version of *Indianerlandschaft*.

And yet there is a more relaxed, less portentous side to Walter Sanden that is much more appealing to me. Using mimeographed duplication, he produced his own comic cartoon and textual commentaries on refugee life-experiences in Bolivia, amusing booklets in a style clearly influenced by the drawings and rhymes of *Max und Moritz*'s creator, Wilhelm Busch. Unlike Busch's sardonic and castigating humor, however, Sanden's comic sense is kinder, less judgmental, more self-mocking. In *Tante Berta wandert aus: ein Abenteuer (Aunt Berta Emigrates: An Adventure)* he depicts the problems of a fictional refugee in Bolivia, Tante Berta—a woman not only caught in a clash of misunderstanding with her new physical surroundings and the lifeways of its indigenous inhabitants, but also confused by the attitudes and reconstituted practices of her fellow immigrants.[23] Hers is a cultural encounter in which newcomer and resident both seem vulnerable, both look "funny" to the other, both seem

Sucre-Mercado   Walter Sanden

La Cumbre   Walter Sanden

Sorata   Walter Sanden

Cover of *Tante Berta wandert aus* (*Aunt Berta Emigrates*) by Walter Sanden

Aunt Berta, quite fit and sound/for there, she lived mostly underground/received from her nephew in South America/a visa to become a planter./But this she could not understand,/since her only farming were chives in a flower stand/or, perhaps a radish when times were hard/and also a cactus—but that's going too far!/So she packed toothbrush, comb, and garters/also clothespins and pajamas/into what may be called her valise./–So, have a good trip, Auntie—please (My free translation)

On the train, Auntie did not feel too well/Four days and four nights, the Devil in hell!/It was crowded and smelly paying second-class fare,/She didn't expect what strange customs were there./And the passing scenery was hardly enticing./Not much else, except cactus and endless horizon (My free translation)

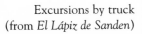

Admiring Mount Illimani

Excursions by truck
(from *El Lápiz de Sanden*)

confused. Where Dr. Stern had cast himself as the lonely, melancholy, romantic stranger within a human and physical landscape he fears to engage, Sanden casts Tante Berta as a comic figure who appears as alien to the Bolivians as they do to her, and who can laugh at her own inadequacies and foibles.

In *El Lápiz de Sanden* (*Sanden's Pencil*), which he produced not long after the end of the war, Sanden presents a series of sketches satirizing various refugee activities in Bolivia: excursions into nature in overloaded trucks on treacherous mountain roads; efforts to jump on packed tramways; frustrations of shopping in crowded markets and confusing stores; their obsessive desire to paint and photograph the same scenic view of Mount Illimani.[24] Here again, contrary to the emotive, highly mediated perspective in his more serious lithographic art, his relationship to his material is more intimate and involving. His often self-deprecating humor permits him to establish a less formal yet more reciprocal connection both with people and with his surroundings. Here, he is neither the superior outsider disdainful of the "primitivism" of his new environment nor the European artist perceiving it through distorting filters brought from a forcibly abandoned home. Instead, in revealing this seemingly lighter side of himself, he is highlighting yet another heritage carried by the refugees to their new land: that particular kind of joking, self-reflexive, and accepting humor known as "Jewish humor"—an engagement with circumstances that, in even the direst of times, proclaimed an intense love of life and a will for survival. It is a strange and often amusing world to which I have come, Sanden seems to be saying. But perhaps it is no stranger than I am. Let's get on with it.

A page from the family album

APPEARANCES

Two young children, holding hands, are standing in a yard by a house. There are plants near them—not in the ground, but in large tin cans. Nature contained. In the background, a woman wearing a dress and apron and holding a pot is partially visible, her shoulders, neck, and head cut off by the top edge of the photograph. One of the children is Indian. She is dark complexioned, black haired, and is smiling broadly, looking directly at the photographer. A knit cap with ear flaps covers most of her hair, and she wears a torn cardigan over an undershirt, and a soiled, ripped skirt. She is barefoot. The other child, blond, fair complexioned, is wearing a light sweater, striped seersucker overalls with cuffs, shiny black shoes, and has a hand in a pocket. He is also smiling—less broadly perhaps—and his eyes look off to the side, away both from his companion and the camera. The blond boy is Poldi, Leopoldo, now known as Leo. I no longer remember the name of the Indian child.

In my father's handwriting, the printed caption above and beneath the photo in the album reads: "*Sechzehn monate! und hab'einen freund!*" ("Sixteen months! and I've a friend!") *Freund* is a masculine word in German; *Freundin* is a female friend. This curious ambiguity—between the Indian child's gender as identified by my father, and gender as indicated by the worn skirt—is possibly inadvertent. But other uncertainties—involving meaning, not identification—attend this photo. "Every photograph presents us with two messages," John Berger tells us, "a message concerning the event photographed and another concerning a shock of discontinuity. Between the moment recorded and the present moment of looking at [a] photograph, there is an abyss." The photograph's ambiguities reside in this "discontinuity," in this "abyss between the moment recorded and the moment of looking."[25]

What could the event in this photographic image have meant for the young Indian child? What was its meaning for Poldi? For the photographer? For the person later assembling the album? Were we truly playmates—friends—as the caption insists? Or could the photograph and its description perhaps have been really intended as a commentary on *differences*, on our obvious racial and class distinctions, as manifested in our contrasting physical appearances and clothing? Did the picture's placement in the album imply that it was as absurd to maintain the possibility of real friendship between "these children" as it was to declare that, at the age of sixteen months, Poldi could *really* write? Alternatively, did this photo and its caption represent one of my parents' immigrant fantasies—their "fairy tale" of New World acceptance and integration: the child of refugees holding the hand of a child of Bolivia's indigenes? If so, it was a fairy tale marred by a frightening and violent reality. This young Indian, whose name or gender I am unable to recall, was killed not long after our photo was taken, hurled to the street from a second-story balcony by the crazed son of our landlord. Our picture together, smiling, holding hands, may be this child's only image in existence.

The discontinuity between that moment when our photograph was taken and the *now* when I attempt to "read" it extends over a period of fifty years. As I try to make sense of this photo in the larger context of the refugee experience in Bolivia—indeed, as I try to make sense of all the memorabilia I've inherited and documentary evidence I've collected—I once again become conscious of my duality in this project. I am a participant *in* as well as a historian *of* the immigration. I would like to think that the roles can be separated, that my professional self can maintain enough distance from my participant subjectivity to enable me to examine, analyze, and render historical judgments in a dispassionate manner. Yet I know this is impossible. The historian I am tells me that friendship between the Indian child and Poldi will never be, that in this instance as in so many others associated with the refugee experience, layers of meaning complicate the seemingly obvious and matter-of-fact. But I also realize, as participant, that yet another kind of invisible baggage needs to be taken into account. Subjective feeling, the personal realm, and the uncertainty of appearances also inform and enhance what I can know and tell about the past. They make up baggage I would not want to eliminate or ever leave behind.

4

"BUENA TIERRA"

DEEP IN THE JUNGLE . . .
Early 1940s.

They were in a place that they could hardly have imagined only a few months earlier back in Europe: an agricultural colony for Jewish refugees in the Yungas, a humid region of lush semitropical vegetation and astonishing vistas lying in deep, undulating valleys northeast of La Paz, between the immense Andes of the Cordillera Real and the rain forest in Bolivia's northern territory. In the evenings after a long day of hard work, they would often sit together by a kerosene lantern, conversing or reading. "I was one of the few who brought books along," the resident physician Dr. Eduard Blumberg recalled of his stay there. "They were in great demand, and not always returned to me after they were borrowed." The colonists were in an isolated spot, but it was never silent when dusk fell on the thickly forested hillsides surrounding their new settlement. Darkness was a time for monkeys to swing and shriek, for insects to buzz and high-pitched bats to fly in search of them, for rodents to emerge, and snakes to slither through the bushes. Seasonally, for weeks at a time, rain poured down during these evening hours, drumming with deafening loudness on the tin rooftops of their houses—torrential, sometimes frightening, with blasts of thunder and brilliant lightning. But when the weather cleared, the colonists would gather every fortnight or so by the veranda of the doctor's house for a musical evening organized by the settlement's schoolteacher, by the man they affectionately nicknamed "Stoepsel," "the Cork," no doubt because of his inordinate

affection for wine. On the wind-up gramophone and speaker that he had some-
how acquired and brought along to this hard-to-reach outpost, he played his
classical-music records for them. And "tief im urwald," "deep in the jungle" (as
they referred to the settlement), in lantern-illuminated darkness, far from "civ-
ilized" Europe now engaged in war and unmitigated horror, they listened to
Beethoven and Schubert and Mozart in polyphonous engagement with nature's
sounds. "Our mood, in the magnificent tropical night," Dr. Blumberg
observed, "was always festive."[1]

JEWISH IMMIGRATION, AGRICULTURAL COLONIZATION

Born in Germany in the 1890s, Dr. Eduard Blumberg, his wife, Trude, and
their two daughters arrived in Bolivia in mid-1939. Some years before
Hitler came to power in 1933, he had earned a university medical degree
and set up a practice in his home city, Leipzig, where he had provided services largely to workers and families affiliated with the Social Democratic
Party, of which he had been an active member. But with the consolidation of Nazi power and especially after the passage of the Nuremberg
Laws, he and all other academically trained Jews were increasingly
restricted—and finally, in 1938, totally forbidden—from their professions. Blumberg was additionally stigmatized and endangered by his
Socialist affiliation and past work, and he was arrested and sent to
Buchenwald concentration camp in the roundup that followed *Kristallnacht* in November 1938. Only after Trude managed to acquire Bolivian
immigration visas for him, herself, and the children, and had signed over
the couple's capital possessions and given the necessary assurances to Nazi
officials that they would be leaving Germany permanently, was he
released. He had been incarcerated for five weeks and was warned by his
Nazi jailers never to reveal what he had experienced there.[2]

Ironically, upon his arrival in Bolivia, limitations on Dr. Blumberg's
professional activities continued. Despite the country's great need for
medical personnel, Bolivian laws restricted immigrant medical doctors
from entering general practice, which could be done only by Bolivian
nationals or naturalized citizens who had passed a qualifying examination
before a licensing board composed of Bolivian members of a university
medical faculty. The examination was given in Spanish, of course. In

effect, this meant that most of the medical doctors (about a hundred) who came to Bolivia during the peak years of the refugee immigration were legally unable to practice. A few of them got appointments at universities under a stipulation that they would confine their activities to instruction or research; some forty or fifty of them received state appointments as military medical personnel or doctors in government employ sent to work in remote areas of the country where Bolivian doctors were unwilling to practice.[3] Indeed, after an initial short period of unemployment, Blumberg himself was offered a position as medical doctor in the government service and, with Trude (as his nurse), was sent to Charazani, a remote village in the semitropical Muñecas valley of the southern Yungas.

Soon the Blumbergs learned that a newly founded organization, the Sociedad Colonizadora de Bolivia, Bolivian Colonizing Corporation, or SOCOBO—which had some months before been established under the collaborative sponsorship of Mauricio Hochschild, the German-Jewish Bolivian mining magnate, and "the Joint" (the American Jewish Joint Distribution Committee in New York, or JDC)—was looking to hire a medical doctor for a Jewish refugee agricultural colony being established in the north Yungas. Dr. Blumberg immediately applied for the position and was hired. In December 1940 he and Trude left La Paz for the new colony, which its founders had optimistically named Buena Tierra—Good Earth. The couple would remain its resident medical personnel for the next three and a half years, from the heady, idealistic early days of the inception of Buena Tierra to the disheartening and abject moments of its demise.

In the mid-1930s, some years before this effort to establish agricultural colonies for refugee Jews in Bolivia's underpopulated, undeveloped semitropical regions was initiated, officials of the Bolivian government had tried a similar experiment, also with immigrant settlers, but on a nonsectarian basis. Launched after the conclusion of Bolivia's devastatingly costly war with Paraguay over the Chaco borderlands, this venture was one of a number developed to modernize, build up, and transform the nation after its shattering experience. The Chaco War, which lasted from July 1932 until June 1935, had resulted in Bolivia's loss of the potentially oil-rich disputed territory and had produced immense human casualties. More than 65,000 soldiers, mainly Indian conscripts, had been killed in battle or died in captivity—one out of four of Bolivia's combatant forces—fatalities that, as a percentage of a total population of about 3.25 million at the time, were of a dimension equal to combatant deaths suffered by European nations in World War I.[4] All aspects of the Bolivian social reality—its ideological underpinnings, national beliefs, institutional structures, societal divisions, and political and economic arrangements—began to undergo close reappraisal and challenge. Some younger military officers, veterans of the war, termed themselves "military socialists"; they were essentially populist and reformist and wished, as the historian Herbert Klein has put it, "somehow to atone for the Chaco disasters by bringing the nation a new social justice." Two of them, Colonels David Toro and Germán Busch, seized governmental power in a military coup in 1936 and, advancing this radical reassessment of Bolivian society, explored a number of options for national transformation and economic growth. Busch, especially—the son of a Bolivian woman and a German doctor who had emigrated to Bolivia early in the century—became interested in the idea of attracting European immigrants as agricultural colonists to cultivate and exploit the vast, potentially rich, but largely undeveloped semitropical and tropical areas of the country.[5]

To transform this idea into reality, Bolivian consular officials in Europe were instructed to attract prospective agricultural immigrants with an offer of free land, free transportation within the country, and a one-year maintenance allowance. Around 150 to 200 prospective colonists from Czechoslovakia, Poland, East Prussia, and Germany (including a number of political and Jewish émigrés) came to Bolivia as potential agricultural settlers, where they were assigned to one of two nonsectarian settlements being established at the end of 1936—one on the Ichilo River, in Santa Cruz province, and the other, the Colonia Busch, in the Chaparé region in the vicinity of Cochabamba.

Both these colonizing experiments were short-lived failures. The regions selected were malarial, and many immigrants fell ill from this disease and from other tropical maladies for which they had neither immunity nor tolerance, and they were incapacitated during key construction phases. The locations chosen, far from rail or existing road communication to any of the main regional towns, made transportation of produce extremely difficult and costly, and the government's promise to construct roads was not carried out soon enough to save the colonies from economic collapse. Financial difficulties and constraints also led the government to

cut back, and then to renege, on its promise to support the European settlers during their first year. Most of them gradually abandoned Ichilo and
the Colonia Busch and went to seek their livelihood in the cities.[6]

Despite these failures, the idea of establishing productive agricultural
colonies in Bolivia's less developed lowland regions remained very much
alive. Indeed, the Bolivian consular practice of granting "agricultural
visas" (or illegally selling them above the prescribed fee) by means of
which many refugees arrived after the *Anschluss* and *Kristallnacht*, appears
to have derived from Germán Busch's initial authorization. In 1938 to
1940, though, it was individual Jews in Bolivia, and members of Jewish
refugee agencies, who became the main proponents of "Jewish settlement" in agricultural colonies; this concept became a central component
in Jewish efforts to persuade Bolivia's leaders to continue their admission
of Jewish refugees, and to enlarge the number they were willing to accept
as immigrants. Jewish planners viewed settlement in agricultural colonies
as a means to rationalize Jewish immigration and to manage it at a time
when thousands of refugees were streaming into the country.

The principal driving force behind all this was the powerful, influential German-born Jew Mauricio Hochschild. A long-time resident and
naturalized citizen of Bolivia, Hochschild, together with Simon Patiño
and the Aramayo family, had become one of the "Big Three" mine owners and capitalists who dominated the extraction and sale of tin, Bolivia's
principal export product, as well as of lead, zinc, silver, and other minerals. Originally from a small farming village near Frankfurt, Mauricio
(Moritz) followed in the tradition of several other Hochschilds who were
involved in the buying and selling of minerals, and in ore extraction and
mineral production in Europe and various parts of southern and central
Africa, North America, and South America. His cousin, Zacharias
Hochschild, was a founder of Metallgesellschaft, one of the principal
European ore- and metals-trading companies, and his cousin Berthold
helped the business to expand into the United States, where Berthold set
up and, for years, headed the highly successful American Metal Company—which grew into American Metal Climax, one of the largest mining and metal-producing conglomerates in the world.[7] Mauricio, with
some years of experience in mine management and the metals business in
Australia and Austria, settled in South America after World War I, and
in the early 1920s established himself, initially in Oruro and then also in
Potosí and Tupiza, as a direct buyer and reseller of ores mined by small-

scale private operators. Profiting from this type of marketing effort—called *rescate* (recovery) in Spanish—Hochschild decided to pursue the extraction of minerals as well. Instead of starting out as a small-scale miner on his own, however, he persuaded a number of the individual mine operators working the Cerro de Potosí—that fabulously rich mountain which for centuries had been the leading source of silver for the Spanish Empire and that still contained vast amounts of tin—to amalgamate with him, pool resources, and form the Compañía Unificada del Cerro de Potosí under his management. At about the same time, he also influenced a German smelting company, Berzelius, to develop a new process for smelting tin from previously unextractable low-grade ore, a development that enabled him to acquire a series of abandoned mines and to rework old colonial mining dumps from which he profitably recovered minerals that others would have ignored. By the end of the 1920s, he had amassed a fortune that enabled him to branch out, purchasing mines and investing in metal and ore marketing in Chile, Peru, Argentina, and Brazil. By the late 1930s, his Hochschild Company controlled at least one-third of Bolivia's mineral production, and his mines were estimated to contain ores even more valuable than those of his competitor, the leading producer, Patiño.[8]

Mauricio Hochschild's wealth, of course, also gained him power and

Mauricio Hochschild at the Exhibition of Industrial and Handicrafts Products by Jewish Immigrants, La Paz, October 1943 (Courtesy JDC archives)

access to Bolivia's political and military leadership. But his foreign birth—and, no doubt, the fact that he was also a Jew (albeit a nonpracticing one)—also generated intense jealousy and dislike among some Bolivian nationals. Well over six feet tall, of stocky build, with intense dark eyes and a thick mustache, he was an imposing and forceful presence in any encounter—a polyglot who spoke German, Spanish, English, and French with almost equal facility. Although he was strongly opinionated and outspoken about the character and composition of the refugee immigration to Bolivia, his considerable financial contributions for refugee resettlement and his unmatched personal influence with Bolivian authorities in the highest ranks of government and armed forces, including Presidents Busch and, later, Peñaranda, assured his central position as a consultative—often decisive—figure in all Bolivian considerations relating to refugees throughout the late 1930s and early 1940s.

In January 1939 Hochschild, in collaboration with the Joint, founded a refugee-aid committee, the Sociedad de Protección a los Imigrantes Israelitas (better known locally as SOPRO or simply as "der Hilfsverein"). Backed by an initial allocation of $137,500 from the JDC and $25,000 from Hochschild, SOPRO set up offices in La Paz, in Hochschild-owned quarters, under the administrative direction of Enrique Ellinger, a relative of Hochschild and junior partner in the Hochschild firm. Within a few months, branch offices of SOPRO were established in Cochabamba, Oruro, Potosí, Sucre, and Tarija. In each of these cities, the organization provided either allowances or loans to subsidize new arrivals in need of support, and gave them beds or rooms in SOPRO-leased housing until they could find living quarters of their own. In La Paz SOPRO also established a twenty-bed hospital and a children's home with a day-care center and kindergarten, and in Cochabamba it set up and administered a home for the aged and a vacation and recuperation retreat for refugees needing respite from the high altitude of La Paz or the mining cities of Potosí and Oruro.[9]

In spite of SOPRO's efforts and successes, it quickly became clear to Hochschild, and to the officials of the Joint who visited Bolivia on fact-finding and advisory missions, that the Bolivian "opening" for Jewish refugee immigration was precarious. Both the further acceptance of additional refugees, and the continuing welcome of those already in the country, were being endangered by economic and political factors, as well as by the activities of the refugees themselves. Still recovering from the

SOPRO children's home and kindergarten, Miraflores, La Paz, 1944

Residents and radio at Recoleta, SOPRO Home for the Aged, Cochabamba, in the early 1940s (Courtesy JDC archives)

expenses and immense losses incurred in the Chaco War, Bolivia's national economy was in a particularly serious slump in 1938 and 1939.

How and where the newcomers were to fit and be integrated economically without creating additional hardship and dislocation was thus a key question. How would they make their living without displacing Bolivian workers and tradespeople? Where in Bolivia would they reside to minimize competition and conflict? Though many of their visas specified their conditional admission as "agricultural immigrants," most of the adult Europeans were city-dwellers with no vocational knowledge of farming and little experience of rural life other than as hikers or holiday sojourners. In Europe, before the implementation of Nazi restrictions against the employment of Jews, they had worked in commerce, business, law, medicine, the teaching professions, or the arts—or, like my father and others in my family, they had been "retrained," with Jewish agency help, to be proficient in some type of skilled manual labor.

At first, most of the Jewish immigrants chose to live in La Paz or in Cochabamba, where they tried to get jobs in which their previous work experience, professional training, or vocational skills might be sought and wanted. But the professionals, especially lawyers and artists, were blocked by differences in legal tradition and by barriers of language and custom, and had virtually no chance. Commercial employment, moreover, was hard to find during this period of economic recession. German firms in Bolivia, in sympathy with Nazi practices in Europe, refused to hire Jews, while English and U.S. companies tended to hire their own nationals or, justifiably, people who could read, write, and carry out business in English and Spanish. As for Bolivian enterprises, they sometimes hired immigrants, but, as Mauricio Hochschild pointed out to directors of the Joint early in 1939, they were "loaded with as many refugees as they can hold."[10]

There were, then, few apparent options. Because of the incredibly low wages paid to unskilled Indian laborers, and the harsh exploitation these workers (often referred to as *peones*, or peons) customarily endured, Europeans were largely excluded from the realm of unskilled manual employment. Work could be found for skilled laborers—plumbers, electricians, carpenters, mechanics—and for technicians and engineers, and many refugees found employment, or eventually set themselves up independently, in these fields. Others tried to start businesses of their own, opening small restaurants, inns, pastry and coffeehouses, tailoring and hatmaking shops, retail and used-clothing stores, watch and jewelry repair shops, lending libraries: establishments that generally did not compete with businesses owned by Bolivians and that filled a void or "need" within the Bolivian entrepreneurial landscape.

But it seemed apparent to Hochschild and to his people at SOPRO in

La Paz that the refugee immigration into Bolivia was out of control. Refugees were arriving in larger numbers and more quickly than could be accommodated. In La Paz, Hochschild observed, unemployed refugees "fill the streets, the coffee houses, and the few hotels . . . and naturally create antisemitism." This was exacerbated, he wrote at the time, by the fact that the incoming refugees also included "persons of the wrong kind," "thieves and other crooks," as well as "less refined . . . Polish Jews, for which there was no necessity whatsoever." Like so many other Jews from Germany and Austria, Hochschild did not hide his prejudices against *Ostjuden*, East European Jews, whom he collectively considered inferior in culture and breeding to the more highly assimilated German speakers. These "undesirables," he argued, blemished the reputation of Jews in general among Bolivians, placed the continued acceptance and residence of the refugees in Bolivia in question, and endangered the future of the immigration itself. A few Bolivian newspapers were already, he said, publishing articles and editorials that were anti-immigrant in content and anti-Semitic in overtone, generally arguing that too many immigrants were being allowed to enter the country, that some officials were enriching themselves from the sale of visas (which was indeed true), and that "immigrants on agricultural visas should be compelled to satisfy the condition of their admission, to abandon the cities, and to take up work in agricultural settlements."[11]

After considering all these factors, Hochschild himself soon concluded that the establishment of productive Jewish agricultural colonies and the resettlement of Jewish refugees away from La Paz and Cochabamba—in more remote and less populated areas—would be the most rational and effective response to the seemingly unbridled refugee influx and the problems associated with it. He decided to initiate a pilot project as quickly as possible using SOPRO as his implementing agency: an agricultural training farm, "Caiconi," in the Miraflores suburb of La Paz accommodating twenty-five refugee "pupils" in its first training session. This "model farm" expressed Hochschild's dual goals explicitly: to adapt "to agricultural life . . . young people who aimlessly and without occupation fill . . . the streets of La Paz," and to "instruct them in the cultivation of vegetables" before their transfer, as agricultural colonists, into the interior of the country.[12]

At the same time, SOPRO, again with Hochschild funding, set up a second agricultural training center—initially with eight men—near Todos Santos, in the subtropical Chaparé zone, some two hundred kilo-

Hochschild visiting Finca Caiconi, the agricultural training farm for Jewish refugees in Miraflores, 1940 (Courtesy JDC archives)

meters northeast of Cochabamba. Founded on the basis of an exploratory plan drawn up by a refugee agronomist, Otto Braun, and a follow-up site-study by F. Saphir, an agricultural engineer "lent" to SOPRO by the Jewish Colonization Association (ICA) in Buenos Aires, it was hoped that this settlement would serve as the regional nucleus for a much larger colony for about 5,000 Jewish families. Eventually, its planners optimistically estimated, the fertile and potentially productive soil of the Chaparé zone (which Saphir had described as "a paradise") could sustain "a minimum of 17,000 families"—or about 50,000 Jewish immigrant settlers, eight to ten times the total number of refugees in Bolivia at that moment![13]

Hochschild and his SOPRO associates realized, however, that practical implementation of any large-scale Jewish colonization scheme in the Bolivian hinterland could not come about without the sanction and substantive support of two key parties: Bolivian government officials at the highest level, including President Busch; and the directors, in the United States, of the American Jewish Joint Distribution Committee. Hochschild lobbied each of these energetically and, for the most part, quite skillfully. President Busch and other "modernizers" in the Bolivian government—on the basis of their own post–Chaco War colonization plans—were, of course, already aware of some of the potential benefits that productive agricultural settlements would yield to the national economy. But in his private meetings with the president, Hochschild wanted to extract pledges from him for a grant of land for the immigrants from Europe to settle and develop, and for the continued acceptance of additional refugees. He thus not only reiterated the longer-term economic and political advantages Bolivia would reap by fostering immigration and agricultural production, but also held up the possibility of additional, more quickly earned rewards. Bolivia was highly dependent on substantial imports of vegetable foodstuffs from neighboring countries and from overseas, he pointed out—wheat from Argentina and Canada, rice from India, sugar from Java, coffee from Brazil and Colombia. Domestic agricultural production replacing foreign purchases could save approximately $6.5 million annually, which could be invested within Bolivia, which would gain independence and self-sufficiency from this transformation, less vulnerability to the fluctuations in international market prices. And more immediate benefits were also likely. Hochschild explained that the refugee agricultural communities would in large part be underwritten with capital from the Joint in New York and from North American bankers and financiers. If an agreement could be worked out, substantial funds would be sent to the government in short order as an initial indication of their sponsors' "serious intent." And continued cooperation by the Bolivian government in accepting and settling refugees would certainly also ensure favorable results in its transactions with U.S. banking, lending, and investment agencies—goodwill and aid that Bolivia definitely needed during this moment of economic difficulty.[14]

In reporting his conversations with President Busch and government leaders to the directors and administrators of the Joint—and in his effort to win their financial support—Hochschild underscored a topic that officials in the refugee agency were most eager to hear about. He indicated the possibility of continued large-scale refugee immigration into Bolivia, noting that Busch had personally assured him "on various occasions" that 20,000 to 30,000 *additional* refugees would be accepted—if they would colonize undeveloped areas of the country and act as agricultural pioneers. In making this pledge, Busch had promised him land near the Chimoré River in the Chaparé zone "without costs" but had indicated that additional land would have to be purchased.

The establishment of agricultural colonies for Jewish refugees was thus not only an enabling condition for the acceptance of many new refugees in Bolivia, but a mitigation to the potential growth of anti-Semitism there, since it would redistribute Jews, especially those on agricultural visas, away from the cities and into the hinterland. Moreover, the very success of agricultural production in these settlements—and Hochschild repeatedly stressed the importance of demonstrating success as quickly as possible—would be not only beneficial for Bolivia, but profitable for the immigrants. "I am of the opinion," he wrote Paul Baerwald, chairman of the JDC, "that even if Jews who have never done any farming . . . [are] put on the land here, with one or several agronomists who teach them farming and stay with them some time, they will be able to make money and a very good living . . . [within] three years' time."[15] Most important, a successful agricultural effort in Bolivia would influence neighboring countries—particularly Peru and Chile—to follow suit. They, too, might then be willing to expand their acceptance of Jewish immigrants from Europe.

The scale of the agricultural settlement project that Hochschild presented to the directors of the Joint in New York—its estimated cost, chances for success, potential benefits, and the long-range financial commitment the JDC would have to make in order to realize it—stimulated much discussion among them, as well as a desire for further study and evaluation. Hochschild had requested an initial $100,000 from the Refugee Economic Fund of the Joint (and had pledged an additional $25,000 of his own capital) as up-front "show money" to ensure both the ongoing interest and support of Bolivian government officials, and to keep the country's doors open for additional immigration. However, the estimated investment required to expand the Chaparé training center into a colony sustaining 5,000 families came to $7 million, which though certainly not out of the realm of possibility for the financial backers of the Joint, could not be agreed upon without additional investigation and careful consideration. Paul Baerwald wrote Hochschild in April 1939:

> We are all keenly interested in your Bolivian farm settlement project for refugees. So much depends on the success or failure of such enterprises, not only in the country where they are being tried, but also by the ricochet [rebound] action of these results in other potential immigration countries, that one of our experts on colonization has said: "It is wiser not to do it at all than to make a wrong start."
>
> Jewish farm settlement . . . is a much more difficult problem than settlement of peasants of other nationalities. With the latter, it is merely a process of

acclimatization in the new country. With our people, it's a double process: acclimatization and psycho-physiological retraining and readjustment. You cannot drop Jewish settlers on the farm as you could peasant families and leave them to take care of themselves. Without a competent technical organization inspired by a genuine human interest in the matter to guide and direct them, Jewish settlers have a much greater chance to fail than to succeed.

It was thus not until March 1940, after nearly a year's delay marked by an on-site investigation by a Joint expert and additional negotiations between Hochschild and JDC officials, that the Sociedad Colonizadora de Bolivia (Bolivian Colonizing Corporation) was finally founded in La Paz. SOCOBO was intended to see to the "settlement, training, oversight, and management of refugees in agricultural colonies," and was set up as a corporate entity able to enter into contracts and formally take over settlement-related matters that had previously been carried out on an ad hoc basis through SOPRO.[16]

By this time, the war in Europe that had begun seven months earlier had virtually closed off the possibility of refugee emigration from the German Reich, and the many German Jews who had found temporary asylum in neighboring European countries as well as new victims seeking refuge from the Wehrmacht's push into Poland and Eastern Europe became a central focus and concern of the Joint and other refugee-aid organizations. Within Bolivia itself, much had occurred in the course of that year that directly affected the original colonization plan, as well as the future of the refugee immigration itself. The initial site in the Chaparé, which had been chosen because of its potentially productive soil and envisioned as the "entirely suitable" location for the settlement of thousands of refugee colonists, had proven less than ideal. Some of the problems that had crippled and finally destroyed the Colonia Busch, the earlier government-sponsored settlement in this area, recurred. Endemic diseases and access difficulties because of deficient or unfinished roads were major impediments to growth here as well, and money to mitigate or overcome these obstacles remained unavailable.[17] And moreover, in an event that had profoundly shocked the nation, Bolivia's president Germán Busch had died in August 1939 under mysterious circumstances—allegedly by suicide. The man who, on the basis of his personal power and through his personal word, had repeatedly promised that thousands of additional Jewish refugees could come to Bolivia as agricultural settlers, and who had pledged land to enable this possibility, was dead.[18]

When SOCOBO came into existence, therefore, the plan to establish the settlement in the Chaparé was indefinitely shelved, though Hochschild and his associates believed that the establishment of a functioning colony was now more than ever a necessity. The reluctance of the directors of the Joint to commit themselves beyond an initial $100,000 for this purpose irked the mining magnate, and he wrote to James N. Rosenberg, chair of the JDC Trustees for Agro-Joint:

> We have brought in, mostly into [La Paz], between 9,000 and 10,000 Jews against the promise to the Government that they would be colonized on the land and that the funds necessary [for this] would be put at our disposal by the Jews of the United States.
>
> Unfortunately, we have not been put in a position to comply with that promise, with the result that the . . . Jews now in La Paz are filling the coffee houses, the few available dwellings and, in order to make some sort of a living, are doing some peddling. Besides, quite a number of them have proved to be of a pretty bad character and some of them are crooks.
>
> When I arranged with the Government that we could bring in a total of 30,000 Jews for colonization, I fully realized that we would have some anti-semitism in Bolivia, but I never dreamt of what has come since. However, we cannot only blame the Bolivians for this state of affairs. It is not for nothing that I have begged all along . . . [for cooperation to] build up that colonization project . . . But only the insignificant amount of $100,000 has been placed at my disposal, and with that we can but colonize about 100 to 150 families—or perhaps 400 people out of the thousands who are already here . . .
>
> Where I formerly had expected that we would make a real big colonization in Bolivia . . . [and] set an example to the surrounding countries that would induce each of them also to take tens of thousands of Jews . . . the lack of money [has made this impossible].[19]

Nonetheless, even before SOCOBO's legal incorporation had been achieved, its administrators in La Paz hired an agronomist, Felipe Bonoli—a naturalized Argentine of Italian-Catholic origin who had founded a very successful agricultural colony for Italians in Argentina—to help them locate a new site for a settlement, and to be its manager and agricultural authority. Bonoli headed to the Yungas, in the semitropical lowlands northeast of La Paz. Here, by the Guarinilla River, in a division called Pacallo, he was shown three adjoining haciendas—Charobamba, Santa Rosa, and Polo Polo—on which coffee, cocoa, mangoes, oranges, tangerines, bananas, and coca had once been cultivated but which had now largely fallen into neglect and were being offered for sale. Based on Bonoli's expert advice that the rich soil on these old haciendas could be reclaimed and their agricultural production further expanded, the properties were purchased by SOCOBO and collectively renamed Buena Tierra. The total area purchased for $16,291 had initially been estimated at some 4,000 hectares. After a proper survey, it turned out to be only 1,000 hectares, of which only some 425 were fit for cultivation; the remaining land—virgin forest on rocky soil—was virtually uncultivatable.[20]

Early in April 1940, the first thirty-five Jewish settlers arrived at the site of the depot for the erection of the future agricultural colony. Together with Indian contract workers hired from nearby settlements and from as far away as villages near Lake Titicaca, they began to recondition the old hacienda residences, build new housing for incoming settlers, and to reclaim previously cultivated land for replanting. By the end of July, wives and families who had stayed behind in La Paz began to join the first colonists. Walter Weiss, who visited the settlement then as a field investigator of the Joint's Refugee Economic Corporation, was immensely impressed by the energy and enthusiasm manifested by Felipe Bonoli and these "pioneers," and he was awed by the physical beauty of Buena Tierra's site. "Not only is the soil long-rested and fertile," he wrote, "but there are more level areas than are usually found in the region, and numerous fresh mountain streams running in abundant quantities. At every point, there are beautiful views—nowhere in our far West have I seen more wonderful panoramas![21] The capacity of the new colony was estimated at 250 to 300 families (1,000 to 1,500 persons), and Weiss was optimistic that many among the refugees then in La Paz and other Bolivian cities—enticed by possibilities of low-cost housing, land, and the opportunity for a new livelihood in a "paradisaical setting"—would soon begin to be drawn there.

He was to be profoundly mistaken.

THE PROMISED LAND

The journey to the colony was often a nightmare, particularly in the initial years. The road to Coroico . . . was in questionable condition at the time, especially during the rainy season when it was frequently blocked by mud slides. When this happened,

everyone—chauffeurs as well as passengers—had to descend and begin to shovel.
And since traffic was generally backed-up by the mud slide, it was not unusual to see
a hundred men working to clear the road.[22]

Even today, when one travels by auto from La Paz to Coroico, the tranquil village in the north Yungas that was the largest urban settlement near Buena Tierra, the journey can be a terrifying one. The highway, mainly used by buses and trucks loaded with goods and packed with passengers, initially climbs from the capital city to a high point over 15,000 feet at La Cumbre, and then begins its steep descent, often through layers of white clouds, into green, lushly vegetated valleys that slowly reveal themselves far below. In large part the road of hard-packed rock and dirt is still unsurfaced, and except for an occasional pull-out is still only wide enough for one vehicle. The vertical scenery is stunning, breathtaking to those with nerve enough to look down to admire it. Snaking its way downward, bend after bend, toward the semitropical lowlands, the road passes under dangerous rocky outcroppings and small waterfalls that can rapidly swell during the rainy season and set off mud slides, and it is edged by sheer drop-offs thousands of feet deep. In numerous spots along the way, it is marked by monumental crosses—memorials to accidents that one waggish writer of travel guides identified as "Bolivian caution signs," and which, in their grim fashion, attest to the fact that travel on this road is not an easy journey to undertake.[23]

To reach the old Charobamba hacienda and the nucleus of Buena Tierra, as the first Jewish settlers and, later, Dr. Blumberg and his family and others had done, one got off one's motor transport (generally, a truck) at a place called Achachicala, some miles past Coroico on the road to Caranavi—where a large storage depot used for the colony's building materials and supplies was located—and then set off on foot or mule-back for an approximate hour-long climb on a path to the colony. Less than sixty miles from La Paz as the crow flies, Buena Tierra was some five to six hours removed in actual travel time, and worlds apart in its climate and physical environment.

From the very beginning, the construction of an automobile road network between the colony and the depot, linking it up with the La Paz–Coroico highway, and between the three haciendas that together made up Buena Tierra, was considered an essential priority. Eventually,

Road construction to Buena Tierra colony, 1941. With the caption "The Road to Independence," Joint officials used this photo to solicit monetary contributions for refugee-relief projects in Latin America during the war years (Courtesy JDC archives)

but more slowly and with much greater difficulty than had been anticipated, portions of this auto roadway—as well as several bridges—were built and brought into service. During the dry season especially, they eased some of the difficulties in transporting produce, goods, and laborers in and out of Buena Tierra, but even then, travel time between La Paz and the colony was still impossibly long, and the settlers felt a profound physical isolation.[24]

Dr. Blumberg, his wife, Trude, and their two girls were assigned to live in the old Charobamba hacienda building, initially sharing the public spaces in this house with Ludwig Capauner, the expert in charge of lumbering and the sawmill, and with the land surveyor, Jaime Gottlieb. Dr. Blumberg saw his patients, and occasionally did surgery, in a renovated small adobe hut nearby that had once been inhabited by an Indian family, and only occasionally had electricity from the diesel generator that supplied power to the entire settlement. He had brought his own medical instruments along to Buena Tierra, including a microscope he had managed to bring out of Germany, which he used to identify and verify some of the tropical illnesses afflicting his patients. Since his patients included all the settlers in Buena Tierra, as well as the Indian laborers working for SOCOBO, he was in considerable demand—frequently to solve problems for which his European training and his Leipzig practice had certainly not prepared him. When smallpox broke out among Indians living near Buena Tierra, he inoculated the entire population of the colony and the neighboring Indian settlements against the disease—only to learn, to his great chagrin, that the vaccine the Ministry of Health had sent him was old and only partially effective. He treated cases of malaria and tropical skin diseases, and once, with Trude and the settlement's dentist, Mrs. Altman, assisting him, he amputated fingers from the shattered hand of an Indian youth who had been playing with road-construction dynamite. A few times during his years at the colony, he was also called upon to circumcise Jewish male babies.

But, as Dr. Blumberg later wrote to a relative, despite his very rudimentary medical office and the challenges he faced in treating illnesses for which he had little or no previous training and experience, he felt "happy and lucky to be able to practice his profession legally." His positive attitude extended into his family life and was shared by his wife and daughters. "Our personal life there, mine and the family's, was exceedingly happy," he recalled. "By origin and education we were city people, but with a liking for nature and country life. It was evident to us that in a place like Buena Tierra, we would have to make some sacrifices."[25]

While Dr. Blumberg and his family, and a handful of others with administrative jobs, lived in housing that antedated the establishment of Buena Tierra, other settlers lived in new housing especially constructed for them. Families, or pairs of single settlers, were assigned small houses built of adobe (a mixture of loam and manure), with cement floors and roofs of corrugated zinc-plate; each had two rooms, a terrace, kitchen with running water, sanitary installations, and an outside shower, and each—"solidly built, rain proof, spacious, and airy," as Manfred Wihl of SOCOBO described them—was furnished with beds, a table, chairs, a lamp, and tools and implements for the agricultural work. Every household received a stock of ten to twelve chickens, five to six ducks, and cash to buy a mule, needed for local transport and work. SOCOBO also subsidized settlers with a monthly payment of 1,000 to 1,200 bolivianos per family (42Bs in 1940 equaled roughly U.S. $1), a small clothing allowance, free medical treatment and medication, and free transportation from the colony to La Paz. In addition, SOCOBO also installed a

pulpería (company store) in Buena Tierra, where settlers, colony administrators, and the company's Indian workers could buy foodstuffs and articles at reduced prices and on limited credit. Within a short time, other
small service establishments—a bread bakery, shoe-repair shop, carpentry, and a metal and mechanical workshop—sprang up as well.[26]

Day by day, the sense of removal and physical isolation that the settlers
felt about living in Buena Tierra—combined, perhaps, with the sense of
shared adventure and "special experience"—acted like a bonding agent,
drawing colonists of different ages, origins, and social backgrounds
together into a close, mutually supportive community. "They get along
well with each other," reported Walter Weiss of the Joint after visiting the
colony a few months after its inception, an assessment that was repeated
nearly four years later by David Stern, another Joint evaluator. "Their discipline . . . is excellent [and I] witnessed no grumbling or bickering of any
kind. They live together like a large family." "Communal life, especially
among the women, was quite lively," observed Dr. Blumberg. "People visited each other often, and when they lived far apart within the colony [in
Charobamba, Polo Polo, or Santa Rosa] they rode on mule-back to meet
and socialize. The young people had their own camaraderie and social life
which, in some cases, led to life-long friendships, even romances. It was
in this way that [my daughter] Ruth found in Laci Dornbush her life's
companion, as did Marianne Capauner in Walter Emmerich."[27]

The wind-up gramophone and the recordings that "Stoepsel," the
schoolteacher, had brought to Buena Tierra not only drew people together
on the Blumbergs' veranda for subtropical evenings of European classical
music but entertained them with lighter fare on Saturdays, with Vienna
waltzes and "old-time" popular music to which they occasionally danced.
Every so often, Mr. and Mrs. Kahnemann, who had both been actors in
their previous life in Germany, performed skits and did dramatic readings.
("They are good actors, but not suitable for work as farmers," was David
Stern's judgment of them in his 1944 report.) People also gathered to listen to European war news and national news on the shortwave radio
installed in the Charobamba hacienda, which functioned only during the
limited hours when the generator was operating. Stimulated by the radio
reports or by an article in *Rundschau vom Illimani* reaching Buena Tierra
from La Paz, discussions of events in Europe occasionally took place as
well. "Jewish problems," particularly regarding anti-Semitism and what
the future might entail for Jews everywhere, were the topical focus of many

In its solicitations, the Joint Distribution Committee captioned this photo: "Jewish Pioneers in South America: Amid the primeval wilderness on the slopes of the Andes Mountains in the far interior of Bolivia, 123 men, women and children, refugees from Europe, are building new lives in the colony of Buena Tierra. One of these refugee families is shown at a meal consisting of the products of the farm they have carved out of the wilderness. Facilities for many more refugees are available at Buena Tierra" (Courtesy JDC archives)

Clearing for a new poultry farm, Buena Tierra, 1943 (Courtesy JDC archives)

The carpentry shop at Buena Tierra, December 1941 (Courtesy JDC archives)

At work at Buena Tierra, January 1943. The original JDC caption read: "Shedding Their Woes: On their farm in the Bolivian mountains, distant, both physically and spiritually, from the Nazi persecution and bestiality, Jewish immigrants are shown husking corn, one of the products of their agricultural toil" (Courtesy JDC archives)

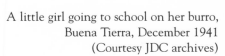

A little girl going to school on her burro, Buena Tierra, December 1941 (Courtesy JDC archives)

of these group gatherings. Still, "the majority of colonists were not very devout," related Dr. Blumberg, "and Jewish practices tended to remain the private concern of a few families."[28]

But even though little predilection for organized Jewish *religious* activity seems to have existed among the settlers, religious holidays gave them opportunities for social gathering and communal interaction. Twice a year, on the Jewish High Holidays of Rosh Hashanah and Yom Kippur, they congregated for services in the rooms of the Charobamba house set aside as the colony's school and teacher's residence, and on the eve of Passover, they came together for a communal Seder. Sabbath services—with readings from a Torah scroll that had been brought to the colony—were also held from time to time.[29]

In their collective encounters, as well as in smaller groups and at home, the refugee settlers primarily spoke German with one another. German was also the predominant language of instruction in the two-grade colony school—although the teacher, himself a recent immigrant, also taught in Spanish. The reliance on German, of course, was initially based on necessity. Few recent refugee arrivals in Bolivia spoke Spanish with any fluency—and certainly none who went as colonists to Buena Tierra knew Aymara, the principal and, oftentimes, only language spoken by the Indian contract-laborers. But for the settlers here, as for many of their fellow refugees from Central Europe in La Paz and other Bolivian cities, communication in German also reinforced their cultural connectedness and helped to mitigate differences in background. It strengthened their sense of common identity and community within a physical and cultural environment in which they were indeed strangers.

Despite the language barriers, Dr. Blumberg and a number of his contemporaries noted that relations between the Jewish refugees in Buena Tierra and the indigenous country-folk in the colony's workforce and surroundings were generally positive. "The [colonists] work well with the Indians," Walter Weiss reported to the Joint, "and that is very important."[30] Spanish was the language of communication between the two groups, Blumberg recalled—which sometimes created misunderstandings, since neither group was proficient in it. Indeed, he noted, colonists frequently addressed the indigenous people in German—or in German laced with Yiddish—with amusing results, as when he overheard an Indian man using this linguistic mixture to call his mule, "*Kommherien, meschuggener Fisch!*" ("Come in here, you crazy fish!").[31]

The lack of hostility and the ability of settlers and Indians to "work well with each other" did not mean, of course, that the cultural and social distance between the two groups narrowed or that anything beyond a most superficial understanding of each other's life worlds resulted. Living in a colony within a subtropical rain forest, in a realm of lush nature and high humidity inhabited by strange insects, snakes, monkeys, colorful birds, and wild animals, the settlers maintained their own sense of "civilization"—of "culture," "modernity," "advancement"—with few, if any, sojourns into a realm they generally contrasted with their own, and often dismissed as "primitive," "backward," and "less civilized." Far from their origins in Europe, excluded and persecuted in their own homelands, compelled to emigrate and live in a place that at an earlier time would have been difficult to conjure up even in some of their wildest bouts of imagination, the Jewish settlers in Buena Tierra were determined to preserve their "Europeanness," a semblance of European cultural life and existence they nurtured and deeply cherished. Few references to Indians appear in their surviving letters, reports, or other documentation, and no contemporary indigenous perceptions of the European newcomers seem to have been recorded. But clearly, much of the same hierarchical order that characterized "white" dominance and Indian subordination throughout Bolivia and much of South America also existed in the Yungas at the time, and the Jewish refugee-settlers, despite their own social and economic "inferiority" as virtually penniless newcomers in the land, were certainly the racial beneficiaries of this status arrangement.

A FADING DREAM

Before the settlement of Jewish refugees at Buena Tierra had actually begun, Mauricio Hochschild and the various "experts" and officials of SOCOBO and the American Jewish Joint Distribution Committee had assumed that, "with systematic and efficient work," its "pioneers" would become self-supporting agriculturists within a year.[32] The soil had been judged excellent, the property was naturally and abundantly irrigated by fresh and pure mountain streams, insects were "not bothersome," and the climate, despite the humidity during the rainy season, was generally thought to be, as Walter Weiss effusively reported to the JDC, "delightful, with sunny and hot days and pleasantly cool nights."

Felipe Bonoli, the Italian-Argentine agronomist who had selected and assessed the site and was the colony's first manager, had expected that Buena Tierra could produce four "main crops"—bananas, pineapples, tangerines, and coffee—all of which would be shipped and sold in Bolivia's cities and, possibly, exported to neighboring countries. Production and sale of other fruits and vegetables, as well as of cacao and coca from pre-existing orchards, and of lumber from the colony's woodlands, were also foreseen. In addition, Buena Tierra's planners thought that each settler family might eventually raise goats, sheep, and some dairy cattle (dairy products were rare and expensive in Bolivia, and this enterprise potentially quite profitable). Poultry, especially chickens, ducks, and geese for eggs and meat, were also to be raised and marketed.

As late as 1944, David Stern (who had considerable experience with Jewish agricultural settlements in the Middle East), again suggested that each settler might keep goats, sheep, and cattle "on his own plot in a stable similarly as it is done in the mountains of the Lebanon and Djebel el Druse and the hilly areas in Palestine where cattle is kept in the open or in stables permanently without pasture and fed only on green fodder and supplementary concentrate feeds." He recommended cattle "of the best quality"—East-Friesian cows "such as are raised with great success in Ecuador and Colombia and also in [parts of Bolivia], with very good results in milk and fat production."[33]

When a major agricultural exposition was held in Buenos Aires not long after Buena Tierra was established, SOCOBO imported fertilized Rhode Island and Leghorn-type chicken eggs from Argentina to the colony, as well as Peking duck eggs, in order to introduce premium poultry into this region of Bolivia. Trude Blumberg became especially adept at raising the Rhode Island breed, harvesting and selling the eggs, and generally supervising poultry farming and the improvement of the quality of poultry stocks within the colony.[34] And yet, despite early optimistic conjectures and plans concerning the growth and productivity of this Jewish agricultural colony inhabited by refugees, a combination of misjudgments and difficulties led to a steady shrinking in expectations for its well-being and ultimate success.

Building the infrastructure for Buena Tierra had been problematic and slow going from the very start, and launching the colony's operation took much longer than had been anticipated. Intermittent delays and problems with weather, workers, and the arrival of essential supplies squelched the hopes that Hochschild and other advocates had articulated: that positive and highly visible results would be achieved at Buena Tierra in short order. They had expected that a good first crop, efficiently cultivated and harvested, would lead Bolivia's "highest authorities" and the Bolivian public at large to recognize the benefits of Jewish immigration.[35] After Charobamba, Santa Rosa, and Polo Polo were purchased, however, the remaining months of 1940 and the first few months of 1941 were mostly taken up by "technical preparations": road and bridge building, land clearing, repairing of existing structures, and new housing construction. Only late in January and in February 1941 was actual planting begun, and then on a much smaller scale than had been anticipated—limited to only 2.5 hectares of pineapples and 3 hectares of bananas and plantains out of the 425 hectares that were believed fit for cultivation.[36]

The truth is, the unfavorable topography of Buena Tierra's land and the difficulty of access to it seem not to have been taken into sufficient account by Felipe Bonoli when he investigated and selected the site. Much of the ground was hilly, not flat like the Argentine pampas, with which Bonoli had first-hand experience. And like virtually all agricultural land worked by the people of the Yungas and the Andean valleys and lowlands in its vicinity, Buena Tierra's soil required contour cultivation in order to avoid erosion. It was virtually impossible to use agricultural machinery, and all work had to be done manually with machetes, hatchets, picks, hoes, and shovels. It took grueling physical labor to reclaim the soil and to farm here—backbreaking, tiring toil that was much more difficult than any of the planners had anticipated, and that few of the immigrants could do without substantial help from the Indian workers.

Based on his experience in Argentina, Bonoli had conceived of Buena Tierra—and had begun to organize it—as a SOCOBO-owned "large-scale plantation" that would be worked collectively by its settlers. But the feasibility of such an idea was soon challenged and categorically dismissed in a report submitted to SOCOBO directors by Otto Braun, another agronomist in SOCOBO's employ. To connect Buena Tierra's various landholdings and prepare them for "big plantation" cultivation was unrealistic, he argued, in light of the area's topography, and would require hundreds of additional laborers from the altiplano—at a cost far exceeding the resources that officials would be willing to invest for such an undertaking. He proposed that Bonoli's "collectively-worked large plantation idea" be dropped, and a "concentrated cultivation system," on a smaller scale, be substituted in its stead.

Braun's alternative plan—which he presented to SOCOBO's directorship, and which gained him Bonoli's position as Buena Tierra's agricultural administrator—called for the assignment of ten-hectare agricultural lots to each settler (or settler-family), and the subdivision of each of these parcels into "three manageable sections" for the cultivation of coffee, bananas, and citrus fruits. But despite the implementation of his suggestions, Braun was no more successful than his predecessor in turning out marketable produce and profitable returns in relative short order. The first crops of bananas and citrus fruits grown under his direction were of poor quality, and the coffee plants (which SOCOBO officials had considered the potentially most lucrative product from Buena Tierra) showed virtually no yield. Braun had no previous personal experience with coffee—which, newly planted, requires careful nurturing and several years to bear fruit—and SOCOBO was unable to hire and bring a resident "coffee expert" to the colony to guide the settlers in its cultivation and supervise its production. Downhearted about his inability to invigorate Buena Tierra and demonstrate concrete results and promising growth in its agricultural productivity, Braun resigned in June 1942, thirteen months after he had taken his job.

After Braun's departure, SOCOBO had great difficulty in engaging a new agricultural expert and managerial supervisor for the settlement. Buena Tierra was thereafter managed in a more or less improvised manner, initially by using the experience of local employees, and eventually through hiring two Bolivians, Luis Solis and Luis Gamarra, who owned neighboring farms in the area.

On-the-spot management difficulties were hardly the most pressing ones concerning Buena Tierra's existence, however. The colony's remoteness from the cities of the immigration, and the fact that many of the German-speaking refugees there thought of it as somewhere "deep in the jungle," made it hard to lure settlers to it. Few Jewish refugees went voluntarily to Buena Tierra as enthusiastic pioneers eager to achieve success in a new venture. Even at its peak, in 1943, there were never more than some 180 adult Jews in the colony. At first, refugee-aid officials of the Hilfsverein in La Paz and Cochabamba had tried a form of coercion, compelling individuals and families who were unemployed and had no earned income to transfer from the cities to Buena Tierra—or, at the very least, to another place in Bolivia less populated by recent immigrants. These nearly destitute refugees "who had nothing to do, and little or nothing to lose," Walter Weiss reported to the Joint, were "fully dependent on the refugee-aid organization, SOPRO, for support." They were, therefore, vulnerable to "resettlement pressures" and to the argument that working in agriculture in the new colony would at least allow them to contribute in part to the cost of their maintenance.

Yet Weiss also stressed that more than pressure was needed to motivate more Jewish refugees to come to the subtropical Yungas. In order, as he put it, "to find the right raw materials for the colony," stimulate new, voluntary applications for resettlement, and to *keep* potential settlers on the land once they had gone there, he recommended that SOCOBO work out and articulate an attractive long-range new "deal" concerning housing, land, and monetary earnings.

Ultimately, however, it was dissatisfaction with the premises of the *already existing* "deal" that led to the demise of Buena Tierra. When the colony was first established, SOCOBO's managers and board had expected the settlers to subsist on little more than the housing facilities and weekly monetary stipend they received. Implicitly, they viewed the colonists in the category of "company employees" with no legal title to land or dwelling at Buena Tierra. They saw them as people who might eventually become self-supporting and gain greater financial rewards for their labor—but only after crop production and market sales had earned the colony enough surplus income to enable the Joint and Hochschild to recover at least some of their investment. Yet, on their part, many colonists were displeased with the small amount of cash they were paid each week for their extremely arduous work. They complained that they labored long hours farming the land, raising chickens and ducks, and doing work for the economic and social well-being of the settlement, but were neither given nor promised a "satisfactory arrangement" that would provide them with an accelerated possibility of higher earnings and a personal stake in the colony's future.[37]

The Buena Tierra colonists, like so many other refugees during the war, tended to be ambivalent about their long-term plans—worried about a possible German victory, about their ability (or desire) to remain in Bolivia, and about their own and their family's life chances, yet some settlers did want to formalize a new arrangement with SOCOBO that would allow them to own their houses and their assigned lots. Since they also consistently requested a guaranteed minimum income from company officials until earnings from farm production could sustain them, however, they and SOCOBO's directors were unable to reach a formal agreement.

A circular impasse, with extremely negative consequences for the survival of Buena Tierra, thus emerged. Given what seemed like an unpromising future for themselves, most of the settlers eventually abandoned the colony. Some, who were artisans or tradesmen by profession, went back to the cities, where possibilities for personal advancement seemed greater—especially during the early years of the war, when the economy of Bolivia in general, and the cities in particular, enjoyed an upswing.[38] The steady departure of colonists, and the inability to replace them and to entice additional willing and qualified settlers, diminished the colony's chances to improve its yields and to increase market earnings. This, in combination with Buena Tierra's increasingly apparent limitations—its less than favorable topography, its hard to reach location, and its ongoing transport difficulties—significantly discouraged officials at the Joint from continuing their financial support.

Mauricio Hochschild was still convinced that Buena Tierra had merit and that the project deserved additional backing. "I am not only in favor of going on with it," he wrote to Charles J. Liebman, president of the Refugee Economic Corporation of the Joint, in February 1943, "but am also absolutely certain that it will turn out a success in every direction."[39] And yet his definition of "success," at this point, already showed how the idea had been transformed. He still conceived of Buena Tierra as a valuable colonizing experiment, a model settlement whose existence would facilitate additional large-scale refugee immigration to Bolivia after the war, as well as to Bolivia's South American neighbors. But Buena Tierra's primary function in this respect, he now argued, was not, as he had initially anticipated, to absorb large numbers of settlers itself but, rather, its contribution should be assessed in terms of the fact that *its very existence* "reflected well on Jews." Bolivian newspapers, he indicated, had thus begun to write about it in very glowing terms. "So appreciable will be the benefit derived from the work of the Jewish agricultural colonizing society," summarized an article in *Ultima Hora*, which Hochschild enclosed in his letter to Liebman, "that it merits encouragement from the Government, its officials, and from Bolivians in general who are increasingly coming to realize that the old prejudice which maintained that Jews are by nature not agriculturists is a vile, hateful, and repugnant slander."⁴⁰ The colony will prove itself an outstanding achievement, the mining magnate predicted to Liebman, "not only for the settlers and the people who put up the money, but also—and this is at least as important—it will show Bolivia and the surrounding nations what Jews can do . . . The people in Bolivia will not fail to recognize the great progress [Jewish colonization brings] to the country, and Jews in general will benefit from this awareness."

Hochschild himself paid a visit to Buena Tierra toward the end of 1943, and Dr. Blumberg recalled the occasion vividly:

> He brought along an entire entourage of high-ranking Bolivians, including government ministers, as well as diplomats like the American ambassador and the papal nuncio. An impressive personality with great charm, Hochschild delivered an enthusiastic speech to the assembled colonists who responded in similar measure. He asked the children what it was that they most wished for, and they responded "a swimming pool"—which he immediately approved for construction . . . But I had the impression that Hochschild failed to recognize the difficulty of the problems we were facing. He offered to purchase a motor-cycle for my medical rounds. This was, of course, senseless [given the terrain and lack of adequate roads]. I would have been much happier if, in its stead, he had authorized a good riding mule for my use.⁴¹

Few people at this time would have guessed that the visit of Hochschild and his companions to Buena Tierra marked the colony's high point, that within a very short time the elation of this occasion would be followed by dejection, abandonment, and worrisome insecurity. Political events in Bolivia were significant in effecting this quick downward turn. In late December 1943, President Enrique Peñaranda, who had steered the nation into its support of the Allies in the war, and who had been recognized as sympathetic both to the continued presence of Jewish refugees and to the possibility of future expansion of Jewish immigration, was overthrown in a coup, led by military officers espousing a reformist agenda and a vaguely Fascist ideology. The new junta initially positioned itself in opposition to the old regime's sympathetic relationship with mine owners, the United States, and middle-class intellectuals and politicians. Hochschild was arrested, imprisoned in a military barracks, and threatened with execution. Although he was freed after a few weeks thanks to the intervention and pressure exerted by diplomats from other Latin American nations and the United States, he left Bolivia immediately after his release and never set foot in the country again.⁴²

By mid-1944, the ruling junta—perceiving that the Axis powers were losing the war and that its own negative attitudes to interests associated with the United States threatened dire economic repercussions for Bolivia—moderated its stance. But the consequences of the instability and fright that had been generated by the coup and its aftermath were fatal for Buena Tierra and for the future of Jewish agricultural colonization in Bolivia. With Hochschild gone, financial backers and supporters of the project fell away for good, and Buena Tierra withered and further declined. Increasingly pessimistic about any chances for recovery and their own economic survival, most of the remaining settlers left the colony—Dr. Blumberg, Trude, and their daughters among them. When David Stern visited the settlement in November 1944, only nine colonists and their families (a total of twenty-one people) remained, and three of these families were awaiting visas to emigrate to Argentina and Palestine. All settlers were now concentrated in the Charobamba hacienda, the adjacent (and least developed) Santa Rosa having fallen into total disuse, and Polo Polo, including its eighteen houses and cultivated land, having been leased out by SOCOBO for seven years to Luis Gamarra, the Bolivian hacienda owner who had briefly been the colony's agricultural administrator.[43]

A little more than a year afterward, all but one of the remaining Jewish settlers had abandoned Buena Tierra. The last, Hans Homburger, who had been employed by SOCOBO since the inception of the colony, was now left as the on-site company representative to watch over the property and to supervise the local Indian sharecroppers who, in return for housing and the use of the land, worked for SOCOBO two days a week. In this manner Buena Tierra continued to exist as an incorporated SOCOBO-owned property for many years, surviving even through the agrarian reforms and land redistribution that accompanied Bolivia's national revolution of 1952. Ironically, however, when it was finally legally dissolved in 1960, the Indian sharecroppers who had worked the land—and who, in effect, had successfully grown and harvested the products anticipated in the Jewish colonizing experiment—received none of the property as compensation for their labors.

Nowadays, even with the help of local inhabitants, it is difficult to find and to identify some of the landmarks referred to in the documents and recollections of the Buena Tierra colony. None of the bridges constructed in the 1940s, and no piece of the auto roadway, still exist; they are casualties of time and the wash of the heavy rains. No one any longer seems to know precisely where they were located. Standing in this site, looking at the lush green semitropical hillsides and the cliffs that envelop it, feeling the humid air flowing on the skin and the moist, rich soil in one's hands, it is difficult not to be taken in by the beauty of the place and by its apparent abundance. Truly, this does seem like *buena tierra*, like good earth, and it is easy to forget that this, in fact, is a domain of failure.

The main hacienda building in Charobamba with its veranda—the building where the Blumbergs lived and where musical evenings and dances were held—still stands, run-down and in disrepair but transformed into a school for children of rural folk in the vicinity. Many of the houses built for the Jewish settlers are in ruins, others virtually unrecognizable, yet a few seem to remain much as they were described or appear in photos. They are now inhabited by Indian families—given new life, providing simple, austere shelter much as they were intended to do when they were first constructed decades ago.

A MATTER OF *YEKKES* AND *POLACOS*

There is an additional episode in this story of failed Jewish agricultural colonization efforts in Bolivia. In July 1939 a letter written in Yiddish, not German, and signed by thirty-seven people, was sent from the European Cooperative Colony "Piña" in Samaipata, province of Santa Cruz, to the headquarters of the JDC in the United States. Addressed to "the only Jewish world institution, 'Joint,' New York," its writers indicated that they represented a group of thirty Polish families who had established "the first Jewish colony in Bolivia" in February 1939. (This was more than a year before SOCOBO was incorporated and Buena Tierra founded.) "We are now going through a very severe crisis," they declared. "This being our first year, the fields have as yet yielded nothing and we are now employed in planting the fields and building our homes." The reason they were appealing directly to the Joint for aid, they explained, was that they were being discriminated against by the local refugee-aid society, SOPRO, the Hilfsverein, which, they declared, "has been very cold and uncivil to us, only because we are . . . *poor Polish immigrants and not German immigrants.*" They desperately needed financial help to get them through their difficulties, but the local German-Jewish-dominated aid organization was ignoring their requests.[44]

The Polish-Jewish colony did not manage to survive the year. The Joint did not send any direct aid in response to the appeal, and Piña quickly dissolved when its hapless settlers, virtually destitute, abandoned the area to seek their livelihood elsewhere in Bolivia. To be sure, the allegation of discrimination presented in the letter to the Joint hides the fact that SOPRO had indeed initially lent the group 50,000Bs (approximately U.S. $1,000) to buy real estate and agricultural equipment in Samaipata, and then had given its members another 5,000Bs for seeds. The settlers' letter also fails to reveal that SOPRO had granted these loans on the stipulation that a first mortgage be issued to the refugee-aid organization for the Samaipata land—and that SOPRO had cut off additional funding because the settlers had ignored this proviso, and failed to present any other documentary evidence that a land purchase had in fact taken place.[45]

Still, the issue of German-Jewish discrimination against East European Jews that was raised was a real and troubling one. German-speaking refugees of course made up the large majority of the immigrants to Bolivia in the late 1930s and the first year of World War II; a minority were of Eastern European origin, many of them from East Prussia and areas of Poland claimed by Germany. East European Jews had also been at the core of the smaller Jewish immigration to Bolivia earlier in the 1930s. (A second wave of Eastern European Jewish immigration to Bolivia, many of them camp survivors, occurred after the end of the war.) And despite the virulence of anti-Semitism in Europe at this time—despite the persecutions, expulsions, and the ongoing threat that Nazi ideology and expansionism posed for Jews everywhere—the old rift continued between the German-speaking Jews from the Austro-German *Kulturkreis* and the predominantly Yiddish-speaking Jews from Poland, Russia, and other parts of Eastern Europe.

In Bolivia, as in other places in the world, this division between the *Yekkes*, as the German-speakers were called by the East Europeans, and the *Polacos* (or, in German, *Polacken*), as the Eastern European Jews were termed by the Central Europeans, was certainly based on cultural and linguistic factors.*[46] And here, too, the prejudices accompanying this division derived from differences in the nature and reach of Jewish emancipation and assimilation in nineteenth- and early-twentieth-century Europe, and from hierarchical valuations assigned to these differences. German-speakers, *Yekkes*, were seen by Jews from Eastern Europe as arrogant, condescending, patronizing, snobbish, as highly assimilated and privileged people hopelessly intent on aping the manners, customs, cultural values, dress, and language of the non-Jewish bourgeois establishment. Central European Jews, on the other hand, tended to look on their Eastern European co-religionists with open disdain as culturally backward primitives who were loud, coarse, and generally untrustworthy. They viewed them as embarrassing embodiments—and reminders—of less enlightened, negative traits associated with "ghetto Jewry" from which they had tried to distance themselves through the process of assimilation.

In the case of the Polish-Jewish colony in Bolivia, many factors besides the alleged discrimination of *Yekkes* against *Polacos* were involved in its rapid demise and dissolution. Inadequate preparation, lack of familiarity with local soil and climatic conditions, distance from markets, poor leadership: all these were clearly present, in addition to undercapitalization and a lack of financial subvention. But judging from the negative attitudes against Polish Jews that influential German Jews like Mauricio Hochschild and SOPRO's managing director, Manfred Wihl, expressed in their letters, prejudice may also have had something to do with the refusal of additional "life-line" financial support for the Polish settlement.

One cannot help wondering. Had things turned out differently, had Jewish agricultural colonization experiments in Bolivia like Piña and Buena Tierra lived up to some of their promise, would more Jews indeed have been allowed to come to Bolivia and take refuge there? Knowing what we now know about the catastrophic fate of so many millions of East European Jews, the small story of Piña takes on larger dimensions, and it becomes an emblem of rescue opportunities missed. That this was so makes this particular story of failure truly ironic, and sad.

---

*On the derivation of the word "Yekke," Jack Wertheimer has written: "Mordechai Eliav has noted four possible etymologies for the term *Yekke*, while admitting that none is very satisfying: (1) it derives from the *Jacke*, 'jacket,' sported by German Jews in contrast to the caftan commonly worn by East Europeans; (2) it serves as an acronym for the Hebrew words *Yehudi Kashe Havana*, 'a dim-witted Jew'; it is a derivative of (3) *Jeck* or (4) Jacob, terms that denote fools, according to German dialect."[47]

5

A N D E A N

W A L T Z

The Masai when they were moved from their old country . . . took with them the names of their hills, plains and rivers; and gave them to the hills, plains and rivers in the new country . . . carrying their cut roots with them as a medicine.
—Isak Dinesen, *Out of Africa*

Nostalgia is memory with the pain removed.
—Herb Caen in Fred Davis
Yearning for Yesterday

When the brass band on the shore strikes up the jaunty mazurka rhythms of the Polish anthem, I am pierced by a youthful sorrow so powerful that I suddenly stop crying and try to hold still against the pain. I desperately want time to stop, to hold the ship still with the force of my will. I am suffering my first, severe attack of nostalgia, or *tesknota*—a word that adds to nostalgia the tonalities of sadness and longing. It is a feeling whose shades and degrees I'm destined to know intimately, but at this hovering moment, it comes upon me like a visitation from a whole new geography of emotion, an annunciation of how much an absence can hurt.
—Eva Hoffman, *Lost in Translation*

Photos taken at the Austrian Club in La Paz, Bolivia, in 1947, two years after the end of the war, show my mother, father, and friends at a Dirndl ball. My parents and the others are dressed in Austrian folk costumes—my mother and the women in full-skirt peasant dress and tight bodice, and my father and the men in lederhosen, white and tasseled Alpine kneesocks, and Tyrolean hats. They all seem happy, perhaps a little tipsy, and enjoying the party.

Other pictures of the same vintage come from an Austrian Club banquet. Scores of people in semiformal dress, including my parents, are seated at long set dinner tables, apparently enjoying the occasion with wine, plentiful food, and smiling conversation. In the background one can see the club's wall hangings—two Austrian flags, a lithograph of Old Vienna—and lampshades emblazoned with the Austrian republican coat of arms. No precise date is marked on

The "Dirndl Ball" at the Austrian Club, La Paz, 1947. *Left to right:* Gisi Helfer, Liesl Lipczenko, Eugen Spitzer, Rosie Spitzer, Heini Lipczenko, Stefi Kudelka, Otto Helfer, Walter Kudelka

A banquet at the Austrian Club, La Paz

the photos; the occasion being celebrated is not indicated. The attendant music can only be imagined.

I see these photos first as visual examples—accessible, direct, even amusing—of the reproduction of "Austrianness" in Bolivia by refugees who had fled or been expelled from their country. I view them as photographic manifestations of cultural memory and national identity, of nostalgic remembrance acted out in national costume, cultural practice, and symbolic representation. They seem to record performances marked by Heimweh and Sehnsucht, homesickness and longing, feelings commonly expressed in refugee discourse. Yet the photos also seem discordant to me: so removed from the Andean physical and cultural setting in which they were located as to appear almost quaint and ingenuous in their incongruity and difference. And they come laden with irony. Taken two years after the conclusion of the war—after Auschwitz, the death camps, and confirmation of Austria's extensive involvement and collaboration in the Final Solution—the enthusiastic celebrations of Austrian nationality strike me as disturbing and distressing examples of denial, if not amnesia.

Over time, my initial responses to these pictures are not eradicated. But, in my efforts to understand the photos more precisely and more historically, I realize that they also express an implicit political dimension. For the refugees to proclaim "Austrianness"—to reclaim an identification with an Austrian republic after the Anschluss, Nazi rule, and the defeat of the German Reich—was also to reassert their rightful belonging within a body politic and cultural tradition from which the Nazis had severed them. You have failed, they seem to assert. We survive. We have a claim on the best of the past, and we welcome the future! Beneath the surface comicality of the lederhosen, dirndl, and Tyrolean outfits lurks the reality that Jews had been legally forbidden to dress in these national costumes when the Nazis came to power. Nostalgic memory, cultural reconnection, ethnic mimicry—their surface readings—take on an additional dimension. Defiance, resistance, victory—these, too, are being proclaimed.

NOSTALGIC MEMORY

Literally translated, the German word *"Heimweh"* means "home hurt" or "home ache," and its sense is closest to the English term "homesickness." Few people nowadays, perhaps, would think of homesickness—"missing home," "the desire to return to one's native land"—as a medical problem, but that is exactly how it was considered for almost two centuries after Johannes Hofer, an Alsatian, first coined the word "nostalgia" in a 1688 Swiss medical thesis. His intent was to translate *Heimweh*, the familiar emotional phenomenon then primarily associated with exiles and displaced soldiers languishing for home, into a medical condition.[1] By formally identifying it as a disease, "nostalgia" (from the Greek *nostos*, to return home, and *algia*, a painful feeling) could thus be opened to rational inquiry and possible cure. Learned physicians would soon observe that the "melancholic," "debilitating," "sometimes fatal" symptoms of nostalgia could be triggered in its victims through the associations of memory—

sounds, tastes, smells, and sights that might remind them of the homes and the environments they had left behind. A "homecoming" and return to familiar and local circumstances could be restorative, ending the problem and curing the affliction.[2]

But in the years after its first coinage as a medical term, the meaning of nostalgia, as well as that of *Heimweh*, expanded and shifted. By the nineteenth century nostalgia was transformed, in David Lowenthal's words, "from a geographical disease into a sociological complaint."[3] Although its association with absence or removal from home and homeland remained one manifestation, nostalgia now also defined "loss" in a more general and abstract way, including the yearning for a "lost childhood," for "irretrievable youth," for a "world of yesterday" from whose ideals and values one had become distanced and detached. In this usage, nostalgia became an incurable state of mind, a signifier of "absence" and "loss" that could in effect never be made "presence" and "gain" except through memory and the creativity of reconstruction.

For the Central European refugees fleeing Nazi persecution who arrived in Bolivia in the late 1930s and early 1940s, *Heimweh* and the nostalgic look back were certainly common afflictions, which often combined yearnings for a lost homeland, cultural milieu, and past existence with the bitterness of rejection and expulsion. A poem published in La Paz in *Rundschau vom Illimani* in 1939 declared,

> The dark dread-filled nights lengthen,
> yet my longing seeks the distant shore,
> only in dreams can I still see your image,
> your streams, your woods, your meadows,
> FATHERLAND!
> . . . torments of homesickness I never knew
> before,
> only now do I truly understand the painful affliction,
> having not laid eyes on you for so long a time,
> FATHERLAND![4]

"Despite the pain, and my anger for what we had been made to endure there," wrote my grandmother Bertha Wolfinger in the early 1940s, "I still have strong feelings for the Vienna in which I spent so many years, and I miss small pleasures I was forced to give up."[5] Bruno Stroheim, brother of the actor Erich von Stroheim, narrated in the *Rundschau* in February 1940:

> In an unassuming Bolivian store my eyes suddenly caught sight of a poster on the wall.
>
>   How amazing that in Bolivia, practically at the end of this side of the globe, one could see a poster depicting a woman dressed in Tyrolean costume . . . a poster that also displays mountains, a snow-covered field in bluest sunlit sky, skiers, and a one-word inscription: Austria! And in a flash, like an electric shock, I am transported back . . . Within seconds a film whirs before my eyes— a film whose title should be *Verlorene Heimat! Lost Homeland!*[6]

Commenting on the character and pervasiveness of the refugees' nostalgic memory in Bolivia with some irony, Egon Schwarz noted how often his fellow immigrants began their sentences with the phrase "Back home in Germany . . . " or "Back home in our country . . . ," and how one man conversing with him had actually exclaimed, "Back home in our concentration camp . . . "[7] The negativity reflected in this darkly humorous recollection was, of course, specifically connected to the refugees' circumstances and not intended as a critique of nostalgic memory as a general phenomenon. But the overall practice of nostalgia, and the societal functions and effects of nostalgic memory in general, have been the subject of sharp reproach by many social critics. Detractors—especially those in the Marxist vein—have denounced it as "reactionary," "escapist," "inauthentic," "unreflexive," and as a "simplification" if not "falsification of the past." Christopher Lasch termed nostalgia "a betrayal of history," and saw "nostalgists" as "worse than . . . reactionary," "incurable sentimentalist[s]" who are afraid both "of the future" and "to face the truth about the past."[8] In Britain, Robert Hewison viewed nostalgic memory as a tool of the "heritage industry" and as a "spurious . . . uncreative. . . miasma" that counterfeited "authentic memory."[9] For Raymond Williams, it was an opiate with dysfunctional consequences, enticing people to take refuge in an idealized past while avoiding a critical examination and engagement with their present. It induced acceptance of the status quo and impeded social change.[10]

But nostalgic memory has also been seen in more positive light. That nostalgic memory allowed for an "escape from the present," for example, was interpreted by the French sociologist Maurice Halbwachs as one of its great virtues, not as one of its defects. Nostalgia, he argued, frees individuals from the constraints of time—in effect, it enables them to transcend the irreversibility of time—permitting them to stress positive experiences and aspects of the past selectively.[11] It recalls, in Suzanne Vromen's words, "a world from which the pain has been removed." In so doing it is neither dysfunctional nor reactionary because it presents a benign past as a contrast to the present and enables a "pleasantly sad dialogue" between them.[12] As a "retrospective mirage" constructed through hindsight, nostalgic memory thus serves an important comparative and, by implication, animating purpose. It sets up the *positive* from within the "world of yesterday" as a model for creative inspiration and possible emulation within the "world of the here and now." By establishing a link between a "self in present" and an image of a "self in past," nostalgic memory also significantly helps to reconstruct the continuity of individual and collective identity.[13]

Nostalgic memory—employed to connect the present to a particular version of the past—certainly did serve the thousands of Central European refugees in Bolivia as a creative tool of adjustment, helping to ease their cultural uprootedness and sense of alienation. No sooner had they arrived in South America than a process began by which they recalled, negotiated, and reshaped their memories of Europe in light of their new circumstances. Concretely, in their everyday practices and in the economic, social, and cultural institutions they established, or symbolically, in the names they selected to give to these, they re-created a version of a way of life and of a cultural reality that they had previously known. Nostalgic memory, creatively reconfigured, became one source through which they built a new communal culture and constructed a new collective identity to serve their changed needs.

They did not, of course, physically reconstruct a "Little Hamburg" or "Little Vienna" in the Andes, as one of the refugees jokingly referred to the German and Austrian communities established in La Paz, Cochabamba, Oruro, and Sucre.[14] But a glance through the pages of *Rundschau vom Illimani* in 1939 and 1940, or of the *Jüdische Wochenschau*—the Buenos Aires German-Jewish weekly that covered Bolivian immigrant news once a month during this period—illustrates both the range of the immigrants' economic and institutional adjustment in Bolivia and confirms the character of their symbolic reconnection with Central Europe. Advertisements for the Café Viena, Club Metropol, Café-Restaurant Weiner, the Pension Neumann, Pension Europa, the Lebensmittelgeschäft Brückner & Krill (a food store), and other eateries and gro-

A posed photo depicting a "Refugee Enterprise" in La Paz during the war years. Like those taken at Buena Tierra and other JDC-supported sites, this photo was used to raise funds in the United States to aid Jewish refugees

The cover and production program for "Radio Wien Sendet"

ceries like them promise food at moderate prices: coffee, Bolivian-produced "European" sausages, pastries, delicatessen items, and lunch and dinner menus identified with culinary pleasures from "back home." *"Saûfst, stirbst/saûfst net, stirbst a. Also saûf!! aber, 'Imperial!' "* "If you booze, you die. If you don't booze, you also die. So booze!! but at the 'Imperial!' " reads an ad in Viennese dialect for a newly established Café-Restaurant Imperial—which also pledges a pleasant dining experience and daily musical entertainment. Made-to-order clothes cut in the "latest European styles" are featured in advertisements for the Haberdashery Berlin, the Casa Paris-Viena, and the Peletería Viena; secondhand European men's and women's apparel, brought from overseas and sold by refugees through the Lipczenko brothers' Casa Wera, is offered as an affordable alternative as well. The *Buchhandlung* La America, a bookstore, listing German editions of authors such as Franz Werfel, Paul Zech, and Bruno Weil, is regularly publicized in the weekly papers, as is the

German-language rental-library Osmaru, which lends out a wide range of secondhand fiction and nonfiction books at very low fees. The Kleinkunst-bühne (cabaret theater) presenting scenes from Schnitzler, von Hoff-mansthal, Beer-Hoffmann, as well as readings of German classics and Viennese dialect skits, advertises often, as does the refugee-organized Colegium Musicum, with its chamber-music concerts and recitals of Mozart, Beethoven, and Schubert played by musicians trained at conservatories in Vienna, Prague, and Berlin. In each issue, starting in late August 1939, the *Rundschau* also carries a weekly schedule for the daily hour-long German-language program on Radio Nacional, a Bolivian radio station: the broadcasts, produced and staffed by refugee actors and performers, include brief news summaries, lectures and recitals, dramatizations of German plays, radio-mystery stories, and live and recorded performances of European classical and Viennese dance music.[15]

In my own memories of childhood in Bolivia, I often recall the many occasions when my parents took me along to the Austrian Club—the Hogar Austriaco (Austrian Home), as it was generally known in Spanish, or the Federación de Austriacos Libres en Bolivia (Federation of Free Austrians in Bolivia), as it was officially called. With special fondness, I remember family meals taken in the club's dining room, a large multipurpose room, convertible into a theater or cabaret hall, with a small stage curtained in the red and white colors of the Austrian flag located at one end. My favorite dishes there, as well as at home, were the icons of Hapsburg cuisine: Wiener schnitzel with potatoes and cucumber salad (*"Wiena Schnitzel mit Erdäpfel und Gurkensalat"*) or Hungarian goulash with '*Nockerl* (dumplings), made complete with *Apfel-strudel* for dessert. I also recall a number of entertainments at the club—piano and violin recitals, theatrical skits, and a magic show in which Heini Lipczenko, playing a flute and wearing a turban in imitation of a Hindu swami, "charmed" a snake out of a basket to perform a rhythmic dance.

Sifting through memorabilia of which I became the keeper when my mother died, I discover a Hogar Austriaco cabaret program, undated but clearly from the early 1940s. It introduces a show, *"Radio Wien Sendet: Ein Wunsch kabarett"* ("Radio Vienna Broadcasts: A Cabaret on Demand") and lists, among its entertainments, *"In einem Wiener Vorstadtvarieté"* ("In a Viennese Suburban Music Hall"), *"Ein Maederl aus Moedling"* ("A Lass from Moedling"), *"Frauen sind zum Kuessen da"* ("Women Are Made to

Collage from contemporary program notes, showing only a few of the many theatrical productions in German mounted by refugees in Bolivia in the early 1940s. Erna Terrel, Rosl Kupferstein; Alfred Brecher; Fritz, Ernst, and Heinz Kalmar; Hans Kulka; Heinrich Neumann; Josef Pasternak; Max Sommer; and Bruno Stroheim performed in pieces generally directed by Georg Terramare

Be Kissed"), and various other skits in Viennese dialect. A German poem in an Austrian Club publication declares:

> "The wanderer, astray in a distant land,"
> Site of strange animal, tree, and plant,
> Site of a strange night and alien stars,
> Site of unfamiliar and lifeless human sound,
> How lonely and displaced he feels.
> But how then, in that strange land, his heart rejoices
> When suddenly he comes upon
> A speaker of his language,
> A brother, native of his home.[16]

Feelings of nostalgia, I realize, lie at the core of my own memories of the Austrian Club, which are layered and quite complex. They are not merely about the club's importance in my parents' communal life or about the happy childhood hours I spent there with them. They also involve the cultural universe to which I connected *through* the club: to food, music, and theater certainly, but also to lively adult group conversation in the German dialect spoken by Austrians, and to a mode of cultural communication—to jokes, conventions, etiquette, and a world outlook that derived from the language and cultural background the club's refugee members shared with one another. It connected me, in that sense, to a reconstructed version of Viennese bourgeois culture in particular and to Austro-Germanic *kultur* more generally, a cultural environment and discourse I had never known in its actual setting but encountered only as an already nostalgic reconstruction in a situation of displacement. Indeed, I now recognize that the nostalgic memory engendered in me—*nostalgia about nostalgia*, so to speak—was precisely one of the aims of the founders of the Austrian Club in 1941. In a Festschrift published in 1944, celebrating the club's activities in its first three years and reaffirming the collective mission of its members, this goal is explicitly indicated: "to provide to the older generation some type of substitute ('Ersatz') for that which they had lost [through emigration], and to the young, some rendering of a native cultural education they had been forced to give up or miss altogether in their displacement from [their Austrian] 'home.' "[17]

In using nostalgic memory for this creative function—the recall and recreation of aspects of the past within an institutional ambiance that would reinforce the refugees' sense of cultural and historical continuity—the Aus-

trian Club was effective but hardly unique. Other organizations, with many
of the same participants, did similar work. The desire to establish and nur-
ture a German-*Jewish* communal identity in Bolivia, for example, emerged
early among the refugees, and familiar Jewish institutional structures that
had served as centers of Jewish communal life in Europe were used as models. It was no doubt from their recollections of the various Israelitische Kultusgemeinden in the cities of Central Europe that one of the first centers of
collective immigrant activity, the Comunidad Israelita, was founded in La
Paz in 1939 by Jewish refugees from Germany and Austria. (A Círculo
Israelita, founded in 1935 by Polish and Rumanian Jews, had been the first
Jewish community organization in Bolivia. It continued as a separate entity
throughout the war and, in the 1950s, absorbed the by then much diminished Comunidad. But it was the Comunidad with its then larger membership and affiliated institutions that dominated Jewish community life in La
Paz.)[18] This communal organization established a Jewish temple in which
religious services were held, an old people's home, and two institutions that
I attended: a Kinderheim serving as kindergarten, boarding, and day-care
center, and a school, La Escuela Boliviana-Israelita. And from its inception,
the Comunidad also fulfilled a less utilitarian social function: its quarters in
the city, and its Sunday "garden retreat" in rural Obrajes, became meeting
places where Jewish refugees could eat meals, read newspapers, play cards,
chess, or Ping-Pong, where they could gossip, socialize, exchange information, and reminisce about their lives, loves, and the past. The Comunidad's
quarters, in other words, like those of the Hogar Austriaco (but less identified with a single country of origin), became a version of an institution that
many of the immigrants certainly remembered with a fond nostalgia: the
Klublokal, or coffeehouse of Central Europe.[19]

Children of refugees like me, especially during the early years of the
immigration, received both formal and informal tuition strongly influenced by cultural memories of Europe. In La Paz, Cochabamba, and
Sucre, there were, of course, Bolivian state schools that immigrant children could attend, as well as Catholic private schools or the Colegio
Americano, where English was the secondary language of instruction and
the curriculum was modeled on North American private-school offerings.
But in La Paz, most refugees initially sent their children to "their own
school," the Escuela Boliviana-Israelita. The school's purpose had been
twofold: to offer courses in Spanish so that recently arrived or Bolivia-
born children of the immigrants might learn the language of the land,

An end-of-year award day at the Escuela Boliviana-Israelita: Dr. Perschak, principal (*standing*); Señor Aaron at portable piano; Señor Arebalo, Bolivian history teacher, by tree

and to teach them to read, write, and do mathematics. The Israelita also gave optional supplemental instruction in basic elements of Jewish religion and history. But although Bolivian officials required it to hire at least one Bolivian teacher to teach local and national history—what the Bolivians called *educación cívica*—the pedagogical philosophy and curricular content of the Escuela Boliviana-Israelita differed little from those employed in elementary schools in Germany and Austria before the rise of Nazism.[20] The referent examples the immigrant teachers used derived, as one might have expected, from their Central European cultural background and experience.

Looking back through my report cards for grades one through four from the Escuela Boliviana-Israelita, and focusing on my grades in geography, I recall that I was in my second year of school when Dr. Ascher first taught us to locate on a map of Europe the Blue Danube, the Rhine "with its many castles," and the "beautiful Austrian Alps." And finding a "*satisfecho*" (satisfactory) mark as my final grade in music at the end of my third year of school reminds me that our teacher, Mr. Aaron, playing on a portable piano or an accordion, taught us to sing German folk songs.

CRITICAL MEMORIES, LAYERED IDENTITIES

Whether some type of nostalgic affect—in tone of voice, gesture, or sigh—was ever evident or apparent to me in school I am unable to remember with any certainty. I find it difficult to imagine, however, that such expressions of longing and bittersweet remembrance would have been altogether *absent* from the teachers' faces and bodies, as they instructed the children of fellow refugees about a European world they had been forced to abandon. And yet, as I think back to Mr. Aaron, Dr. Ascher, the Escuela Boliviana-Israelita, the Austrian Club, and the refugee environment I was raised in, I am also wary of privileging nostalgia too much, and mindful of simplification and distortion. The culture and community created by the refugee immigrants in Bolivia should certainly not be misrepresented as merely a curious, somewhat ironic reconstruction in the Andes of a sanitized Central European culture and past, one from which Hitler, and the persecutions and policies that had led to refugeehood, were obliterated. The immigrants were, after all, *refugees* and not voluntary émigrés. Before their departure from Europe, each and every one of them had been identified as undesirable and stripped of citizenship and possessions. Their "present" in Bolivia, the "here and now" from which they looked back upon the past and confronted the future, had come about as a consequence of oppression and expulsion, and it was indelibly marked by painful loss, separation, and ongoing war. Within that present, nostalgic memory certainly did help the refugees to transcend the negativity of their recent history by reconnecting them to broadly shared values and social practices that had characterized the Austro-German bourgeois culture to which they had belonged or aspired to belong. When the future seemed darkest to them, as the news of Nazi military victories and Nazi atrocities against Jews enveloped them, and their own life chances seemed most precarious, they turned to the past as a way to gain some sustenance and stability in their present. In this respect, however, the creative communal reconstruction engendered by nostalgic memory showed their cultural resistance and cultural survival, a denial of success to Nazi efforts to disconnect and expel them from the Austro-German *kulturkreis* in which they had played such an integral part.

But nostalgic memory, the selective emphasis on what was positive in the past, was only one layer of recall. Critical memory, memory incorporating what was negative and bitter from the immediate past, was always present as well. As nostalgia's complicating "other side," it, too, became a prominent creative force and influence within Bolivia's refugee society.

Critical memory of persecution "experienced" and "remembered" was, of course, the overarching framework of refugee collective identity in Bolivia. Within a present clouded by displacement, insecurity, and war, this was the connective tissue of their "refugeehood," the ubiquitous bond that obliterated many differences among them. It also added a distinctly *political* dimension to their institutions and to their culture and community. If nothing else, this political dimension affirmed that, even though they had all been victimized, they had been neither crushed nor extinguished. "Every day, we came together at a park bench in the Plaza 14 de Septiembre," commented Eva Markus about a practice that became a routine in Cochabamba during the 1940s, "and we talked about the war from accounts in the press and radio. We weren't a consistent bunch. The same people weren't always there, and no one stayed very long. But we felt tied together, and our chats sometimes inspired activities—personal or in small groups—connected to the general effort to defeat the Nazis."[21]

Though many of the refugees' differences were submerged within a collectivity sharing a common history of persecution and its critical remembrance, no single political grouping or organization ever emerged among them that expressed their common concerns and interests. "Refugeehood" always remained an amalgam made up of multiple, overlapping histories and identities. In this regard, critical memory also acted as an instrument of much more specific recall and reaction, an overall "connector" among the refugees, to be sure, but stimulating a variety of responses to the past, and challenges to the present, that were based on very particularistic "national," "political," and "ethnic" identifications.

Again, the Austrian Club provides a clear illustration. While nostalgic memory had animated and shaped it as a social and cultural institution reproducing elements of a "lost homeland" in the Bolivian refuge, critical memory helped it to be an activist political organization. The formal name of the club, after all, was Federación de Austriacos Libres en Bolivia (Federation of Free Austrians in Bolivia). In its charter document, and in a number of "general assemblies" called during the war years, its members proclaimed the club as "nondenominational" and "above party affiliation": as a democratic organization open to all Austrians—gentiles as well as Jews, persons who were left, center, even monarchist in political-party identification. But members considered two fundamental tenets to be at the very heart of the club's existence and function: its reassertion of an Austrian national identity, distinct from that of Germany, and its political work to reestablish a "free," "independent," "democratic" Austria that would negate Austria's *Anschluss* to the German Reich and battle Nazi domination.[22] Heinz Kalmar, who returned from Bolivia to Vienna after the war, recalls:

> We were politically active on a number of levels. We stayed out of Bolivian national politics, but we did convince Bolivian officials to modify the forms for the "census of foreigners" of 1942 to include a separate "Austrian" category of identification—thus precluding the necessity of our having to identify ourselves as "German" or "stateless." From admission receipts and collections taken at some of our functions, we donated funds and materials for the Allied war effort.[23]

Writing on behalf of the Free Austria Youth Group of the La Paz Austrian Club to the international headquarters of the Austrian World Youth Movement in London in 1943, Heinz Markstein confirmed this activism and patriotic zeal. He declared:

> We have had the opportunity to address Bolivians on radio to explain Austria's plight and to affirm our readiness to fight against Nazi fascism. Some of our men have even volunteered to join the Allied forces on the battlefield but have been refused . . . We thus work to unify all Austrian youth in this country, and to inculcate within ourselves an even greater love for our homeland and for democracy.[24]

In formal gatherings and speeches, club members marked the March 12 anniversary of the *Anschluss*, which they viewed as the commemoration of "Austria's forceful subjugation," as well as the November 9 memorialization of *Kristallnacht*. In November 1942, on the occasion of the fourth anniversary of that infamous event, Dr. Georg Terramare, a Catholic-Austrian refugee, who as novelist, playwright, actor, and director, was one of the club's most creative and engaging members, composed the words for an anthem, "The Hymn of the Free Austrians." Sung to the melody of the last movement of Beethoven's Eroica symphony, this alternative *Exil-shymne* enabled Austrians in Bolivia to avoid the tune of their old anthem—the Haydn melody, which the Germans also employed in *Deutschland, Deutschland, Über Alles*.[25] The Terramare lyrics declared:

In the East a day will come,
And o'er the land
A storm will lift . . .
Newly risen will you be, Austria! . . .

We wish to stand united . . .
And with new strength . . .
rebuild you, sacred land of freedom.
Newly risen will you be, Austria![26]

German refugees in Bolivia, unlike the Austrians, found it much more difficult to join together on the basis of national origin, under a single organizational umbrella. Many German-Jewish and non-Jewish refugees—among them Ernst Schumacher, Willi Karbaum, Ernst Altmann, Hugo Efferoth, Erhart Löhnberg, and Wolfgang Hirsch-Weber—had been politically active in Germany and had been persecuted for their activities in the banned Social Democratic Party (SPD) or in other anti-Nazi political organizations. Scores of SPD members had been helped to emigrate to Bolivia from Germany, or from their interim places of European refuge, by the Social Democratic Refugee-Aid organization, headquartered in Prague before the war.[27] Many of these Social Democrats, as well as other German political refugees, viewed their stay in Bolivia as an exile that would terminate as soon as the Nazi dictatorship was defeated and return to Germany became possible once again. In this respect they differed little from their Austrian counterparts. But members or supporters of competing German refugee political organizations like Freundschaft (Club Amistad), Das Andere Deutschland, Vereinigung Freier Deutschen, and Freies Deutschland refused to coalesce into a larger antifascist "popular front" association. An important effort in this regard—initiated in La Paz in 1942 by Ernst Schumacher, editor and owner of the *Rundschau vom Illimani*—to establish an "above party" Free German counterpart to the Austrian Club, with branches in Sucre, Cochabamba, and Oruro, fell apart.

The failure of German refugees to unify institutionally and to combine and act politically as Germans can in part certainly be attributed to ideological differences and long-standing antagonisms among supporters of competing political factions. The Vereinigung Freier Deutschen in La Paz, like its sister affiliates in Argentina, Brazil, Chile, Uruguay, and Ecuador, attracted refugees who had been Communist sympathizers or members of the Communist Party (KPD) in Germany. Das Andere

Deutschland tended to be left-leaning but non-Communist in orientation—attractive to the considerable number of German refugees in Bolivia sympathetic to the SPD. Freies Deutschland, a third alternative, had a right-of-center appeal and relatively few supporters. Political arguments among German refugees about the Hitler-Stalin pact, the politics of the U.S.S.R., and their divergent expectations for the character and ideological direction of a post-Hitler Germany abounded. This range of political opinion and similar divisions existed among Austrian refugees as well, of course, but the intensity and uncompromising nature of political disagreement among the German refugees was exacerbated by the clash of individual personalities and by what has been termed a "legendary" acrimony among German refugee "leaders," characteristics reflected in many *Rundschau vom Illimani* newspaper columns from the period and noted in several refugee memoirs and accounts. Among German refugees, it would seem, neither nostalgic remembrance of an absent German homeland, nor shared memory of persecution and expulsion, nor the universal desire for Nazi defeat was sufficient to submerge the political divisions and animosities they had imported to Bolivia—and now again reproduced.

But to note only the failure of German refugees to unite, "as Germans," beneath a single umbrella-organization is to distort the multilayered nature of refugee identity in Bolivia, as well as the complexity of refugee responses and adjustments over time. Read more "thickly," taking into account the broader context of the Bolivian immigration, it becomes clear that German refugee responses—like those of other national groups—transcended the boundaries of national origin. Individual refugees from Germany, after all, like all refugees in Bolivia, were identified, and identified themselves, according to a number of other criteria. Their politics, religion, age, gender, class background, and, if Jewish, the nature and strength of their identification with Judaism—all these also influenced and affected their responses and adjustments to their new world. At different moments in time, depending on circumstances, any one or combination of these identifications was primary and influential.

Among Jewish refugees in Bolivia, whether originally from Germany or not, the political dimension of critical memory was displayed in the very assertion of an ongoing Jewish existence and vitality in the public sphere—in the openness of the refugees' collective presentation of themselves "as Jews" both institutionally and symbolically. One could see this in the range of Jewish public organizations established in the late 1930s: synagogues in La Paz and Cochabamba, a Jewish kindergarten, primary and secondary schools, a home for the aged, cemeteries, Jewish cultural and refugee-aid associations, the Comunidad Israelita and the older Círculo Israelita. Each of these, generally identified by a sign or placard in Spanish as well as in Hebrew lettering, occupied physical space in the urban surroundings—acreage, a building, a portion of an edifice—and was a tangible manifestation of Jewish presence and endurance.

Jewish vitality was also expressed in the refugees' participation, "as Jews," in parades and public events celebrating Bolivian national holidays, and in their activities in public athletic and gaming competitions. Carrying the blue-white-blue banner and the Star of David insignia associated with a promised Jewish national homeland, young immigrant women and men in Bolivia's largest cities represented local branches of Macabi, the international Jewish-Zionist sports association that had flourished in Europe before the outbreak of war.[28] They engaged in all kinds of contests open to spectator attendance—table tennis, tennis, soccer, swimming, track and field, chess—competing against one another but also against Bolivian and other Latin American teams.[29]

Clearly, the public presentation of continuing Jewish communal existence and spirit politically negated the images of Jewish degeneration and dissolution projected in anti-Semitic propaganda. During the war years, especially, when news of German military victories and Nazi brutalities and killings brought fearful shudders to so many, they not only proclaimed survival but promised reconstruction and renewal. They displayed Judaism as an enduring religion and living culture, and Jewish communal identity as a basis for the Zionist dream of nationhood.

Still, indisputable differences—social, political, economic, as well as in the degree of connection to Jewish religion and practice—continued to divide the Jewish refugees and Jewish groups. For many Jewish refugees in Bolivia, the tie to Judaism in its broadest communal sense was secondary to other connections and identifications. Was one a Jew *first*, and *then* a German or Austrian? Or was political identification and ideology the primary allegiance—to Social Democracy, to Communism, to some version of internationalism? And what about differences within Judaism? Between the religious and the secular? Between Labor Zionists, other Zionists, and assimilationists? Between Jews from different cultural backgrounds, with distinctly different cultural memories? As the complaints from Polish-Jewish settlers in the failing Piña agricultural colony indicated, cultural distinctions and prejudices imported to Bolivia from Europe helped to maintain a division between the German-speaking Jewish refugee majority from Germany and Austria and the Yiddish speakers from Eastern Europe.[30] The *Yekkes* tended to fraternize with one another and kept their social distance from the *Polacos*.[31] Thus, while *Yekkes* and *Polacos*, Austrian Jews and German Jews, Zionists and assimilationists, the Orthodox and the secular could at any time elide distinctions among them—in the course of their economic and athletic interactions, as well as on those occasions when they rallied together to present themselves to others *as Jews*—the complex character of refugee identity, and the dynamic nature of refugee adjustment, remained a central characteristic of the Bolivian immigration.

LOOKING BACK: THREE VIGNETTES

July 1990. Julius Wolfinger, in the living room of his apartment in Queens, New York:

> For many of us from Austria and Germany, Bolivia was like a hotel. We arrived there, found a safe place to stay for a while, and then many of us packed up again and left. Some didn't go far—maybe to Argentina, or Chile, or Brazil, places in South America that were a little more European. Others, like me and my parents, were able to come to the U.S. after the war. Ferry Kohn and other younger people emigrated to Palestine—Israel—in '48 or '49. And then some, who couldn't be happy anywhere else, actually went back—to Vienna, or to where they had come from in Austria and Germany.
>
> I've been in America for forty-five years, But you know, if I didn't have a bad heart, I would really like to visit Bolivia. I would like to see it again—to eat salteñas,* see the mountains. I was a young man when I was there. We had some good times. Bolivia took us in. I feel a deep attachment to the place. I miss it.[32]

April 1995. Liesl Lipczenko is speaking to me on the telephone. Originally from Vienna, she and her husband and two sons emigrated from Bolivia to New York in 1951 and have lived in Cleveland for more than thirty years:

---

*Salteñas, eaten as a midmorning snack, are a pastry with a filling of beef or chicken with peas, potatoes, hardboiled eggs, olives, and a spicy sauce.

Even though I left La Paz so long ago, I feel a strong connection—everything seems familiar . . . I have such good memories of those years. I wish I was younger and could go there again. I have real Sehnsucht *[longing] for the place. Not for Vienna, not at all. But for Bolivia, I have* Sehnsucht.[33]

A Nostalgic Recollection:

My mother's apartment in Kew Gardens, New York. The framed, artist-signed lithograph of St. Stephen's Cathedral and the Stefansplatz originally acquired in La Paz hangs in the living room. As it had been in our apartment on Calle México, it is again centrally placed. But here, on a shelf beneath the picture, my mother also has displayed an old, one-armed, plaster of paris ekeko—a Bolivian Aymara folk god of good fortune and plenty. Standing on short legs, fat bellied, wearing sandals made from recycled auto tires, a knit Indian cap, and a manta, he is laden with miniaturized versions of wished-for goods and possessions: currency, sacks of grain and sweets, noodles, beans, baskets, utensils, tools, suitcases, and other foodstuffs and essentials. The belief is that ekeko must be "fed" annually by its owner—rewarded with a gift—so that he, in turn, will bring luck and prosperity. Every year, my mother put a fresh cigarette in ekeko's mouth.

6

LOS JUDÍOS
ALEMANES

THE ANAS

Two women—one quite young, in her early twenties, the other wrinkled, older but probably no more than in her late forties—merge in my memory. Both, in my recollection, are named Ana, and I think of them as "the Anas," even though in all likelihood one of them had a different name.

Both of them are cholas, *the Bolivian term for urban-dwelling* mestizas *of Spanish American and Indian American descent, and both dress in traditional Aymara chola style. They wear several layers of short* pollera *skirts tucked one beneath the other like crinolines, a blouse and woolen pullover, a vest-jacket, and a woolen shawl. On the street, they use a richly colored rectangle of hand-woven cloth, the* ahuayo, *as a carryall slung across their back and tied around the neck, and wear a dark green, brown, or black bowler hat—the characteristic item of attire with which* chola *dress is most widely identified.*[1]

The older Ana worked for us first, but I can't recall when my parents first hired her as a servienta—*as an all-around house "maid" to help with the cleaning, laundry, and cooking. I associate them both with our apartment on the Calle México in La Paz, where we moved in 1946, after the war ended, when my father decided to set up a plumbing and electrical shop of his own and our family's economic situation took a turn for the better. Neither one was a live-in maid, but both spent long hours in our house five or six days a week, and both worked for our family for many years. Each used a tiny room in an interior courtyard of the house, near our apartment and my father's workshop, as a* place to rest during the day and to sleep over on those rare occasions when they stayed overnight. Although I don't recall any interdiction about our presence in that room, my sister and I rarely entered it. Yet I do remember it vividly: a room no larger than a pantry, barely able to contain a cot and a stool, with cut-out pictures from magazines pasted on the walls and a small statue of the Virgin of Copacabana and a candle enshrined in a corner. I seem to have been both attracted to and a little frightened by the dark, lairlike quality of the place.

Despite the years that both of "the Anas" worked in our house, and the many hours they spent with our family, especially with my sister and me, almost every day, we knew remarkably little about them and their lives. While the older Ana was most probably married, a mother, perhaps even a grandmother—facts that my parents would certainly have been interested in and informed about—our knowledge and comprehension of Ana's home world and cultural milieu seem to have been superficial and limited. Where she actually lived, what her family looked like, what they did every day, what they thought and spoke about: all this intrigued me as, I am sure, it did my mother and father. But a certain cultural distance remained unbridgeable between the Anas and my parents, reinforced in part by the master-servant, employer-laborer hierarchy of their relationship, and in part by some unspoken, perhaps unexamined, unwillingness by each of them to grant the other more than restricted access to their respective private and collective universes.

In one of our family albums there is a photo of the younger Ana, standing near the street entrance to our apartment with my sister, Elly, and me. Elly and I are dressed in costumes—for Carnival, perhaps. My sister is outfitted to look like an Andean "Indian boy," wearing coarse linen pants, a hand-woven cloth belt, a knit wool cap with ear-flaps, a woven cloth ahuayo slung across her shoulder. I am costumed as a "Mexican Indian peasant," with wide-brimmed "sombrero," poncho, pants tucked into boots, and I am carrying a miniature guitar. Ana, dressed normally in her everyday chola style but with her dark bowler hat set on her head at a rakish angle, is between the two of us. She is laughing broadly, without apparent resentment—seemingly in good-humored amusement about the imitation "indios" in her company. Looking at the photo, I recall the time when this Ana took me along to see where she lived in a part of La Paz where I had never been before, a crowded area of small stores and houses quite far from our apartment and the main concentration of refugee settlement. There, in the midst of her kinfolk, neighbors, and numerous children, I became an object of curiosity and display. I was stared at, examined, touched—a blond, hazel-eyed anomaly in a crowd of black-haired people.

Elly, Ana, and Poldi by the entrance of our house at 134 Calle México, La Paz

"AND THEY LOOKED AT US . . ."

"We looked at them, and they looked at us," Hanni Pinshower responded when I asked her to tell me about her first encounter with Bolivian Indians after she arrived in the country as a young refugee woman in 1939. References to "looking" and "being looked at"—two fundamental and complementary aspects of strangers meeting, and central to the formation of attitudes and the reinforcement of stereotypes—appear again and again in accounts and materials concerning the refugee immigration to Bolivia.

When one focuses on the Bolivian component of that encounter—when one examines how the immigrants (particularly the Jews among them) were actually seen by persons from varying cultural and economic backgrounds in the Bolivian world—a clear issue emerges immediately. The sources on the Bolivian responses to the massive refugee inflow of the late 1930s largely concern the perceptions and reactions of urban-dwelling, literate upper- and middle-class Bolivians, people belonging to a very small segment of Bolivia's total population. It is difficult to find materials from that period that give one more than a surface sense, or secondhand impression, of how the immigrants were perceived by the highland Aymara and Quechua people who first met them, or how they were viewed by people in the indigenous settlements in Bolivia's tropical lowlands. Since most of these indigenous Bolivians were illiterate, their early impressions or reactions remained within the realm of oral discourse and were not transmitted outside the confines of family or small group conversation. Unrecorded in writing or in more widely disseminated forms of popular and artistic representation, little firsthand contemporary information about indigenous reactions has thus been retrievable for analysis.

Quite possibly, of course, the immigrant newcomers made no special impression on the indigenes. Many Quechua and Aymara were themselves only relatively recent immigrants from the countryside in cities like La Paz and Cochabamba, and they may not have noticed the sudden numerical increase in Bolivia's non-Indian, foreign population. They would not necessarily have had many opportunities to interact with the refugees on more than a chance or casual basis. Those who did meet refugees regularly and for longer periods, at a work site or through some form of commerce, would certainly have been exposed to—perhaps surprised by—"whites" of both sexes willing to engage in hard manual labor, and they may have noted qualitative differences in the kind of clothing worn, and in the less than affluent condition of these foreigners. And yet I wonder: beyond perceivable economic differences such as these, could many Indians really have made additional physical or cultural distinctions between the *judíos Alemanes* (as the German-Jewish refugees came to be called), and other European immigrants in Bolivia? On what basis could they have drawn their comparisons? Did this refugee episode, in which so many thousands of Jewish Europeans entered Bolivia and found a haven from persecution, really have any significance at all, or much relevance, for people whose own marginalization and subjugation so restricted and limited their knowledge of an outside world?

But if little can now be learned about early Indian perceptions of the incoming refugees, this is not at all the case when one probes and examines the realm of documentation and memory associated with the more literate groups in Bolivian society. Here, in the discourses of Bolivia's native-born middle sectors and of its native and expatriate elite (particularly in that of the Germans), I found that *judíos Alemanes* were certainly noticed, "looked at," categorized, and discussed. Some of the representations are hardly flattering to the Jewish refugees, indicating the anti-Semitic dangers they had sought to escape were not at all absent from the land they had now come to inhabit.

BIG NOSES AND THE ELDERS OF ZION

In March 1939 the *Revista de Bolivia* published a photo of the first-prize winners in a Carnival contest for most humorous costume.[2] It shows a couple facing the camera: a "husband" dressed in a shabby dark suit, wearing a fedora pulled down over his ears, carrying a large carpetbag, and standing arm-in-arm with his "wife." "She," obviously a man dressed in women's clothing, is wearing a curly-haired wig and hat, dark glasses, smeared-on lipstick, an oversized overcoat, and is carrying an umbrella. The most conspicuous feature in the photo, however, is the "husband's" oversized nose, a beaklike protuberance overwhelming his face. The picture, entitled "Los judíos" ("the Jews"), requires little interpretation. The parody of the forlorn appearance of many a Jewish refugee in Bolivia at the time—the shabby dress, the poverty of material possessions—is clear. But it is the depiction of a Jewish physical stereotype—the grossly enlarged "Jewish nose" on the "husband"—that is undoubtedly meant to trigger the viewer's guffaw. See the funny-looking Jews!

"Los judíos" (reproduced from *Revista de Bolivia*, March 1939)

A year later, in March 1940, a La Paz newspaper, *El Eco Libre*, printed a cartoon on its front page showing two opulent and corpulent Jews, each with a sizable nose, pulling a Bolivian citizen to a cross to crucify him.[3] In Cochabamba, *La Prensa* published a series of editorials and articles in November 1940 decrying the presence of "a Jewish beast," of "rancid" Jews with their "nauseous odor and devilish attitude," and warning of a "Jewish pestilence [brought on by] . . . this race cursed by God and mankind." Focusing on "the typical smell of the Jews, the nauseous smell . . . somewhat stronger than that of the animals of the highlands," Dr. Cesar Herrera argued that this bodily odor revealed Jews to be hereditary carriers of leprosis, potentially fatal sources of infection to unaware Christians with whom they came into contact.[4] "Prostitution, like leprosy, is a racial trademark of Jews," a writer for *La Crónica*, in La Paz, added. "It is a defect they have carried in their veins since the time of Ben Hur."[5]

In letters written during this period, refugees complained that the epithets "*Judío*" ("Jew") and "*Sucio Judío*" ("dirty Jew") were occasionally hurled contemptuously at them, and that they were called "murderers of Christ." They told of being jostled and hassled in the streets, of being ignored or insulted by officials, and of having graffiti—"*¡Basta de Judíos!*" ("No more Jews!") and "*¡Fuera Judíos!*" ("Jews Out!")—scrawled on their doors and walls. Given their generally impoverished condition upon arriving in Bolivia, they found it particularly ironic that some Bolivians considered them "money-grubbers," identifying them with usury, unfair financial dealings, and "international Jewish capitalist" schemes for world economic domination.[6]

Many of these Bolivian anti-Semitic stereotypes of course derived from the long-existent Spanish-Catholic popular tradition of blaming Jews for the killing of Christ and from ancient images depicting Jews as avaricious, physically unattractive, and potentially dangerous "outsiders"; these anti-Jewish prejudices had been brought to South America from Europe centuries earlier. They were in this sense "invisible baggage" carried by Catholic Bolivians in their encounter with the refugees. But since few "real" Jews lived in Bolivia until the mid-1930s, the fact that these stereotypes were retained so vividly and reemerged with such frightening vehemence suggests a peculiar characteristic of religious and economic prejudices against Jews throughout history. In areas influenced by European colonial expansionism, as in Europe, anti-Semitism existed and persisted *even where Jews were virtually absent.*

It was also clear, however, that the virulence of some of this anti-Jewish reaction was inspired by Nazi propaganda and activities, by the efforts of German officials, pro-Hitler German residents, and fascist sympathizers within the Bolivian civilian and military elites. Stirring up anti-Semitic sentiments was a way to further their own political and strategic agendas. Two related examples confirm this.

The first centered on a scandal about the illegal sale of Bolivian visas to Jews in Europe, which was uncovered in 1939, a few months before the death of President Busch. The discovery that a ring of consular officials in Europe, allegedly with the compliance and active involvement of Busch's foreign minister, Eduardo Diez de Medina, had sold thousands of Bolivian immigration permits in the consulates in Warsaw, Hamburg, Genoa, Paris, and Zurich, and pocketed millions of U.S. dollars from their dealings, was seized by a number of Bolivian politicians as a potential propaganda windfall. They utilized this scandal to rally and enlarge popular support against "outsiders" and to stir up nationalist sentiment against foreign domination of Bolivia's natural resources and the economy of the nation. They alleged that Diez de Medina had been motivated by greed and by sympathies stemming from his own "crypto-Jewish" family background (Marrano or New Christian origins were suggested by his surname, meaning "Ten of the Medina"). Implying guilt by association, they hinted at an international conspiracy between Jews and capitalists to control Bolivia's wealth and exploit its people, singling out the German-Jewish tin-mining magnate Mauricio Hochschild's central involvement in the economy, and his role in facilitating refugee immigration, as confirmation of their dire warnings. Pointing to the large influx of refugees who had stayed in the cities in economic competition with Bolivians, some of them called for an immediate cessation of refugee immigration. Others, seeking more drastic measures, demanded the expulsion of all Jewish newcomers. "Jews are an unhealthful element," because of their "selfish social, racial, and moral principles," declared a group of Bolivian Congressional Deputies who introduced an (ultimately unsuccessful) bill in August 1940 to bar Jews from residing in the country. "They should be cast out from the land."[7] The newspapers *La Razón, El Eco Libre,* and *La Crónica* in La Paz, and *La Prensa* and *El País* in Cochabamba joined the attack with an ongoing campaign of anti-Jewish articles and editorials.[8] And in November 1940, when Diez de

Medina was put on trial in the Chamber of Deputies for his alleged role in the sale of sanctuary to European refugees, spectators in the packed galleries above him kept up a steady chant of "Down with the Jews! Death to the Jews!"[9]

Although the anti-Semitic agitation subsided by mid-1941, when President Enrique Peñaranda used the exposure of an alleged pro-Axis plot to overthrow his government as the reason to expel the German ambassador, Ernst Wendler, and crack down on Fascist (as well as left-wing) political critics, it resumed with renewed intensity in September 1942 when the Chamber of Deputies again debated a bill to exclude "Jews, Negroes, and Orientals" from Bolivia.[10] In the course of the debate in the Chamber, Deputy Zuazo Cuenca read aloud portions from *The Protocols of the Elders of Zion*—that ubiquitous and scurrilous forgery implicating Jews in acts of ritual murder—as well as from Henry Ford's anti-Semitic diatribe *International Jew*. Supporting him, Deputy Gustavo Chacón described Jewish immigrants as "parasitic suckers of the national moneys," and warned that they would bleed the country dry. Other deputies denounced the "international character of Judaism" as a potential threat to Bolivian institutions, maintaining that the consistent consequence of Jewish "penetration" anywhere in the world was Jewish domination of the press, banks, and politics. The newspaper *La Calle*, in one of its many editorials supporting the exclusion bill, lamented the "inundation" of the country by immigrants "with very beaked noses": by members of the "Jewish race" who were waiting "to fall like a ravenous invading horde upon the cities of Bolivia," and who were scheming to gain control of the government. Jews, another article declared, were "corrupter[s] of defenseless people," who, if not stopped at the gates, would cast a "noose" over the heads of Bolivians. Jews as "a race," some of these "influentials" within the Bolivian political and press elites concluded, posed a danger to Bolivia's "nationality" and should be expelled.[11]

While it is possible, as some believed at the time, that the documents implicating the German ambassador and Nazi officials in plans for a pro-Axis putsch were fabrications produced by U.S. counterintelligence agents, no such uncertainty exists about the direct and indirect Nazi efforts to stir up anti-Semitic and anti-refugee resentments in Bolivia, and to bolster sympathetic Bolivian nationalist politicians in their pro-German, anti-American, anti-British stance. Ernst Wendler had also been *Landeskreisleiter* (district leader) of the NSDAP (National Socialist

Workers, or "Nazi," Party) in Bolivia that, according to official German records, counted 170 active members and more than eleven hundred supporters.[12] Not long after Zuazo Cuenca read sections from *The Protocols of the Elders of Zion* to the galleries and into the record of the Bolivian Chamber of Deputies, it was revealed that the portions he had "selected" came from a pamphlet published and distributed gratis by the German Office of Propaganda, *Ilustrativo y Informativo Material para Oradores (Illustrative and Informative Material for Orators)*.[13] It was also no secret that the German embassy subsidized the two most malevolent anti-Semitic newspapers in La Paz, *La Razón* and *La Calle*, as well as *El Imparcial*, *El País*, and *La Prensa* in Cochabamba.[14]

German expatriates (other than the recently arrived, predominantly Jewish, refugees) had certainly been present in Bolivia for a long time, and had fostered stout economic and cultural ties with the Bolivian political and military elites. Before the war, German export and import firms had been active throughout Bolivia, extending liberal credit terms, and had reached even the country's remotest areas with many of the latest products of German industry and business. The Cervecería Boliviana Nacional—the country's premier brewery and one of Bolivia's largest businesses—was established and built up by Germans and continued to be managed and, in large part, staffed by German employees throughout the 1930s and again after World War II. Lloyd Aereo Boliviano, the national airline, was founded in 1925 with a plane donated by the German government to celebrate the centenary of Bolivian independence from Spain. Its pilots and principal managers throughout the 1930s were almost exclusively German; its primary network connections were with the German system of commercial airlines in South America (Condor in Brazil and Lufthansa in Peru); and 60 percent of its stock (until the expropriation enacted under President Peñaranda in 1941) was owned by German residents in the Reich and by German businessmen in Bolivia, many of whom were openly sympathetic to National Socialism.[15]

German involvement in the training of the Bolivian armed forces also had a long history, dating back to before World War I, when a German military mission led by General Hans Kundt was invited to help modernize the Bolivian army. Kundt returned to Bolivia after the war as a private citizen to direct the Bolivian military academy and to head the training of the army and its officer corps. A number of German military men, including some who had been in the paramilitary and proto-

Fascists Freikorps after Germany's defeat in 1918, joined him. From 1926 to 1928, Ernst Roehm, who helped to create and organize the Nazi Party's S.A. (*Sturmabteilung*, storm troopers, or brown shirts) and who in 1930 was assigned the leadership of this paramilitary group by Hitler, was in Bolivia as a lieutenant colonel instructing Bolivian army officers.[16] A group of German volunteers served on the Bolivian side in the country's disastrous Chaco War against Paraguay, during which German pilots flew thousands of air missions for Bolivia, transporting supplies to the front and carrying wounded soldiers back to military and civilian hospitals for treatment.

Increasingly in the 1930s—through their diplomatic and commercial involvements in Bolivia, their propagandists, and the efforts of resident German citizens—officials and agents of Hitler's Germany tried to increase support for Nazi ideology and to extend the political and economic influence of National Socialism among dominant sectors of Bolivian society. A number of younger Bolivians entered competitions sponsored by the German embassy in which the winners were awarded paid trips to Germany as prizes. Once there, they were given "information tours" intended to convert them into partisans of the National Socialist regime and propagandists of its "virtues." German clubs in La Paz and Oruro organized dances, fiestas, and cultural and sports events to which Bolivian members of the military and civilian establishment were invited and in which the energy, accomplishments, and transformations reflected in the New German Order were emphatically acclaimed. German-sponsored schools in La Paz, Cochabamba, and Oruro were viewed as key agencies for the dissemination of Nazi propaganda and the implantation of Nazi ideas in the minds of their students—groups that always included children belonging to Bolivia's foremost families. Fritz Kübler, a leader of the NSDAP in Bolivia and director of the Colegio Mariscal Braun in La Paz—"El Colegio Alemán," the largest and "most elite" German school in Bolivia—was quite open and explicit in spelling out the propaganda and ideological functions his school served. In a book entitled *Deutsche in Bolivien* (first published in Germany in 1936 and then translated into Spanish and republished in *La Razón* of La Paz in 1940), Kübler wrote:

> The large public rallies of the NSDAP in Bolivia . . . are in great part organized with the collaboration of the German schools. And German residents

in the country are always profoundly impressed when they see our school's choir—in which the smallness of our contingent of blond, true-German students is a noticeable fact—enthusiastically present the German salute, and when they listen to its beautiful renderings of our national anthem and the marching and folksongs of our new Germany. In every sense, it should be clear, the main goal of the educational work of our schools today is to convey an understanding and esteem for the National Socialist world view. We shall continue to fill the hearts of both our German and non-German pupils with fervor and love for our Fatherland and Führer. The German school in La Paz can already claim much success in this regard. Indeed it was the proudest day in our school's history when, on September 7, 1935, in recognition of our efforts, the German ambassador presented us with a personally signed photograph of our Führer and Chancellor which our school now proudly displays.[17]

The Colegio Mariscal Braun in La Paz, displaying Nazi insignia and a portrait of Adolf Hitler (from F. Kübler, *Deutsche in Bolivien*)

Nazi Party members in La Paz, c. 1935

In the last years of the 1930s and the first years of the war, various military and civilian intelligence analysts, as well as writers sympathetic to the Allied cause, argued that direct or indirect control of Bolivia was a central goal in Nazi Germany's strategic planning in South America—and that the threat posed by Nazi agents, provocateurs, and supporters had to be taken seriously and effectively countered. Whoever exerts its dominance over this "roof of the world . . . and possesses good airdromes and refueling stations" wrote Hugo Fernández Artucio in his *Nazi Underground in South America,* "is in a position to hold mastery of the air in South America from a base which is practically inaccessible."[18] "I believe that the effort to grasp Bolivia as a territory on which to install a puppet-regime discloses a well-contrived and organized plan," declared Oscar Schnake, a Socialist who had been a Chilean government minister. "If we realize that Bolivia lies in the very core of the heart of South America, and that it borders a large number of neighboring states, one can clearly see the significance and potential consequences of the installation of a Nazi-regime in this place."[19] Bolivia's mineral wealth, warned several anti-Nazi publicists—its extensive deposits of tin, and its pyrites, silver, copper, tungsten, bismuth, and potentially rich holdings of oil and natural gas—were coveted prizes that were highly important to the success of the war effort and to the future stability of this region. Germany was dangerous in this part of the world, they maintained, precisely because Germans had such a long history of economic and military involvement in Bolivia, and because the Nazis had cultivated support for their ideology within significant groups in Bolivian society. Given the strong sympathy for fascism and the Axis alliance that already existed in neighboring Argentina, Brazil, and Chile, they worried that much of South America could easily fall prey to the "Nazi octopus" if no significant measures were immediately taken in Bolivia to destroy its growth and expansion.[20]

In reality, of course, many measures were already being taken—and the dire warnings of the anti-Nazi commentators were no doubt part of them. Indeed during the very period when the refugee influx from Central Europe was at its height, both German and Allied governments and their agents in Bolivia were battling behind the scenes and in a propaganda war to undermine each other's positions in the country, and to strengthen their influence over Bolivian decision makers at the highest levels. For the Nazis and Nazi-sympathizers, the arrival of so many Jews in Bolivia, their concentration in the cities, the "visa scandals," and the potential competition offered by immigrants for jobs and scarce economic resources, all served as grist in the mill in the effort to appeal to Bolivian nationalists of both the political right and left. By repeatedly linking Jews with an "international conspiracy" involving Bolsheviks, Communists, "Yankee capitalist bankers," Roosevelt, and Uncle Sam, the Nazis and their supporters hoped to trigger fears about "external invasion" and "outside control," especially the long-residual dread of national domination by that "Colossus of the North"—the United States of America.[21]

Placed on the defensive in trying to counteract the political support these extremist critics seemed to be gaining, President Enrique Peñaranda took formal action to curtail refugee immigration and control the immigrants' presence in Bolivia. He established a commission empowered to oversee immigrant affairs and to conduct a census to record adult immigrants for purposes of taxation. Under the aegis of this commission, all refugees sixteen years and older were required to be photographed to register, and to carry an identification card (*cédula*) in public at all times.[22] But Peñaranda and officials in his government also granted the immigrants great freedom to carry on their personal and communal affairs. While publicizing the measures they had taken to control further immigration and to keep track of the immigrants within the country, the Peñaranda government made no move to interfere with or delimit

President Enrique Peñaranda (in uniform), visiting the Exhibition of Industrial Products and Handicrafts Produced by Jewish Immigrants, La Paz, October 1943

refugee-sponsored cultural events, clubs, religious worship, or even political activities concerned with European affairs. Indeed, throughout his years in office, President Peñaranda himself remained openly friendly and supportive of the work of the American Jewish Joint Distribution Committee and its Bolivian refugee-aid agency, SOPRO. He personally paid visits to the Miraflores agricultural training farm established by SOPRO, as well as to a trade fair that it organized to exhibit furniture, handicrafts, and other articles produced by immigrant trainees. Toward the end of his presidency, he also attended and addressed a large immigrant assembly in La Paz gathered to commemorate the fifth anniversary of *Kristallnacht*. His cynical critics—and even some JDC officials—thought his sympathies were motivated by his own unexamined acceptance of the stereotype of Jewish international power and influence, by his wish to curry favor with leaders of Jewish organizations like the JDC who, he believed, were closely linked to banks and U.S. government agencies able to bestow economic benefits on Bolivia.

True or not, it was certainly also in the interest of the U.S. government to "win" Bolivia to the Allied side in the war against the Axis powers, and the United States offered Peñaranda's government many economic incentives to achieve this. In short order, Bolivia received substantial low-interest U.S. government loans, promises of technical assistance, an agreement for large-scale purchases of tin to build up U.S. wartime stockpiles, and a commitment from the U.S. to continue buying Bolivian minerals at reasonable prices over the long term.[23] The results of all this could not have been more pleasing to U.S. officials—and certainly brought euphoria to members of the refugee community. In January 1942, two months after the United States had entered World War II, the Bolivian government formally joined the Allied side and broke diplomatic ties with both Germany and Japan.[24]

Paradoxically, however, it was not until February 1944, some two months after President Peñaranda was ousted from office, that strict measures were taken to close down and freeze the assets of firms and businesses headed by German residents who had been identified as actively supportive of the Nazi cause. This response was certainly motivated by the fact that the United States and most Latin American countries initially refused to recognize the junta that had ousted Peñaranda, a junta headed by Major Gualberto Villaroel who, himself, was overthrown and killed in July 1946. Given both Bolivia's economic dependency on the United States at the time, and increasing indications that the tide had turned and Germany was losing the war, moderates associated with the government decided that a move against pro-Nazi German residents in Bolivia was politically prudent. The owners and managers of these pro-Nazi German enterprises, as well as a number of teachers at the German schools—all of whom had long ago been placed on a "Fifth Column Black List" by Allied agencies—were arrested and shipped off to internment camps in the United States. The majority of them returned to Bolivia eventually, many within a year or more of the end of the war.[25]

NAZIS IN THE STREETS

"So, tell me more about Bolivia," people have said to me on a number of occasions. "I don't know very much about the place. Isn't that where the Nazis hid out after the war? Isn't Bolivia where the SS criminal lived who was caught and tried in France? What was his name? . . . Barbie? . . . Isn't that where Barbie and other Nazis went into hiding?"

There is certainly irony, if not injustice, in the fact that for many Europeans and North Americans, Bolivia has acquired a reputation primarily as a place sheltering Nazi war criminals, while its role as a saving haven for thousands of Jewish and non-Jewish refugees and displaced persons is virtually unrecognized, if not unknown. In part, this is explained by the widespread lack of knowledge by "outsiders" of Bolivian history and politics, and by even less awareness (or considerable underestimation) of the importance of South America in general, and Bolivia in particular, for refugee and postwar "displaced-person" immigration. But it also reflects the international publicity generated since the early 1960s by the "discovery" of a number of war criminals in South America—especially, in the case of Bolivia, by the identification of Klaus Barbie there and by his extradition and trial in France. The "Nazi hunter" Beate Klarsfeld's confirmation that the man Bolivians knew as Klaus Altmann was indeed the notorious head of the Gestapo in Lyon, Klaus Barbie; the revelations that he and other wanted Nazis had been helped to escape to South America on so-called rat lines by U.S. Army Counterintelligence Corps (CIC) people who had found their wartime anti-Communist "expertise" useful in the intensifying U.S.-U.S.S.R. cold war hostilities; the "protection" that Barbie and other less than savory Germans received from Bolivia's right-wing military dictators: all these had been the focus of numerous journalistic accounts, articles, books, newsreels—and even of an Academy Award–winning documentary film, *Hotel Terminus: The Life and Times of Klaus Barbie*, by the famed director Marcel Ophuls.[26]

Throughout the 1940s and 1950s, many Jewish refugees in Bolivia were of course also convinced that there were "Nazis in the streets." My grandmother Bertha was among them. One morning a few months after the war ended, she returned from the market to our apartment in Miraflores shouting, "My God, I just saw Goebbels near the *mercado*. He is alive!" Those words (did I *actually* hear them spoken on that particular day?) were quoted and the incident mentioned many times in my family whenever the topic of "escaped Nazis" or "Nazis in South America" came up in conversation. On one occasion, my mother—who knew from long daughterly experience that her own "very serious" mother was prone neither to hysterical outbursts nor to spontaneous jokes—was qualitatively supportive of my grandmother's claim. "I'm sure it wasn't Goebbels," she explained to my sister, my father, and me when this "sighting" was mentioned, some years after we had moved to the United States. "But that doesn't mean that Mama couldn't have seen some other Nazi criminal in La Paz." My father, much more skeptical, retorted, "Yes, it was probably Adolf himself, shopping for vegetables in the *mercado*!"

There were, of course, evil apparitions in the new land. Frightening sightings in public spaces. Along with their recipes for *Apfelstrudel* and *Wiener schnitzel*, their few material possessions and their cultural memories, the refugees brought alarming ghosts with them, frightening phantasms from their past. And certainly not all these ghosts were effervescent phantoms or traumatic flashbacks from the recesses of the mind. Some were real flesh-and-blood villains. "Look, there is no question," recalled Heini Lipczenko in 1990, "Nazi criminals came into the country (and probably are still there). They were absorbed into the local German community. They were shielded by Fascist Bolivian military [men]. And they made profitable business deals with Bolivian business people." "If you went into the Café La Paz in the late afternoon," added Liesl Lipczenko, "you would see many of these Nazis sitting there, drinking coffee or beer, eating pastry—laughing, having conversations, quite at home, comfortable. But, of course, no Jew was meant to go into that café."[27]

And yet, despite the widespread perception by "outsiders" and Jewish immigrants that Bolivia harbored numerous Central European Nazis, it is curious that in contemporary sources, and in more recent narrative recollections by Jewish refugees and postwar Jewish residents in the country, one finds no accounts—other than those relating to Klaus Barbie—of person-to-person confrontations or verbal exchanges between Jews and "known" Nazis. Indeed, even when I specifically asked individuals still living in Bolivia (or who had been part of the Bolivian immigration) about their reactions to the presence of Barbie, their responses were for the most part vague. "Until Beate Klarsfeld and others began their extradition campaign," Marek Ajke told me, "most of us were either unaware of who Barbie was, or we knew him as Klaus Altmann—as a German businessman who, among other things, also did business with Jews. For a period of time, he actually lived in the apartment house right next to ours, and we had no idea about him." "Barbie was a *German of that generation*," said Andres Simon. "We were suspicious of *any German* of that generation! Where were they during the war? What did they do? Why are they living in South America? These questions came into my head whenever I ran into any German of a certain age. Other than the fact that Altmann/Barbie had powerful friends among 'influentials' in the Bolivian military and government, he did not seem different to me than other Germans in Bolivia."[28]

But Naftali Fischzang and Salo Frischman, Nazi concentration camp survivors who had emigrated to Bolivia after the war, each had a direct encounter with Barbie after his identity became known—during the period when he still enjoyed the protection of Colonel Hugo Banzer and General Luis García Meza, Bolivia's military rulers. Fischzang relates:

I was at the airport, with my daughter's new in-laws, who were flying out of the country. I looked around and there right in front of me sat Barbie with another German. He had a Bolivian bodyguard with him, a man named Castro, and maybe others—but they were not seated. Suddenly all the past came back to me. Blood rushed to my head! What to do? A scandal! I got up. I started pacing, faster and faster, I paced back and forth in front of him. "After thirty-five years, to be faced by a Nazi criminal": I spoke out loud, repeated that, louder and louder. My fifteen-year-old nephew was observing me. He, too, got up. He approached Barbie, stood in front of him, and motioned to him with the sign of murder: a finger across the throat. Bar-

bie's bodyguard, Castro, then approached my nephew: "What's the problem?" he asked. My nephew, who was born in Bolivia—a Bolivian citizen and native speaker [of Spanish]—began to yell at the bodyguard: "You are a criminal, protecting Barbie! We Bolivians shouldn't be doing this. He is a criminal, a murderer!" The accusations were shouted at Castro and other Bolivians in the lounge. Barbie, meanwhile, just sat there, unruffled. He seemed unaffected by the scene around him. Not moving.

Salo Frischman, a big and still-powerful man, now in his seventies, who spent years in Auschwitz and lost his entire family in the Holocaust, recalled:

One day, Altmann—Barbie—stood right outside my store on the Calle Yanacocha. "This was already after Beate Klarsfeld was here. I couldn't stop myself. I rushed into the street and shouted again and again [in Spanish]: 'Here is a murderer of children—a war criminal!' People gathered. The police came. I didn't care. I did it because I knew, as a victim, what he had done. They took me away. They questioned me. 'What do you want? Why did you make such a scene?' 'I don't want to see him! I'm not responsible for what will happen to him if I see him again!' They warned me, but they let me go. I knew I was now in danger. Barbie had powerful friends. I was playing with my life. But what I felt was that if I could hit him with these hands, then I am happy. And I would say it openly with every blow I give him: 'this one is from my father, from my mother, from my brothers, my sister . . .' I am the only one who survived who could hit such a Nazi criminal, such an SS man!"[29]

It requires no complicated interpretation to conclude that the passions, anger, and pent-up frustration that these refugee accounts express are directed not only at Klaus Barbie, or the past history of Nazi criminality he embodied, or the presence of other "concealed" Nazis and their German sympathizers in Bolivia during this period, but also at Bolivians in general, and at what many refugees perceived as overt or covert anti-Semitism in the willingness of powerful Bolivian officials and businessmen to shelter, assist, and make use of Barbie and, possibly, other Nazi residents in the country. Yet it is important to underscore how exceptional these reactions seem to have been. Neither the real nor imagined harboring of Nazi criminals after the war, nor the various moments in Bolivian history (such as in the early 1940s) when anti-Semitism threatened the safety of Jewish immigrants, seem to have elicited public reactions from Jews that survive in the documentation. Nor has Bolivian anti-Semitism been a major topic of concern in the present-day recollection of the immigrants.

In part, of course, this apparent absence of publicly recorded responses reflects an insecurity and vulnerability that many Jewish immigrants in Bolivia felt (and those still resident in the country still feel) about their acceptance, safety, and political existence. But it certainly also suggests a much more positive conclusion about Bolivian middle-sector and elite responses to Jews—both during the period of intense refugee immigration and afterward. It highlights the fact that by far the most widely held Bolivian reactions to the Jewish presence ranged from indifference, to tolerance, to a welcoming, sympathetic acceptance. During the peak immigration months, many Bolivians forcefully attacked anti-Semitism and came to the defense of the immigrants. Their voices and opinions, expressed publicly in forums and in print, made for a strong counterpoint to anti-Semitic hate mongering, and reassured the refugees of important support within the Bolivian establishment. Indeed, from the earliest days of the refugees' arrival, goodwill and trust characterized the relationship of many Bolivians toward them. Bolivians, in this respect, "made space" for the immigrants, let them set up businesses and enter and participate in numerous entrepreneurial activities. They also "made space" physically and culturally.

Refugee recollections of Bolivia have been universally grateful to Bolivians for saving their lives.[30] In their present-day memory, Bolivian anti-Semitism—despite its persistence in its milder form as Christian religious anti-Jewish prejudice, its economic stereotyping, its expression in slurs and mockery—is usually remembered as a relatively minor episode within a sojourn fraught with challenges and difficulties but also characterized by relative tolerance. No matter how short or long their residence in Bolivia would be, this Andean land inserted itself into the memory of these émigrés as the place that gave them refuge when all others had rejected them. "For better or for worse," Ilse Hertz observed, "Bolivians permitted us to live." It was in Bolivia that the refugees survived the horrors of the Nazi Holocaust. Consciousness of that overwhelming reality is the background against which their present-day memories are constructed. "Here in Bolivia," Salo Frischman concluded, "anti-Semitism is not in the blood, as in Europe. It has to be provoked and incited. I've felt free since I came here. Look at the hands of the people here—of Bolivians. Unlike those of Europeans, their hands don't have Jewish blood on them!"

APARTNESS WITHIN THE CONTACT ZONE

In a recent book, Mary Louise Pratt has used the term "contact zone" to identify the social space that marks the encounter of peoples previously separated by geography and history. Within a "contact zone," members of encountering groups interact on an individual and collective basis, establishing ongoing relations with each other. Relations between encountering groups within "contact zones" have varied over time and from place to place; they have reflected situations of domination and subordination as well as "conditions of coercion, radical inequality, and intractable conflict." But they have also shown significant degrees of cultural reciprocity and hybridity, and the phenomenon of "transculturation"—the way people and groups absorb as well as shape and influence their construction and constitution of each other.[31]

In the Bolivian "contact zone" within which the mutual encounter between Central European refugees and Bolivians occurred, there was significant economic interaction but relatively little cultural reciprocity and hybridity, little breakdown of the cultural, social, and political boundaries between refugee and host groups. Paradoxically, the very institutions the refugees created in Bolivia, and the symbols and memories on which they relied for their collective identity, were instrumental in maintaining those boundaries. While one might have expected some greater degree of social and cultural interaction and interchange between the refugees and those Bolivians closer to them in social background—with the Spanish-speaking white and mestizo middle-classes, and with members of the professional and ruling elites—relatively little in fact took place. The immigrants' reconstituted culture—based on Central European–Jewish bourgeois values, on the German language, on a certain conception of "modernity," literature, music, and hygiene, and on their liberal and materialistic worldview—proved largely irreconcilable with what they perceived to be a deeply rooted Catholicism, intensely private family lifestyle, social conservatism, and industrial "backwardness" of middle- and upper-class Bolivians.

These latter, of course, also maintained largely impermeable barriers. Guarding access to Bolivian citizenship by means of lengthy residency and complex naturalization regulations, they relegated the vast majority of refugees to the legally, much less secure status of "resident alien," which strongly discouraged and in effect generally impeded their participation in politics, which the Bolivian elites controlled. Personally, too, their social interactions with immigrants were largely superficial. Certainly, flirtations and sexual encounters did occasionally occur, but marriages between Bolivians and refugees were extremely rare, and were viewed by members of both groups as eccentric departures from the communal fold.[32] Despite business and professional dealings with the immigrants, moreover, it was highly uncommon for Bolivians to invite them to their house. Culturally and, in many respects, socially, Bolivians and refugees remained each other's "other."

Ella's grave in the Jewish cemetery in La Paz

7

SURVIVING

MEMORY

Generations remain alive only in the flickering memory of a person whose own days are drawing to a close.

—David Lowenthal

Memory is a perpetually actual phenomenon, a bond tying us to the eternal present; history is a representation of the past.

—Pierre Nora, "Between Memory and History: *Les Lieux de Mémoire*"

All those moments will be lost in time, like tears in the rain.   —Batty, in *Blade Runner*

"HOTEL BOLIVIA"

As I had done on previous occasions, near the end of a recent stay in Bolivia I made arrangements to go to the Jewish cemetery in La Paz to visit my aunt Ella's grave. I was expected by the Bolivian caretaker when I arrived because he had been informed of my intention by Salo Frischman, an Auschwitz sur-vivor and postwar immigrant who, for years, had been a member of the Chevra Kadesha (burial society) and who was the person who washed the dead before their final enshrouding and burial. The walled-in cemetery is located in a beau-tiful spot in the Miraflores section of the city, within a large natural terrace, high up on the northwestern side of the mountainous "bowl" in which La Paz is located, on a rising hillside whose summit terminates on the altiplano. From the height of its site, the view of La Paz stretching out below Mount Illimani is stun-ning, and the usual city street noises—accelerating car engines, honking horns, people's voices, barking dogs—seem softened and muffled, masked by the breezes flowing through well-kept bushes and aromatic eucalyptus trees.

Looking at the cemetery this time, its smallness, its many graves, I was impressed more than ever before. Outside its walls, practically to the edge of their perimeter, apartment houses have been constructed—or, still unfinished, are in the process of being erected—leaving the cemetery with no possibility of future expansion.

Ella's grave, from 1943, is among the oldest here. Yet in the part of the cemetery where it is located, it is surrounded by dozens of tombstones from the early 1940s, for the most part of persons much older than she when she died. Her tombstone, of dark tan andesite, is unusual in its coloration, but it shares a stark simplicity with the others from these early years of the immigration, a lack of ostentation that contrasts significantly with many of the more recent marble headstones and family memorials that now predominate. It is certainly easy to notice the increasing affluence of the Jewish immigrant community in La Paz over the years by looking at these tombstones and monuments. The newer, bigger memorials now virtually shut the older ones out from view, overshadowing and dwarfing them almost as if the memorialization and remembrance of the earlier deceased immigrants has become a secondary order of recollection. Indeed, it is apparent that the older graves— generally of persons with German names—receive fewer visitors than the more recent ones: hardly any of the little stones that Jews place on tombstones to mark their attendance and attest to their recital of the prayer of mourning can be found on them.

Few relatives of the people buried in the oldest graves still live in Bolivia. The size of the German-speaking Jewish community—not only in La Paz, but in the country as a whole—dwindled so drastically that none of the cultural and social institutions, and only some of the commercial establishments, founded in the late 1930s still exist. The Hogar Austriaco, the Austrian Club, is no more, and the Comunidad Israelita has gone out of existence—its functions absorbed by the surviving Círculo Israelita. Many German- or Austrian-Jewish business establishments from the 1940s—restaurants, small hotels, clothing stores, and the shops of tailors, electricians, carpenters, and mechanics—have likewise disappeared or been sold to native Bolivians or postwar Jewish immigrants from Eastern Europe. The school I attended, the Escuela Boliviana-Israelita, has been transformed into the Colegio Boliviano-Israelita, moved to larger and much more impressive quarters on the Calle Cañada Strongest (into a building owned by the Círculo Israelita). But, although still partially subsidized by the Jewish community, it is no longer run by Jews on a day-to-day basis, and few German-speaking Jewish immigrants are associated with it. Christian Bolivians, and not the children and grandchildren of Jewish refugees and immigrants, currently make up most of the student body and of its teaching and administrative staffs. Wealthy Jews now send their children to the Lycée Français, or the American Institute, or the Colegio Calvert in Calacoto: elite schools attended by the sons and daughters of the Bolivian social and political ruling class, and by the children of members of the international diplomatic and business community.

Altogether no more than twelve hundred to fifteen hundred Jews still live in Bolivia—and this number, as older members of the community have indicated to me, some of them in a tone of resignation, is shrinking. The *smallest* percentage of this Jewish population, perhaps no more than 100 people, consists of survivors of the panic immigration of the late 1930s. A slightly larger number is made up of children and grandchildren of those refugees—born in Bolivia, for whom the country is homeland. The largest proportion consists of immigrants, mainly of East European origin, who survived concentration or death camps or who lived in Europe in hiding, and who came to Bolivia after the war, usually by choice, to join relatives or acquaintances and to start a new life. They and their offspring are now at the core of Bolivia's Jewish cultural and religious life; their memories and institutions and activities define the character and spirit of the existing collectivity. But that second wave of immigration, bringing hundreds of Eastern European Jews to Bolivia after World War II, was certainly not large enough to compensate for the fact that an outflow of Central European Jews was already ongoing—that far from growing, the total Jewish population of Bolivia continued in its numerical decline.

From their very arrival in Bolivia in the 1930s, many, perhaps most, of the German, Austrian, and other refugees from Central Europe considered Bolivia only a temporary haven—"Hotel Bolivia," as they described it. Some of them, who had managed to flee Europe in large part only because they had been able to acquire Bolivian visas, left soon after their arrival, often crossing borders illegally, reemigrating to Chile, Argentina, Brazil—places with larger and more established European populations, "officially closed" to new immigration but accessible through the "back door." Others stayed a few years longer, generally until after the end of the war, and then left. Many, who managed to get the mandatory affidavit of support and the required quota clearance and visa in the mid-1940s, went directly to the United States. Hundreds moved elsewhere in South America, especially to Argentina, eventually choosing to become permanent residents there, or to wait before emigrating once again either to North America or to Europe. A smaller number, usually people who had considered themselves primarily as "political refugees" in Bolivia—Social Democrats, Communists, and other activist political opponents of the Nazi regime—went back to Germany and Austria. Scores of refugees left for Israel after its establishment as a state in 1948.

These departing refugees, and those others who emigrated from Bolivia later, in the 1950s, 1960s, even in the 1970s, went elsewhere for reasons that they later recalled as being sound and compelling. Thus political refugees returned to Europe "as soon as possible," as one of them, Alexander Deutsch, indicated, intending to participate in "the construction of a new society." The justification he offered for his personal decision to return to Austria echoes the sentiments of many other political emigrants in this respect.

> I returned to Vienna not long after the war because this has always been my real home. I will eternally be grateful to Bolivia and to Bolivians for saving my life. But I thought of myself as in exile, not as an immigrant, in La Paz. I had been in Social Democratic youth circles before the war, and in Bolivia I had been very active in the small "Free Austria" political grouping that we formed there, and which we affiliated with the international "Free Austria" movement, headquartered in London. After the war, and the defeat of the Nazis, I was eager to return here to work and to build a new, Social Democratic, Austrian land.[1]

A sense of mission was a motivation also for those who went to Israel, but the political nature of this mission, and its combined Socialist and Zionist agenda, was not always clear to them. Ferry Kohn explained:

> Although quite a few who left for Israel had belonged to Labor Zionist youth organizations like Ha-Shomer ha-Za'ir in Europe, or had become associated with Zionism in Bolivia during and immediately after the war years, some— like me—who came to Israel after 1948, were young people who had simply felt lost in Bolivia, uprooted, disconnected from things that mattered. My parents and three of my sisters were unable to get out of Austria in time, and my father and mother and the two younger girls were taken and killed by the Nazis in Riga. In La Paz, during the war years, I tried not to think about what might have happened to them. I played cards and gambled at the casino, I womanized, I was an irresponsible *laus-bub*, a charlatan. A move to Israel, I was eventually encouraged to think, would provide me with a purpose. Together with others, I would help to build a homeland for Jews and, at the same time maybe, redeem myself. But little did I know then how truly difficult it would be here during those early years after the state was formed, and how strenuously I would have to work.[2]

Other "departees" provided explanations that generally show an inability—perhaps an unwillingness—to root themselves with any permanence in their Bolivian haven, or to commit and connect themselves more deeply and organically to its people and land. "Bolivia was a dead end for me, socially and professionally," a number of them said. "Before the war, when we were frantic about getting out, I wanted to come to the United States. In America, I believed—and I don't think I was wrong—*real* opportunities exist to start again." "If not me, at least my children needed the chance for the kind of education and professional training that was only available outside of the country." "Bolivia was politically too unstable, there were too many revolutions, too many *golpes* [coups]. One never knew, from one day to the next, what might happen politically—and the instability did not inspire confidence." "We always felt like outsiders in relation to Bolivians of the middle and, especially, upper classes—like *judíos tolerados* [tolerated Jews]: accepted, even encouraged to participate in some areas of the economy, but from whom a certain distance would always be kept."[3]

Within my own family, the emigration from Bolivia occurred in stages. My maternal grandparents, Bertha and Nathan, left first, early in 1946, for New York—where Regi, their oldest daughter, her husband Ernst, and son, George, had managed to immigrate a few years earlier after an intermediate period in Trinidad. Julius, my uncle, departed soon afterward and joined them. Ferry Kohn, my cousin, left for Israel in 1949. My paternal grandmother, Lina, and I then went to the United States in March 1950, where my mother, father, and sister, Elly, joined us six months later.

If I could now ask my parents to give their reasons for leaving Bolivia, I would assume that they would include many of the same factors recalled by other Central European departees: the seemingly greater possibilities for improving their "life chances" elsewhere, the unpredictability of Bolivian politics, the difficulties in bridging cultural differences, and their inability "to feel" as though they genuinely belonged and were truly a part of Bolivian social and political reality. Yet, in my parents' case—as in that of so many other refugees who left Bolivia after the war—the desire to rejoin surviving members of a family from whom they had been separated, to reconstruct some version of familial life in the aftermath of dispersal and destruction, was no doubt the most important motivation. Certainly by the late 1940s, most of the members of my family who had survived the war—my father's half-sister Kathe in England, my cousin Frieda (who had been in a British-run "displaced persons" camp after almost four years in Nazi concentration camps), my grandparents, my aunt and uncles in the United States, and my parents in Bolivia—seemed to have decided that vigorous efforts would be made to reconstitute ourselves as a family group in one place.

I don't remember ever being asked to voice an opinion in the decision to leave Bolivia, and I am uncertain how it was ever determined that the United States (instead of Bolivia, or some other Latin American or European country) would be the place for our regathering. I do recall that when my parents decided to send me with my grandmother Lina after she received her U.S. visa early in 1950, it seemed totally natural to me—a matter of course, what *had* to happen next—as though I had always been prepared for that tomorrow to arrive. In my memory of the years between the end of the war and our actual departure from La Paz, my parents, grandmother, sister, and I always lived like sojourners: temporary visitors in Bolivia, not permanent residents. Even when it was clear that my father's plumbing and electrical business was doing quite well, he was hesitant to commit himself to large or long-range building contracts that were offered him. We acquired no car, no apartment or house, no material possession that might tie us down.

I was going with my grandmother, my parents assured me, in what must certainly have been their effort to instill responsibility as well as pride in me, because I could serve as my grandmother's escort and interpreter. Knowing Spanish, German, and a little English, I could translate for her (she spoke German and Hungarian but virtually no Spanish) on the land and sea voyage north, and could make sure that all went well when we transferred ships, from the Italian liner that would take us from Arica to Panama, to the United Fruit Company freighter in which we would then travel from Colón to the United States. But I was *really* going because my elderly grandmother was extremely reluctant to make the voyage to the United States by herself, her visa would lapse if she didn't leave within a stipulated period, and my parents, having regained their Austrian nationality and passport after the war, still had to wait some months before *they* could get entry visas under a U.S. quota restricting the annual admission of Austrian immigrants. I, on the other hand, could enter the United States without difficulty on the basis of my Bolivian birth and Bolivian passport.

Thus when I left Bolivia as a ten-year-old—left the country where I was born but in which I had been encouraged not to deepen my roots—I left willingly, not thinking about the meaning or consequences of the break I was making. It seems to me I believed then that I might never return to Bolivia. Friends I was leaving behind, the spectacular beauty of the place, its cultural life, music, foods, its air, colors, and smells. I seem not to have allowed myself to feel and to express the profundity of the rupture. I don't recall shedding tears when the train pulled out of the station on its way to our port of embarkation in Chile. I was going to live in the United States of America. That would be my future. My parents and sister would join me there in a few months. We would all be together— what remained of the family would be reunited. Already I seemed to think of Bolivia as a concluded chapter. Time to turn the page.

MEMORY AND BOLIVIA AS EXPERIENCE

Early in 1991, four decades and some months after I arrived in the United States from Bolivia, I placed an advertisement in German in the *Aufbau*, the German-Jewish newspaper published in New York that, since 1934, has served the Central European immigrant community in America as a primary vehicle for world and communal news, and for information about German-Jewish rescue, immigration, and life events.[4] "For a book project, 'Surviving Memory,' " I wrote under the heading BOLIVIAN IMMIGRANTS, "I am seeking interviews with persons who emigrated to Bolivia in the 30s and early 1940s from Germany or Austria."[5] My hope was to reach people in the New York–New England region who were outside the network of ex-Bolivia refugees with whom I had become acquainted through my parents and family members—possibly to meet them and videotape their recollections.

I was quite surprised by the enthusiastic response the ad generated. Scores of people contacted me by telephone and mail—either after having read it themselves in the *Aufbau* or after being apprised of the ad by a friend or relative who had seen it. At first, the responses came mainly from people in the New York–New England area, but soon I was also contacted by people elsewhere in the United States—the Midwest, West, Florida, and the South. Then people from outside the United States also began to get in contact with me: Canada, Brazil, Argentina, the United Kingdom, Germany, Austria, and Israel. All were eager to reminisce about Bolivia: some were willing to meet with me and have their accounts taped, others to send me written materials and to respond to specific written questions. A number of these respondents had kept in touch with each other over the years. They told me that recollections of their time in Bolivia—or of particular incidents from the years they resided there—came up in conversation among them. But others noted that they had few if any connections with other "ex-Bolivianos," and what had compelled them to respond to the *Aufbau* ad was a combination of curiosity ("why would anyone be interested in memories of what happened to them during those years?") and a desire to remember and relate their "Bolivia experience" to a willing listener.

Once I began to interview people—to meet and talk with them and to note or tape their accounts—the content of what they said spotlighted for me the power of remembrance in re-creation. It led me to confront questions about the past and how we know it; about the character of memory and its relationship with place and time; about the differences, but also the interconnecting links between memory and history. For what is meant by the "Bolivia experience"? I asked myself. Can one speak of it collectively, as something shared by the refugees over the years, as something (almost like an object?) that is knowable, with definable characteristics, agreed upon by all those who were part of the refugee emigration to this Andean land. In other words, does a collective memory identify it? Or was this experience highly personal, in fact, the construction of individual memory, differing from person to person and within individuals over time?

In the broadest possible terms, of course, certain general elements were incontrovertibly part of the "Bolivia experience"—characteristics that everyone who gave me oral recollections, or whom I came to know through writing, would agree were central to its identification. Its participants had all been refugees displaced by Nazi persecution. After crossing from Europe to South America, they had been admitted as strangers into a land that in its culture, climate, and physical geography differed profoundly from the places from which they had come. All of them had, at minimum, spent a part or all of the war years in Bolivia—and many had lived there much longer (well into the 1950s, even the 1960s and 1970s). Despite their arrival with few if any material resources, they had (either as individuals, or as members of family units) managed to survive economically—some of them with great success—through earnings from employment, commerce, business, or for services rendered. Though they had interacted economically and, to a lesser degree, socially with Bolivians of various class and ethnic backgrounds, their primary social and cultural connection was with other refugee immigrants. They socialized in informal gatherings, frequented immigrant establishments, and participated in refugee-initiated cultural events and organizations.

But beyond these broadly shared general components, what constitutes the "Bolivia experience" in their later lives—recalled over time and observed from different places—is much less clear-cut. The reason for this has to do with the very workings of memory, its rendering of "experience," as well as with the character of experience itself. For memory is certainly, on the one hand, intensely personal as a form of awareness. As David Lowenthal notes: "for someone else to know about my memory is not the same as having it." Many aspects of the past are recalled as "some particular event [that] happened to me."[6] The content of such personal remembrances may include "minute and intimate details of past events, relationships, and feelings," elements that cannot be fully shared and, oftentimes perhaps, cannot even be articulated in words—emotions, sensations, physical imprints such as those which Charlotte Delbo, in *Days and Memory*, an account of her survival during the Holocaust, has labeled "deep memory."[7]

Transmitting the past through memory is problematic in another way: the recollection of any event or "experience"—as well as "forgetting it"— is a socially constructed act undertaken from the perspective of "a present." Factors like "where" the remembering takes place, its cultural context, the social and political background of the rememberer, his or her gender, age, economic situation, and perception of future—as well as narrative strategies and the discernible and invisible influences of ideology— all these affect recollection and the shapes of memory. Memory is, in this sense, what Natalie Z. Davis and Randolph Starn have termed "an instrument of reconfiguration and not of reclamation or retrieval."[8]

And since recollection occurs within a particular "present," since it is situated in time, memory itself is susceptible to "change over time." It too has a history. What, for example, individual refugees would recall about the "Bolivia experience" in 1941 or 1945 or after the Bolivian Revolution of 1952, or more recently, might differ considerably not only among them but within each person as well.

The differences between observations in the early 1940s of the threat of anti-Semitism in Bolivia, and more recent, much more benign recollections of its importance offer a clear illustration of this constructed nature of memory. They point to some of the multiform ways in which individuals and groups recall, reorganize, and distort their present memory to represent the past.

In perhaps more direct and explicit fashion, my own background and the nature of my involvement in this work have also illuminated for me the discursive, historicized construction of memory. As the Bolivia-born child of refugees, I am both a participant in and historian of "the Bolivia experience"—an interlocutor extracting recollections and shaping what I hear through my own projections. Many impulses and feelings feed my activities in this respect: curiosity about the past and my own family's role within it; desire to document the life stories, and reclaim the memories and discourses, of ordinary people who might otherwise remain hidden from history; responsibility to the many individual voices and documentary traces to which I have had access; ambivalence about my ability to render into a fluent yet coherent narrative the diversity, richness, and emotional complexity of what I have been told or discovered. The people who gave me oral accounts or entrusted me with their personal memoirs—their "little stories," as some of them put it—became witnesses in this process of creation. I became a medium for their testimony, who would take aspects of their "little stories" and, through the filter of my own memories and present consciousness, embed them in yet another story. The process involved in this construction reveals the contingent nature of "experience" and the fluidity of its multiple interpretations. And what ultimately emerges as the "Bolivia experience" has no singular manifestation, no fixed meaning. Like experience in general, to use Joan W. Scott's words, it "is at once always already an interpretation *and* something that needs to be interpreted."[9]

If this is indeed the case, if the many oral, written, and visual recollections of refugeehood in Bolivia, and my account of this history, affirm the multifaceted character of memory and the many meanings of the "Bolivia experience"—if the refugee community in Bolivia has virtually ceased to exist and no collective memory of their "Bolivia experience" has emerged—what energizes the witnesses to testify and narrate? What drives them (and me) to recall and tell? Why do we share a profound need to keep memory alive?

TRANSMISSION

It is mid-July 1991 and I am back in La Paz for the first time since my initial return visit to Bolivia (a brief stopover seventeen years earlier, when I was on my way to Brazil). I am here for two purposes. I am engaged in historical research: videotaping oral histories about the European refugee immigration and examining archival materials relevant to it. And, because Marianne and two of our children, Alex and Gabriel, will be with me for a part of my stay, I also want to introduce them to Bolivia, to show them La Paz, the city where I was born, as well as its surroundings, and to travel with them to Cochabamba and Sucre, where I also lived when I was a child.

On this day, however, only my first in La Paz since my arrival, I am on my own. I slept badly the night before, no doubt from the effects of my body's efforts to adjust to the altitude, and I am taking an early walk in the bright sunshine and the brisk, brilliantly clear, blue-thin air that still characterize winter mornings in this Andean capital. Despite its increasing physical transformation into a city of tall buildings and glass skyscrapers, and its inundation by thousands of exhaust-emitting autos, trucks, and minibuses, it is difficult not to be awed by the spectacular beauty of La Paz's natural setting. Illimani, with its three peaks, looms in the near distance, and is totally revealed in its full three-dimensionality in today's morning light—a giant volcanic mountain of dark rock capped by the whitest of snows. And the city's early-hour scents and noises—of strong coffee and freshly baked rolls (marraquetas), of church bells, newspaper vendors, and people making their way to work—emerge sharply in the clarity of the atmosphere, reminding me of mornings like this when I was a child.

I am drawn, like a moth to a flame, down the Calle México to the building where we lived at number 134 for many years. From its intersection with the Calle Otero de la Vega, close to our apartment, to the Plaza del Estudiante near the University, Calle México is on a downward incline, and as a child I spent hours on my scooter, wheeling down to the plaza, walking back up to our house, then again scooting downhill, down and up the street, until boredom or exhaustion led me to take up some different activity. But now such childhood sport would be incredibly dangerous, if not impossible, because Calle México has become a major traffic thoroughfare. As I walk down the street, making my way toward the house we lived in, crossing back and forth a number of times to look more closely at places that seem vaguely familiar, I am keenly aware of speeding cars and accelerating engines. And yet I realize that even though numerous new buildings now dominate the street, and that the process of demo-

Elly on her tricycle and Poldi on his scooter, wheeling down the Calle México to the Plaza del Estudiante

lition and replacement seems to be ongoing, more than a few of the older houses are still standing—somewhat harder to recognize because of the commercial establishments that have been installed on the ground floor of a number of them, and because they have been painted in different colors from what, in my mind's image, I remember. I thus cannot identify the entrance to the patio-type housing where that eccentric refugee lived who used to tutor my father in algebra— a man whom my father admired for his erudition and mathematical talent, but about whom we nonetheless joked because he always wore his pants belted high above the hips, much too short on the bottom, and because he moved in extremely long strides that seemed calculated to place the minimum amount of wear-and-tear on the soles of his shoes. Nor am I able to find the small tienda that was located almost across the street from where we lived, to which I was often sent to buy morning rolls, matches, or other sundry items, and where I also purchased my "pelis" ("peliculas")—individual frames of 35mm film cut from movie stock that we children collected, traded, and gambled in a game of chance we invented. A camera shop, with a modern display window, occupies the site where the tienda had existed.

And yet on reaching what used to be number 134 Calle México, the entranceway to the place where we used to live, I immediately recognize the address despite its renumbering and change in paint and its metamorphosis from residence into a carpentry shop (on this day, "closed"). There is no mistaking the large, latticed window facing the street, close to where my bed once stood, or the high step from the street into our home, where we often sat. And the old colonial-style carved double door, which led to the interior courtyard of the main house of which our flat was a part, is still there as well, quite dilapidated, its blue-gray paint faded, its wood cracked and failing.

Standing in front of this wooden door this morning, no other person nearby, I notice that it is slightly ajar, and on an impulse I crack it open further, step over the threshold, and squeeze sideways into the interior of the building. Only the light from the street passing through the opening in the doorway illuminates the darkness inside. The stone stairs, which had led up to the apartment where my friend Willi Crocker and his parents lived, are still vaguely discernible in the nearby shadows, but most other light that had once passed into an open interior courtyard that had been located beyond the stair-case—and where I had spent numerous hours playing and pretending to be Robin Hood or an American pilot of a fighter plane—has been shut out by a windowless wall and a roof. In this darkness it is impossible to make out details of this enclosure with any certainty—to know if the entrance to what had been my father's electrical and plumbing shop is still there, or if the room under the stairs that was used by the two Anas remains, or if it is still possible to get to what had been the back of our kitchen and our living room. The places where these would have been located, in an L off the hall where I am standing, is now in pitch-blackness, spooky in its impermeable obscurity. "No. You can't see in there. It's not the same. You can't find anything." I speak out loud, needing to break the silence. And I know that I am unable to walk farther into the building, unwilling to remain in this dark place where I do not belong, eager to leave. With a shiver I turn to exit, and I notice the old electrical fuse and power box near the door that had been used for our apart-ment. For the briefest of moments my mind flashes back through the years: my mother is there in that very spot, standing on a chair, temporarily replac-ing a burned-out fuse with a coin. I recall her ingenuity with a smile, walk past my reverie with diminished dread, open the door, and step into daylight and the present.

"Down those incredibly steep steps," I tell Gabriel, Alex, and Marianne some days later, as I point to the stone-stair passageway between the Prado and

the Calle México, "an American soldier, probably drunk, drove a jeep on a dare, all the way from top to bottom . . .

"See that terrace on the Hotel Sucre. I sat there with my parents in 1948 to view a giant display of fireworks to celebrate the four-hundredth anniversary of the founding of La Paz. It was incredible! . . .

"There is where I went to school for first grade." I point to the second floor of a building on the Prado that now houses California Doughnuts and California Burgers. "The synagogue was also located up there. I remember when we received our first report cards. I was so proud I could write in script that I signed my father's name on my report, and the appropriate parents' names on reports for a handful of impressed classmates. Our teacher did not appreciate the generosity of my impulse or my talents as a scribe! . . .

"A stray bullet penetrated the window of that house during the street battles here in La Paz in July 1946 and accidentally killed a boy, my age—someone I used to play with, a child of refugees. At one point during that 'revolution,' when one side was trying to bomb various public buildings, my parents hid Elly and me in a makeshift shelter, under my sister's crib. . .

"Here, I believe, is where the Austrian Club used to be," I say, indicating with some hesitation, pointing to the shut gate of a walled yard that now contains parked trucks and vans. "It seems to have disappeared when most of the Austrian refugees departed. I spent many Sunday afternoons here."

"What do you think about these delicious salteñas*?" I eagerly ask Marianne and the children, who seem less than enthusiastic about tasting the spicy, piping hot Bolivian midmorning snack that I have long adored—and somewhat suspicious about the true identity of the meaty ingredients inside its doughy shell. "What kind did you get, chicken or beef?" My query is addressed to the three of them. "Alpaca, I think," Alex responds, without even a hint of a smile.*

I am eager to take them all around the city: to show them the (now renovated) Plaza Abaroa, where I learned to ride a bicycle, and the location in Obrajes of the no longer existent refugee-owned Quinta Elma, where my parents occasionally took me for afternoon strudel and a Papaya Salvieti. I take them to the Cine Tesla where I saw Pinocchio, *my first film. I point out the white marble Colón statue on the Prado, with its curious Latin inscription "Navigare Necesse Est, Vivere Non Necesse," and explain to them how different and uncrowded the Prado and this spot used to be when Elly and I and the Lipczenko boys chased one another around it. To place after place I lug*

*them, seemingly oblivious to the fact that they have only recently arrived and
are not yet used to the effects of the city's high altitude. Quite relentlessly, I
want to share "my La Paz," as I remember it to have been, with them.*

Years later, as I review highlights of my guided tour on a videotape we
made on that day, I notice an eager, almost anxious, tone in my voice.
There is pleasure in my face from having Marianne and the boys with me.
I smile often, laugh with enjoyment. Yet there is also an intensity in my
efforts to lead them into my past through the sites of my memory, a kind
of frustration about my sense of blockage by an invisible and insurmountable barrier to transmission. How could I convey a past to them
that even for me, at that moment, was far removed in time—a past whose
traces were only identifiable like layers within an archaeology of change,
a shadowy past that, except in deepest personal memory perhaps, was
gone, forever unrecoverable? And in thinking about my efforts to connect to my own "Bolivia experience," and to pass aspects of it on to my
children, I realize that my conduct on that day is not so very different
from that of the many persons who recalled and recorded their "Bolivia
experience" for me in response to my ad in the *Aufbau*. I was perhaps a
more knowing listener to their accounts than Marianne, Gabriel, or Alex
could be to mine—a participant who had been there, albeit as a child,
when they were there as well. My parents and many in my family were
their fellow refugees. I could relate better to details in their narratives. I
knew many of the places about which they spoke, even some of the persons whom they mentioned. I could follow-up with questions, and ask for
further elaboration. And yet, in some fashion, for them as for me, the gap
between the past and the present memory of it, compounded by a sense
of intransmittability—of incompleteness, of difficulties with language, of
not really being heard, of not truly being understood—emerges in every
account. A feeling of loss is certainly a component of this sense of
intransmittability—a kind of mourning that is perhaps only qualitatively
less intense, less wrenching than the yearning for a lost homeland that so
many of the refugees expressed on their voyage of displacement. It is a
feeling, I think, infused with the kind of sadness I felt when I last visited
Ella's grave in the Jewish cemetery in La Paz. In the not too distant future,
I realized most profoundly at the time, the generation of refugees who fled
to Bolivia will no longer be alive. And those of the next generation, children of refugees like me, are middle-aged, preoccupied with their own

transition into seniority and the accelerated passing of time. If the traces fade and lose their meaning, and transmission is so difficult and incomplete, how will memory survive?

I realize, of course, that the fullness, the richness, the depth, the multidimensionality of the "Bolivia experience," like any experience, will forever remain beyond recall and complete narrative reconstruction. Indeed, in time this episode may fade even more into the background of history: a small story, composed of thousands of smaller ones, that may shrink to a paragraph, a sentence, even to a footnote within the larger story of Nazi persecution, the Holocaust, and the rescue of the displaced in the era of World War II. The willingness of so many people to record their memories of emigration and time in Bolivia, and my own eagerness to remember and convey my recollections to my children, is most certainly connected to an understanding of this evanescence, and to a desire to combat it. And despite the incompleteness of transmission, despite its failure to capture and convey experience through memory, transmission is surrounded by values and lessons that transcend its inherent limitations—values and lessons that can indeed be passed on from person to person, from generation to generation over time. My children, and theirs, will never truly be able to "see" what I have seen; from the vantage of my present, I can no longer truly "see" that past myself. But, perhaps some elements of this experience—of its scope and meaning—will touch them and remain within them, and be recalled. At the very least, they would have heard from me, as I heard from my parents and those around me, about the realities and consequences of exclusion and persecution, and the need to battle against them; about survival and the capacity for renewal as expressed in so many refugee lives; about decency and compassion, such as Bolivians of all backgrounds manifested toward immigrants whose culture differed so greatly from their own. Ultimately, they might also come to understand and learn from my very eagerness "to tell," as I have learned from the many "tellers" for whom I acted as "medium," that transmission is itself a meaningful act—a value worth nurturing and passing on.

POSTSCRIPT

NOTES FROM A RECENT RETURN

La Paz's main boulevard, Avenida 16 de Julio, better known as El Prado, has changed considerably over the years since my family left Bolivia to come to the United States. The most visible changes occurred after the mid-1970s, when many of the street's stately private homes and public buildings, with their massive, carved wooden doors, ornate stained glass windows, and elaborate iron latticework and balustrades, were razed and replaced by large hotels, tall office buildings, and by numerous shops and eateries advertised with electric signposts and flashing placards. The Prado's impressive central promenade still remains much as I remember it, with its trimmed flower beds, its elaborately designed burnt-orange and white-tiled walkway lined by trees and white-bubble lampposts, its French-designed fountain displaying a statue of Neptune in its center, and with its monuments honoring Cristóbal Colón and Bolivia's heroic founder, José Antonio de Sucre. But the once genteel promenade and avenue is now thickly crowded until the late hours of the evening with pedestrians and street-hawkers—a reflection of La Paz's immense population increase during the last two decades—and its roadway is often packed bumper-to-bumper with cars and loud minibuses. Gone is the slow-moving electric tramway that ran on tracks on the Hotel Sucre side of the Avenida 16 de Julio—the tram that I often took to school, and the steel rails on which we children placed bottletops to be flattened into objects of play. And the whitewashed turn-of-the-century building that housed the synagogue and my first-grade classroom now stands boarded up, seemingly ready for demolition, having failed in its most recent function: as a hamburger and fast-food restaurant.

The Confitería Elis, however, owned by an Austrian Jew who had emigrated to Bolivia in 1939 on the same ship with my parents, continues to thrive on this street. It advertises its longevity and quality on signs in its showcase and on its printed menu—as an establishment specializing in excellent European meals and baked goods for over forty-five years—and although it is now connected by name and ownership to a trendier New York–style pizzeria on the same block that caters to a younger crowd, it has remained a popular restaurant with local Paceños and with tourists who appreciate its well-prepared food, elaborate pastries, and reasonable prices. It offers daily specials and a wide-ranging blend of cuisines: Bolivian chairo, matzo ball soup, Wiener schnitzel, goulash, arroz con pollo. Elis is also the place that continues to attract a regular crowd of "old customers"—mostly Jewish men in their sixties and seventies who came to Bolivia as refugees in the late 1930s, or as Holocaust survivors after the war. The number of Jewish refugees still remaining in Bolivia has dwindled to under a thousand. Every weekday around five in the evening, a group of them come together at Elis, frequently at the same table—the Stammtisch, as one of them calls it—and they order tea, coffee, or juice and try to resist the temptation of indulging in a slice of Mohnstrudel, Apfelstrudel, Streuselkuchen, or in whichever cake or pastry looks most appealing in the confectionery display case near the kitchen. Their conversation is wide-ranging, their opinions strong, and their arguments animated and sometimes loud. They speak to each other in many languages—Yiddish, Spanish, English, Polish, German—but usually in what sounds like a multilingual blend. They discuss business, the value of the dollar, the world situation, the outlook of the future, and they compare recollections of the past. None of them, they tell me, would ever think of returning to Europe. Many of them have sent their children to the United States to college or for professional training, and some have relatives in North America or in other South American countries that they visit occasionally. They feel themselves established in Bolivia, permanent residents, fixtures in the landscape. Like the Confitería Elis that they frequent on such a regular basis, they have maintained much of the old world within them: its memories, its tastes, aspects of its culture. Yet in a very real sense, they are no longer of that old world. Nostalgia for homeland, for Europe, if it still arises within them on occasion, is recognized as nostalgia for irreplaceable loss. But they describe the feeling in more accepting terms—as more akin to leave-taking and final separation than to a yearning for return.

NOTES

PERSONAL
SOURCES

INDEX

NOTES

PREFACE

1. See the detailed account in Herbert A. Strauss, "Jewish Emigration from Germany: Nazi Policies and Jewish Responses," in *Leo Baeck Institute, Yearbook* 25 (1980), Part I, pp. 313–61, and 26 (1981), Part II, pp. 343–409. Although a large number of refugees were admitted to Bolivia conditionally, as *agricultores*—with visas stipulating that they settle in rural areas and engage in agriculture or related occupations—the majority, coming from urban backgrounds, managed to remain and settle in Bolivia's towns and cities.

2. It is difficult to know with certainty how many refugees actually entered Bolivia in the years between Adolf Hitler's rise to power in Germany in 1933 and the end of 1940, when emigration from Europe came to a virtual halt. Estimates vary incredibly widely, ranging from a low of 7,000 to a high of 60,000. Official registration of refugee-immigrants by Bolivian authorities did not begin until mid-1940. My estimate of 20,000 is based on a tally of immigrant census sheets from this 1940 effort, located in the Archivo de La Paz. This census did not count immigrant children under sixteen years of age and no doubt missed refugees who came to Bolivia only briefly, using it as a staging place for further "back-door" emigration to Argentina, Brazil, and Chile. Perhaps as many as 3,000 people may thus have been omitted from the count altogether. See chapter 6 for additional discussion of this point, and for the political reasons that existed for undercounting them. Estimates of the size of Jewish refugee immigration were made periodically in the late 1930s and during the war years for the American Jewish Joint Distribution Committee (hereafter cited as JDC) in New York. See JDC, Index, pp. 422–23, JDC, File 1,075 (16 January 1940), File 1,076 (13 May 1943). Patrik von zur Mühlen, *Fluchtziel Lateinamerika: Die deutsche Emigration 1933–1945: politische Aktivitäten und soziokulturelle Integration* (Bonn: Verlag

Neue Gesellschaft, 1988), pp. 46–48, summarizes refugee immigration estimates for Latin America. Also see J. X. Cohen, *Jewish Life in South America: A Survey for the American Jewish Congress* (New York: Bloch, 1941), pp. 119–20; Judith Laikin Elkin, *Jews of the Latin American Republics* (Chapel Hill, University of North Carolina Press, 1980), pp. 147–48; Marek Ajke, "Colectividad y Vida Comunitaria Judía en Bolivia," in Círculo Israelita, *Medio Siglo de Vida Judía en La Paz* (La Paz: Círculo Israelita, 1987), p. 20.

3. The name Diez de Medina, for example. The name Sucre itself, of course, has been the subject of some controversy. The "Liberator" and first president of Bolivia, Antonio José de Sucre, after whom the city of Sucre was named, is sometimes traced back to a Jewish ancestor named Zucker who is said to have emigrated to Alto Perú from Uffenheim, Bavaria, in the eighteenth century. See "Bolivia," in Comité Judío Americano, *Comunidades Judías de Latinoamerica, 1971–1972* (Buenos Aires: Editorial Candelabro, 1972), p. 101. For early Jewish settlement in Bolivia see Jacob Beller, *Jews in Latin America* (New York: Jonathan David, 1969), pp. 211–12; Cohen, *Jewish Life in South America*, pp. 111–21; Elkin, *Jews of the Latin American Republics*, pp. 3–24; Marc J. Osterweil, "The Meaning of Elitehood: Germans, Jews and Arabs in La Paz, Bolivia" (Ph.D. diss., New York University, 1978), pp. 55–58; Jacob Shatzky, *Comunidades Judías en Latinoamerica* (Buenos Aires: 1952), pp. 100–101.

4. See Günter Friedländer, "Bolivia," in Morris Fine, ed. *American Jewish Year Book*, vol. 59 (1958), pp. 410–11; Beller, *Jews in Latin America*, pp. 211–12; Ajke, "Colectividad y Vida Comunitaria Judía en Bolivia," pp. 17–18.

5. See Haim Avni, *Argentina and the Jews: A History of Jewish Immigration* (Tuscaloosa: University of Alabama Press, 1991); Jeffrey Lesser, *Welcoming the Undesirables: Brazil and the Jewish Question* (Berkeley: University of California Press, 1995), pp. 1–46 and passim; Susane Worcman, ed., *Heranças e Lembranças: Imigrantes Judeus no Rio de Janeiro* (Rio de Janeiro, ARI: CIEC: MIS, 1991); Elkin, *Jews of the Latin American Republics*, passim; chapters by Victor A. Mirelman, Anita Novinsky, Haim Avni in Judith Laikin Elkin and Gilbert W. Merkx, eds., *The Jewish Presence in Latin America* (Boston: Allen & Unwin, 1987), pp. 13–68.

6. Videotaped interviews with Renate Schwarz, Hanni Pinshower.

7. Telephone interview with Dr. Walter Guevara Arce Sr.

1. DESPERATE DEPARTURE

1. See Gombos, Gruber, Teuschler, eds., ". . . *und da sind sie auf einmal dagewesen": Zur Situation von Flüchtlingen in Österreich. Beispiel Rechnitz* (Eisenstadt: Burgerländische Volkschulen, 1992).

2. G. E. R. Gedye, *Betrayal in Central Europe: Austria and Czechoslovakia, The Fallen Bastions* (New York: Harper and Brothers, 1939), p. 284.

3. See Gedye, *Betrayal*, 292. See also Mark Wischnitzer, "The Martyrdom of Austrian Jewry: A Year of Trials, March 1938 to March 1939" (March 1939), and N. Bentwich, "Council on German Jewry: Report on a Visit to Vienna" (August

17, 1939), in JDC, File 439 (Austria). Herbert Rosenkranz, *Verfolgung und Selbstbe-hauptung: Die Juden in Österreich 1938–1945* (Vienna: Herold, 1978), pp. 20–23.

4. Rosa Eisinger letter 5 January 1939, in *Allgemeines Verwaltungsarchiv Wien, Bestand Reichskommisar für de Wiedervereinigung Österreichs mit dem Deutschen Reich. Karton 195*, reproduced in Hans Safrian and Hans Witek, eds., *Und Keiner War Dabei: Dokumente des alltäglichen Antisemitismus in Wien 1938* (Vienna: Picus, 1988), p. 31.

5. See Elisabeth Klamper, "Der schlechte Ort zu Wien. Zur Situation der Wiener Juden vom "Anschluss" bis zum Novemberpogrom 1938," in *Der November-pogrom 1938: Die "Reichskristallnacht" in Wien* (Vienna: Wien Kultur, 1988), p. 36. See also Rosenkranz, *Verfolgung*, p. 27.

6. Gedye, *Betrayal*, 293.

7. Jewish Telegraphic Agency Bulletin (hereafter cited as JTA), Vienna, 18 March 1938, pp. 1–2.

8. Rosenkranz, *Verfolgung*, p. 23.

9. Gedye, *Betrayal*, p. 297.

10. For photographs, reproduction of documents, and essays concerning these events see *Wien 1938*, Catalog of Exhibition at the Historisches Museum der Stadt Wien (Vienna: Wien Kultur, 1988).

11. See Gedye, *Betrayal*, p. 299, for a report of one such objection.

12. Klamper, "Der schlechte Ort zu Wien," p. 34.

13. See "Ordenlicher und unordenlicher Terror" and "Unorganisierte und organi-sierte Umverteilung," in Safrian and Witek, eds., *Und Keiner War Dabei*, pp. 39–158; Jonny Moser, "Die Apokalypse der Wiener Juden," in *Wien 1938*, pp. 286–97.

14. Gedye, *Betrayal*, 299; Rosenkranz, *Verfolgung*, pp. 22–23, *The Jewish Chronicle* (London), 25 March 1938.

15. *The Jewish Chronicle* (London), 1 April 1938. Rosenkranz, *Verfolgung*, especially chapter 2; Safrian and Witek, eds., *Und Keiner War Dabei*, and *Wien 1938*, passim.

16. Klamper, "Der schlechte Ort zu Wien," pp. 36–37.

17. This argument is detailed in Gerhard Botz, *Wien vom "Anschluss" zum krieg: Nationalsozialistische Machtübernahme und politisch-soziale Umgestaltung am Beispiel der Stadt Wien 1938/39* (Vienna: Jugend und Volk, 1978), pp. 107–11.

18. Klamper, "Der schlechte Ort zu Wien," p. 36.

19. Helmut Genschel, *Die Verdrängung der Juden aus der Wirtschaft im Dritten Reich* (Göttingen: Musterschmidt, 1966), pp. 144 ff. See also Jonny Moser, "Depriv-ing Jews of Their Legal Rights in the Third Reich," in Walter H. Pehle, ed., *November 1938: From "Reichskristallnacht" to Genocide* (New York: Berg, 1991), p. 124.

20. JTA, Vienna, 27 March 1938; Karl A. Schleunes, *The Twisted Road to Auschwitz: Nazi Policy Toward German Jews, 1933–1939* (Urbana: University of Illinois Press, 1990), pp. 157–60; Avraham Barkai, "The Fateful Year 1938" in Pehle, ed., *November 1938*, p. 102; Klamper, "Der schlechte Ort zu Wien," p. 40; Leni

Yahil, *The Holocaust: The Fate of European Jewry* (New York: Oxford University Press, 1991), p. 107.

21. See Gerhard Botz, *Wien vom "Anschluss" zum Krieg,* pp. 96–98; See also "Telegramm RMDI Berlin 21.3.38" in Safrian and Witek, eds., *Und Keiner War Dabei,* pp. 98–99 for text ordering restrictions against these actions—but restrictions to be undertaken after the April 10 "Volksabstimmung," which would provide the electoral underpinning for the *Anschluss.*

22. JTA, Vienna, 14 March 1938.

23. Jonny Moser, "Die Apokalypse der Wiener Juden," p. 291.

24. Other estimates place the numbers of arrests at between 50,000 and 75,000. See Wolfgang Neugebauer, "Das NS-Terrorsystem," in *Wien 1938,* p. 224; Gedye, *Betrayal,* p. 311.

25. See Neugebauer, "Das NS-Terrorsystem," pp. 231–33; Rosenkranz, *Verfolgung,* p. 37. For Mauthausen, see Hans Marsalek, *Die Geschichte des Konzentrationslagers Mauthausen* (Vienna: Österreichisschen Lagergemeinschaft Mauthausen, 1980, 2nd ed.), pp. 31–32. Mauthausen became a camp with gas chambers and a crematorium in which some 100,000 persons met their death. Despite its origins in the aftermath of the *Anschluss,* of the more than 200,000 people who eventually were sent to Mauthausen, fewer than 2,000 actually originated in Austria: inmates were primarily Polish, Soviet, Hungarian, French, Yugoslav, Italian, and Spanish prisoners of war transported to Austria.

26. *Reichsgesetzblatt,* I (Reich Law Gazette, cited hereafter as RGBl, p. 245. GBl. f. Ö. 3/1938. The curtailment of voting was specified for the referendum on 10 April 1938 in which the Austrian unification with Germany was to receive its popular approval. Since no other vote was held until after the end of World War II, Jews were in effect stripped of their political rights with this action. Also see Jonny Moser, "Die Katastrophe der Juden in Österreich, 1938–1945," in *Der Gelbe Stern in Österreich: Katalog und Einführung zu Einer Dokumentation* (Eisenstadt: Roetzer, 1977), passim.

27. For a comparative discussion of emancipation and assimilation and for bibliographical details on these topics see my *Lives in Between: Assimilation and Marginality in Austria, Brazil, West Africa 1780–1945* (New York: Cambridge University Press, 1989), especially chapters 1 and 3 and pp. 200–5, 214–18. See also Jacob Katz, *Out of the Ghetto: The Social Background of Jewish Emancipation 1770–1870* (New York: Schocken Books, 1978). For a memoir and meditation on emancipation, assimilation, and exclusion in Austria, see Stefan Zweig, *The World of Yesterday* (Lincoln: University of Nebraska Press, 1964).

28. Peter Gay, Introduction, in Ruth Gay, *The Jews of Germany: A Historical Portrait* (New Haven: Yale University Press, 1992), p. ix. See also Jehuda Reinharz and Walter Schatzberg, eds., *The Jewish Response to German Culture: From the Enlightenment to the Second World War* (Hanover: University Press of New England, 1985); H. I. Bach, *The German Jew: A Synthesis of Judaism and Western Civilization, 1730–1930* (New York: Oxford University Press, 1985); Steven E. Aschheim, *Brothers and Strangers: The East European Jew in German and German*

Jewish Consciousness, 1800–1923 (Madison: University of Wisconsin Press, 1982); Jack Wertheimer, *Unwelcome Strangers: East European Jews in Imperial Germany* (New York: Oxford University Press, 1987).

29. An excellent summary of the implementation of the racial laws in Germany and of their content can be found in Yahil, *The Holocaust*, pp. 67–73. The eagerness of Austrians to conform with Germany in the implementation of these laws was reported in the JTA, Vienna, 18 March 1938: "Minister of Justice Hueber announced to-day that racial legislation would receive first consideration as his department sets to work on the wholesale legal alterations necessitated by the merging of Austria into the Reich. He declared that the 'tempo' with respect to race laws would be 'speeded up.' "

30. RGBl, 1938, pp. 922, 1044, 1342.

31. For a contemporary summary, see Wischnitzer, "The Martyrdom of Austrian Jewry." See also RGBl 1938 pp. 969, 1403 and the discussions in Moser, "Depriving Jews of Their Legal Rights," pp. 124–26, and Sebastian Meissl, "Wiener Universität und Hochschulen," in *Wien 1938*, pp. 197–209.

32. *Völkischer Beobachter* (Vienna edition), 16, 19, 26 June, 14 May, and 21 August 1938.

33. Volksgarten, Stadt- und Rathauspark,
Ihr Frühling war noch nie so stark.
Den Juden Wiens ist er verboten.
Ihr einziges Grün wächst bein den Toten.

Quoted in Klamper, "Der schlechte Ort zu Wien," p. 33.

34. A contemporary report on the failure of the Socialist workers' uprising, its effect on Jews, and an excellent summary of Jewish institutional life and politics in Austria during the early 1930s is contained in the report by B. Kahn, "The Situation of the Jews in Austria" to the JDS, 28 February 1934, File 439.

35. Ibid.

36. Stefan Zweig, who lived in Salzburg in the early 1930s, writes movingly of Austrian knowledge of everyday actions against Jews in Germany in his chapter "Incipit Hitler" in *The World of Yesterday*, pp. 358–89.

37. P. G. J. Pulzer, "The Development of Political Antisemitism in Austria," in Josef Fraenkel, *The Jews of Austria: Essays on their Life, History and Destruction* (London: Vallentine, 1967), pp. 441–42; F. L. Carsten, *Fascist Movements in Austria: From Schönerer to Hitler* (London: Sage, 1977), pp. 249–315.

38. Jean Améry, *Örtlichkeiten* (Stuttgart: Klett-Cotta, 1980), pp. 25–27. My translation.

39. Mark Wischnitzer, "Jewish Emigration from Germany 1933–1938," *Jewish Social Studies* 2 (1940), p. 26; Yahil, *The Holocaust*, p. 91; Herbert A. Strauss, "Jewish Emigration from Germany, Part I, pp. 330–31, and Part II, pp., 346–47. In addition, emigrants went to Canada, Mexico, Costa Rica, Guatemala, Nicaragua, Honduras, El Salvador, Cuba, Dominican Republic, Haiti, Argentina, Brazil, Chile, Colombia, Ecuador, Peru, Uruguay, Paraguay, Venezuela, Egypt, Algeria,

Tunis, Morocco, Kenya, Union of South Africa, South-West Africa, Southern Rhodesia, Angola, China, Manchukuo, India, Siam, the Philippines, Persia, Netherlands, India, Syria, Turkey, Cyprus, Australia, New Zealand.

40. Wischnitzer, "Jewish Emigration from Germany 1933–1938," p. 27.

41. Videotaped interview with R. M.

42. Schleunes, *The Twisted Road to Auschwitz*, p. 185; Hermann Graml, "Die Auswanderung der Juden aus Deutschland Zwischen 1933 and 1939," in *Gutachten des Instituts für Zeitgeschichte* (Munchen: Instituts für Zeitgeschichte, 1958), pp. 79–80.

43. Strauss, "Jewish Emigration," Part I, p. 330.

44. Wischnitzer, "Jewish Emigration from Germany 1933–1938," p. 28, based on materials from his report *Die Arbeit des Hilfsvereins der Juden in Deutschland 1934–35* (Berlin, 1935). See also Strauss, "Jewish Emigration," Part I, p. 331.

45. Wischnitzer, "Jewish Emigration from Germany 1933–1938," p. 29, summarizing statistics in his report *Die Arbeit des Hilfsvereins der Juden in Deutschland 1935–1936* (Berlin, 1936), pp. 13, 14.

46. Schleunes, *The Twisted Road to Auschwitz*, pp. 178–213; Yahil, *The Holocaust*, p. 103–106.

47. Wischnitzer, "Jewish Emigration from Germany 1933–1938," p. 30.

48. For accounts of the politics of Jewish emigration to Palestine during the Hitler era see Strauss, "Jewish Emigration," Part II, pp. 343–57; Schleunes, *The Twisted Road to Auschwitz*, pp. 179–81, 196–99; Yahil, *The Holocaust*, pp. 97–104; Tom Segev, *The Seventh Million* (New York: Hill and Wang, 1993), passim.

49. Strauss, "Jewish Emigration," Part I, pp. 349–58.

50. For excellent accounts of two such countries, see Avni, *Argentina and the Jews* and Lesser, *Welcoming the Undesirables*.

51. I am indebted to Mark Wischnitzer for the clearest presentation of this demographic reality. See his "Jewish Emigration from Germany 1933–1938," pp. 30–31.

52. I owe this summary formulation to Yahil, *The Holocaust*, p. 105.

53. Testimony of Dr. Franz Meyer, former chairman of the Zionist Organization in Germany, at the Eichmann trial, quoted in Yahil, *The Holocaust*, p. 106.

54. Interview with Julius Wolfinger. Dorit Bader Whiteman presents a very similar first-person account in *The Uprooted: A Hitler Legacy, Voices of Those Who Escaped before the "Final Solution"* (New York: Insight Books, 1993), pp. 45–46.

55. For detailed descriptions of the emigration procedures, see Ernst Löwenthal, ed., *Philo-Atlas: Handbuch für die Jüdische Auswanderung* (Berlin: Jüdischer Buchverlag, 1938), passim. See also Christian Kloyber, "Man Gab Ihnnen den Namen 'Emigranten' " in *Wien 1938*, pp. 299–309; Whiteman, *The Uprooted*, pp. 46–49.

56. Konrad Kwiet, "To Leave or Not to Leave: The German Jews at the Crossroads," in Pehle, ed., *November 1938*, p. 145.

57. "Jewish Youths Seek Visas for Australia," JTA, Vienna, 22 March 1938; "Jews Still Thronging British and American Consulates for Visas: 6,000 Applications Received for Australian Visas in Last Four Days," JTA, Vienna, 28 March 1938.

58. "American Consulate in Vienna Stormed by Would-be Emigrants," JTA, Vienna, 25 March 1938.

59. See Herbert A. Strauss, *Essays on the History, Persecution, and Emigration of German Jews* (New York: K. G. Saur, 1987), p. 207.

60. A composite of various refugee accounts.

61. Videotaped interviews with Julius Wolfinger, Frieda Kohn Wolfinger, Regi Wolfinger Frankl.

62. "Unser Los," signed manuscript written in pencil, no date, in my possession. My free translation.

63. Videotaped interviews with Julius Wolfinger and Ferry Kohn. For an excellent account of Swiss official and unofficial responses to refugees fleeing Hitler's Germany and Austria, see Alfred A. Häsler, *The Lifeboat Is Full; Switzerland and the Refugees* (New York: Funk & Wagnalls, 1969). Also see "Switzerland the Lifeboat," in Yehuda Bauer, *American Jewry and the Holocaust* (Detroit: Wayne State University Press, 1981), pp. 226–27. Since Ella's beau, later husband, did not wish his real name used, I refer to him as Peter C. throughout this chapter.

64. Videotaped interview with Julius Wolfinger.

65. Videotaped interviews with Julius Wolfinger, Frieda Kohn Wolfinger, Regi Wolfinger Frankl.

66. Videotaped interview with Julius Wolfinger; notes of an interview with Peter C., Los Angeles, 16 March 1991.

67. Notes of an interview with Peter C., 16 March 1991.

68. His mother turned down this opportunity because she believed she had the alternative option of joining her daughter in Palestine. Tragically, however, she was unable to acquire this permission and, delaying too long, she was unable to leave Vienna once emigration was restricted in 1941, during the war. She was eventually transported to Poland and died in the Holocaust. Interview with Peter C., Los Angeles, 16 March 1991.

69. Angelika Bammer, "Mother Tongues and Other Strangers: Writing 'Family' Across Cultural Divides," in *Displacements* (Bloomington: University of Indiana Press, 1994), p. 97.

70. A mohel is the ritual practitioner of circumcision. Peter C. interview.

71. Videotaped interviews with Julius Wolfinger, Frieda Kohn Wolfinger, Regi Wolfinger Frankl.

72. Videotaped interview with Julius Wolfinger.

73. Ella Wolfinger, loose pages from an unpublished journal, in my possession.

74. As refugees who had themselves been admitted to the United States only a few months earlier, neither Regi nor her husband, Ernst, could help her.

75. Videotaped interview with Frieda Kohn Wolfinger.

76. Transports from Vienna had begun in mid-February 1941 but were halted in mid-March after some 5,000 of the approximately 60,000 Jews remaining in Vienna had been sent to the ghetto in Lodz. When they resumed again in October, the primary destinations were Riga and Minsk, although Theresienstadt also received a steady stream starting in mid-1942. See Yahil, *The Holocaust*, pp. 289–90, 294,

396–98. See also "The Jews in Austria at the End of 1939," "Report of the Vienna Jewish Community, 1st–30th November, 1939," "Special Report on the General Situation of the Jews in Vienna (February 1, 1940)," "The Activity of Emigration and the Budget of the Jewish Community for the Year 1940," "Confidential Report on Jewish Life in Vienna in 1941," "Mass Deportations of Viennese Jews (March 12, 1941)," and JTA Bulletin, 2 November 1941, "5,000 Jews Deported from Vienna to Poland; Suicides Reported," in JDC, File 439–40 (Austria).

77. Letter from Dolfi Schneider to the family in Bolivia, 24 October 1941, also letter of 29 July 1941. Seventeen letters from Dolfi, starting in August 1939 and describing the increasingly difficult circumstances of survival in Vienna until the deportations, are in my possession.

2. THE CROSSING

1. The Italia Line was formed in January 1931 by the consolidation of Cosulich, Lloyd Sabaudo, and Navigazione Generale Italiana Lines. See Eugene W. Smith, *Passenger Ships of the World: Past and Present* (Boston: George H. Dean, 1963), p. 716.

2. For a critical discussion of the concept of the "affiliative look" and of the "familial narrative," see Marianne Hirsch, *Family Frames: Photography, Narrative and Postmemory* (Cambridge: Harvard University Press, 1997).

3. For a concise but extremely thorough and informative discussion of Jewish mourning practices, see [A. Ro.] in *Encyclopaedia Judaica*, XII (Jerusalem, 1972), pp. 485–93.

4. Arthur Propp, "[Auto]Biography to the End of the Stay in Sucre," *Propp Memoirs*, typescript at the Leo Baeck Institute, New York, p. 131.

5. "Unser Unglückschiff 'Virgilio,' der verwünschter Transport wo unser unvergesslicher Vater starb"; "Traurige Seereise"; "Vorderdeck des verwünschten 'Virgilio.'"

6. Quoted in Christian Kloyber, "Man gab ihnen den Namen 'Emigranten,'" in *Wien 1938*, p. 299. My translation of: "Immer fand ich den Namen falsch, den man uns gab:/Emigranten./ Das heisst doch Auswanderer. Aber wir/ Wanderten doch nicht aus, nach freiem Entschluss/ Wählend ein anderes Land. Wanderten wir doch auch nicht/ Ein in ein Land, dort zu beliben, womöglich für immer./ Sondern wir flohen. Vertriebene sind wir, Verbannte./ Und kein Heim, ein Exil soll das Land sein, das uns afnahm."

7. León and Rebeca Grinberg, *Psychoanalytic Perspectives on Migration and Exile* (New Haven: Yale University Press, 1989), p. 74.

8. Because of the heavy passenger bookings after war broke out to Bolivia and to those few countries on the western coast of South America still accepting refugees, the larger *Augustus* was taken from its North Atlantic service and rescheduled for Central American and Latin American sailing in December 1939. See "Circulaire, Paris 10 Nov. 1939," HIAS-HICEM Archive at YIVO, Series II, France I, File #390. The *Augustus*, 32,650 tons, was the largest motorship (as opposed to steamship) ever built when it was launched in 1926, with a capacity

for well over two thousand passengers. In 1943 it was renamed *Sparviero* and converted into an aircraft carrier by the Italian Navy, then scuttled by the Germans at Genoa in September 1944. See Smith, *Passenger Ships of the World*, p. 23.

9. Julius Wolfinger transcript of telephone conversation and videotaped interview.

10. Grinberg and Grinberg, *Psychoanalytic Perspectives*, p. 67.

11. Smith, *Passenger Ships of the World*, pp. 23, 355, 438, 498, 716, 723; I've derived the *Virgilio's* passenger-crew capacity from figures published for the *Orazio*, which was only 49 gross tons smaller. The *Virgilio* became a war loss in 1944.

12. JDC File 1,084 (Bolivia: 1939–40/March), "Letter from a German Refugee, September 27, 1939"; videotaped interviews with Egon Taus and Heinz Pinshower.

13. Built in 1914, this 15,507-ton ship normally carried 190 passengers in first class, 221 in second class, and 476 in third class. Its normal itinerary was Liverpool, La Rochelle, Bahamas, Jamaica, Cuba, Cristóbal, Buenaventura, Callao, Arica, Valparaiso. See Smith, *Passenger Ships of the World*, pp. 438, 439, 731, 736.

14. Egon Schwarz, *Kine Zeit für Eichendorff: Chronik unfreiwilliger Wanderjahre* (Königstein: Athenäum, 1979), p. 62. My translation.

15. For a summary discussion of refugee exit routes, I am indebted to Patrik von zur Mühlen, *Fluchtziel Lateinamerika*, pp. 25–28. Also see Arieh Tartakower and Kurt R. Grossmann, *The Jewish Refugee* (New York: Institute of Jewish Affairs, 1944); Mark Wischnitzer, *Visas to Freedom: The History of HIAS* (Cleveland; World Publishing Co., 1956); Herbert Agar, *The Saving Remnant: An Account of Jewish Survival* (New York: Viking Press, 1960).

16. Cecilia Razovsky, "Bound for Nowhere," Report to the National Coordinating Committee for Aid to Refugees and Emigrants Coming from Germany," March 9, 1939. In JDC, File #1059 (1937–39 April. South America, General).

17. For the *St. Louis* see Gordon Thomas and Max Morgan Witts, *The Voyage of the Damned* (New York: Stein and Day, 1974); Yehuda Bauer, *My Brother's Keeper: A History of the American Jewish Joint Distribution Committee 1929–1939* (Philadelphia: Jewish Publication Society of America, 1974), pp. 278ff; Mark Wischnitzer, *To Dwell in Safety* (Philadelphia: Jewish Publication Society, 1948), pp. 197ff. See also "The Voyage of the St. Louis" in Michael Berenbaum, *The World Must Know* (New York: Little, Brown, 1993), p. 58.

18. See von zur Mühlen, *Fluchtziel Lateinamerika*, p. 26.

19. For the Shanghai emigration see Ernest G. Heppner, *Shanghai Refuge: A Memoir of the World War II Jewish Ghetto* (Lincoln: University of Nebraska Press, 1993); James R. Ross, *Escape to Shanghai: A Jewish Community in China* (New York: Free Press, 1994); David Kranzler, *Japanese, Nazis and Jews: The Jewish Refugee Community in Shanghai, 1938–1945* (Hoboken: KTAV, 1988); Marvin Tokayer, *The Fugu Plan: The Untold Story of the Japanese and the Jews During World War II* (New York: Paddington Press, 1979).

20. For an excellent study of this, see Michael R. Marrus and Robert R. Paxton, *Vichy, France and the Jews* (Stanford: Stanford University Press, 1995), especially pp. 215ff. Also, see *L'internment des juif sous Vichy* (Paris: Centre de documentation juivre contemporaine [1996]).

21. For refugees on the Iberian peninsula see Haim Avni, *Spain, the Jews and Franco* (Philadelphia: Jewish Publication Society, 1982) and Bauer, *American Jewry and the Holocaust*, pp. 46–48, 196, 206–10. See also von zur Mühlen, *Fluchtziel Lateinamerika*, pp. 27–28; Yahil, *The Holocaust*, pp. 600–602; Herbert Agar, *The Saving Remnant*, passim.

22. Adolf Kronberger, "Ein Augenzeugen-Bericht vom Untergang der 'Orazio,' " *Rundschau vom Illimani*, 29 March 1940. My translation.

23. "At the same time that France permitted refugees to pass through its territory on their way to the Americas, still other refugees with visas for the Western Hemisphere were taken off Italian boats in the French ports and interned as 'German nationals.' HIAS-ICA intervened on their behalf and obtained arrangement whereby the French Admiralty permitted passage of emigrants on lists submitted by HIAS-ICA. These lists were prepared by the HIAS-ICA committees in Italy, which was a neutral country until June 1940." From Wischnitzer, *Visas to Freedom: The History of HIAS*, p. 162.

24. See "Das Drama der 'Orazio,' " *Rundschau vom Illimani*, 26 January 1940 and Kronberger, "Ein Augenzeugen-Bericht vom Untergang der 'Orazio,' " 29 March 1940. See also letter from M. Katzenellenbogen of the Comité Central d'Assistance aux Emigrants Juifs, Marseilles office, to HICEM, Paris, 29 January 1940. Katzenellenbogen reported that the seven men taken from the *Orazio* all had J stamped on their passport and were *"juifs authentiques,"* while the women, one of whom was a Jew and the other a convert from Judaism, were both perfectly able to prove their origins.

25. Kronberger, "Ein Augenzeugen-Bericht vom Untergang der 'Orazio,' " *Rundschau vom Illimani*, 29 March 1940. Captain Carli's account is included in "Das Drama der 'Orazio' " 26 January 1940.

26. In videotaped interviews, Ferry Kohn, Heinz Pinshower, Julius Wolfinger, Liesl and Heinz Lipczenko all stated that they believed that the *Orazio* sinking was not accidental.

27. See *Rundschau vom Illimani*, 16 February and 8 March 1940.

28. See *Rundschau vom Illimani*, 15 March 1940. Also videotaped interview with Heinz Markstein.

29. My translation of "Orazio von Richard Mossmann," *Rundschau vom Illimani*, 15 March 1940:

> *Vergest, wenn ihr es koennt, das Gestern*
> *Und denkt an Morgen, an die naechste Zeit.*
> *Ihr Vaeter—Muetter—Brueder—Schwestern*
> *Auf, auf zum neuen Kampf seid neu bereit.*
>
> *Verteidigt Menschenrecht und Menschenlieber.*
> *Es leb die Freiheit, es verstumm' der Hass.*
> *Auf dass das Glueck fuer immer bei uns bliebe—*
> *"Volldampf voraus."*
>
> Willkommen in La Paz

NOTES TO PAGES 78–89 · 213

3. INVISIBLE BAGGAGE

1. Wilhelm Busch, *Max und Moritz: Eine Bubengeschichte in sieben Streichen* (Santiago de Chile: Editorial "R. Holzer," n.d.), p. 3. The translation is by H. Arthur Klein and others in the English-language edition published by Dover. Heinrich Hoffmann, *Der Struwwelpeter* (Zurich: Globi, Erste Schweitzer-Ausgabe, n.d.), p. 1. My free translation modifies an anonymous one in *Slovenly Peter or Cheerful Stories and Funny Pictures for Good Little Folks* (Philadelphia: John C. Winston, n.d.), p. 2.

2. Schwarz, *Keine Zeit für Eichendorf*, p. 58, my translation; videotaped interviews with Andres J. Simon and Renata Schwarz.

3. Rudolf Dienst, *Im dunkelsten Bolivien: Anden, Pampa und Urwaldfahrten* (Stuttgart: Strecker und Schroder, 1926); Theodor Herzog, *Vom Urwald zu den Gletschern der Kordillere: Zwei Forschungsreisen in Bolivia* (Stuttgart: Strecker und Schroder, 1923).

4. Hilfsverein der Juden in Deutschland, *Jüdische Auswanderung nach Südamerika* (Berlin: Jüdischer Kulturbund in Deutschland, 1939), pp. 21, 23. My translation.

5. Interviews with Werner Guttentag, Julio Meier, Egon Taus, Heinz Markstein. See Karl May, *Das Vermächtnis des Inka* and *In den Kordilleren*, vols. 5 and 8 of *Karl Mays Werke* (Nördlingen: Grenofürdie Karl-May-Stiftung, 1988). See also Christian Heermann, *Der Mann, der Old Shatterhand war: Eine Karl-May-Biographie* (Berlin: Verlag der Nation, Martin Lowsky, *Karl May* (Stuttgart: J. B. Metzlersche Verlagsbuchhandlung, 1987); Klaus Mann, "Karl May: Hitler's Literary Mentor," *Kenyon Review*, vol. II, 1940, pp. 391–400; Günter Scholdt, "Hitler, Karl May und die Emigranten," *Jahrbuch der Karl-May-Gesellschaft* (1984), pp. 60–91; Ekkehard Koch, "Zwischen Rio de la Plata und Kordilleren: Zum historischen Hintergrund von Mays Südamerika-Romanen," *Jahrbuch der Karl-May-Gesellschaft* (1979), pp. 137–68.

6. Videotaped interview with Heinz Markstein.

7. From videotaped interviews with Heinz and Hanni Pinshower, Renata Schwarz, Werner Guttentag.

8. Schwarz, *Keine Zeit für Eichendorf*, pp. 65–66. My translation.

9. Videotaped interview with Julius Wolfinger.

10. For an example articulating this feeling, see Schwarz, *Keine Zeit für Eichendorff*, pp. 72–73.

11. Heinrich Stern, "Indianer-Landschaft," July 1941, typescript. My translation. See published version in *Rundschau vom Illimani*, 21 July 1941.

12. William Wordsworth, Preface to second edition of *Lyrical Ballads* (London: T. N. Longman and O. Rees, 1800).

13. Stern, "Indianer-Landschaft."

14. For a stimulating discussion of representation in family albums, see Patricia Holland, "History, Memory and the Family Album" in Jo Spence and Patricia Holland, eds., *Family Snaps: The Meaning of Domestic Photography* (London: Virago, 1991).

15. Victor Burgin, "Looking at Photographs," in Victor Burgin, ed., *Thinking Photography* (London: Macmillan, 1982), p. 144.

16. Roland Barthes, *Camera Lucida*, Richard Howard, trans. (New York: Hill and Wang, 1981), pp. 80–81.

17. Susan Sontag, *On Photography* (New York: Farrar, Straus and Giroux, 1988), p. 9.

18. Mary Louise Pratt, *Imperial Eyes: Travel Writing and Transculturation*, (London: Routledge, 1992), pp. 120–26. The original titles of these early works by Humboldt are *Ansichten der Natur wit wissenchaftlichen Erlauterungen* (Tubigen: J. G. Gotto, 1808); *Vues des cordillers, et monuments des peuples indigenes de l'Amerique* (Paris: F. Schoell, 1810).

19. Menahem Savidor, "Maccabi World Union," in *Encyclopaedia Judaica* (Jerusalem, 1972), XI, pp. 664–65; Peretz Merhau and Josef Israel, "Ha-Shomer ha-Za'ir," in *Encyclopaedia Judaica* (Jerusalem, 1972), VII, pp. 1372–76.

20. See Edith Foster, *Reunion in Vienna* (Riverside, Calif.: Ariadne, 1989), pp. 131–32 for an interesting parallel recollection by a Jewish Viennese refugee of the Wandervogel and their hiking songs.

21. See Catherine Lutz and Jane Collins, "The Photograph as an Intersection of Gazes: The Example of *National Geographic*," *Visual Anthropology Review* (Spring 1991), VII, no. 1, pp. 142–43. See also their *Reading National Geographic* (Chicago: University of Chicago Press, 1993).

22. See Frederic Jameson, "Pleasure: A Political Issue," in F. Jameson, ed., *Formations of Pleasure* (London: Routledge, 1983), pp. 61–74.

23. Walter Sanden, *Tante Berta wandert aus: ein Abenteuer mit vielen Bildern von Walter Sanden* (mimeographed booklet, privately published, La Paz, 1947). The first edition appeared in 1944.

24. Walter Sanden, *El Lápiz de Sanden* (mimeographed booklet, n.d., no p.d.).

25. John Berger and Jean Mohr, *Another Way of Telling* (London: Writers and Readers, 1982), pp. 86–87, 89.

4. "BUENA TIERRA"

1. Eduard Blumberg, "Bericht über die jüdische landwirtschafltliche Kolonie der Emigranten in Bolivien, 1940–43," Dr. Eduard Blumberg Collection, Leo Baeck Institute, New York (AR-4818 Loc. A15–7), September 1984, 6 pp. typescript.

2. Eduard Blumberg, "Erlebnisse als Juedischer Arzt und Sozialist in Deutschland," Dr. Eduard Blumberg Collection, Leo Baeck Institute, New York (ME-62), undated 84 pp. typescript.

3. See JDC File 1,085, "Report on Bolivia by Mr. Frederick W. Borchardt," La Paz, 6 December 1944; Dr. Herman Hirsch, 1981 oral interview with Leonardo Senkman. Oral Documents from Latin America (tape and transcript Files 19–20 [17]), Institute of Contemporary Jewry, The Hebrew University of Jerusalem.

4. See Herbert S. Klein, *Bolivia: The Evolution of a Multi-Ethnic Society*, 2d ed. (New York: Oxford University Press, 1992), pp. 193–94. Among the many books on the Chaco War see David H. Zook, Jr., *The Conduct of the Chaco War* (New York: Bookman Associates, 1960) and Roberto Querejazu Calvo, *Masmaclay: Historia política, diplomática y militar de la guerra del Chaco*, 3d. ed. (La Paz: Juventud, 1975).

5. See Klein, *Bolivia*, p. 201.
6. JDC File 1,081, David Stern Report, 4 December 1944 (hereafter cited as Stern Report) p. 4; File 1,078, "Parting words to native workers of F. Bonoli on his departure from 'Buena Tierra,' " 7 June 1941.
7. For Mauricio Hochschild, see Helmut Waszkis, *Mining in the Americas: Stories and History* (Cambridge, U.K.: Woodhead, 1993), pp. 122, 127–29. I am indebted to Mr. Waszkis for information on mining in Bolivia and for Hochschild's role in this industry. Also see Cohen, *Jewish Life in South America*, pp. 114–16; Klein, *Bolivia*, pp. 166, 208. For a fascinating account of Berthold Hochschild's son, Harold Hochschild, a U.S.-born relative of Mauricio and a founding director of American Metal Climax, see Adam Hochschild, *Half the Way Home: A Memoir of Father and Son* (New York: Viking, 1986).
8. See "Bolivia," 13 May 1940, enclosure in JDC File 1,075 (Bolivia) 1939–40; Waszkis, *Mining in the Americas*, pp. 120–26.
9. Between 1939 and 1944, the JDC allocated $737,000 to SOPRO for financial aid and resettlement of newcomer refugees, and Hochschild contributed about $250,000 of his own funds. See JDC, General Index, pp. 423, 427; JDC File 1,075 (Bolivia), letter "Bolivia," 22 May 1939; see also "Juden in Bolivien," in Asociación Filantropica Israelita, *Zehn Jahre Aufbauarbeit in Südamerika, 1933–1943* (Buenos Aires: 1943?), pp. 172–74. Extensive correspondence, reports, and memos concerning SOPRO are in JDC files 1084–87.
10. JDC File 1,077, "Discussion with Hochschild," 7 February 1939.
11. JDC File 1,075 (Bolivia 1939–40), Hochschild to Paul Baerwald, 10 May 1939, 7 June 1939.
12. Stern Report, pp. 1–2. Within a few months, more than a hundred refugees were being trained in Miraflores for agricultural work. See JDC File 1,077, Hochschild letter to James N. Rosenberg, Chairman, JDC Trustees for Agro-Joint, 30 April 1940.
13. See Otto Braun, "Report on the Colonization Possibilities in the Zone of Chaparé," at YIVO: HIAS-HICEM Archives, Series I, File XIII, Bolivia. See also JDC File 1,077 (Bolivia 1939–40), "Discussion with Hochschild," 7 February 1939, and JDC File 1,075 (Bolivia 1939–40), Hochschild letter to Paul Baerwald, 10 May 1939. The Jewish Colonization Association (ICA) in Argentina had been founded in 1891 by Baron Maurice de Hirsch. Its original purpose was to help Jews escape from Russia and Rumania after the pogroms there and to settle them on lands purchased in Argentina and Brazil.
14. See JDC File 1,077 (Bolivia 1939–40), "Discussion with Hochschild," 7 February 1939; JDC File 1,075 (Bolivia 1939–40), Hochschild to Paul Baerwald, 10 May 1939; "Minutes of meeting held at the Office of the Joint Distribution Committee, Friday, July 28, 1939."
15. These and following quotations from JDC File 1,077 (Bolivia 1939–40), Hochschild to Paul Baerwald, 10 May and 7 June 1939, and Paul Baerwald to Mauricio Hochschild, 17 April 1939.
16. See JDC File 1,077 (Bolivia 1939–40), "Resume of Report on the Sociedad Co-

lonizadora de Bolivia by Enrique Ellinger," 6 May 1940. SOCOBO's first board of directors included Hochschild (as president), two senior managers from his firm, two prominent Bolivians, and four U.S. citizens affiliated with the Joint. Responding to suggestions made by Joint officials, Hochschild became vice president, the presidency was offered to Abel Solis, the Bolivian owner of haciendas in the Yungas region, where Buena Tierra was located, and a tenth member, a resident in the U.S. and connected with the JDC, was added.

17. For a contemporary assessment of factors involved in the failure of the Chaparé project, see "Bericht aus Bolivien vom Jahre 1939" in Asociación Filantropica Israelita, *Zehn Jahre Aufbauarbeit in Südamerika: 1933–1943*, pp. 186–87.

18. See Klein, *Bolivia*, pp. 208–11; Porfirio Diaz Machicao, *Historia de Bolivia: Toro, Busch, Quintanilla* (La Paz: Juventud, 1957), passim.

19. JDC File 1,077 (Bolivia 1939–40), Hochschild to James N. Rosenberg, 30 April 1940.

20. Additional material for my discussion of the Buena Tierra settlement derives from an unpublished, unsigned paper given to me by Marek Ajke in Bolivia, "Socobo: Sociedad Colonizadora de Bolivia: Agricultores Judíos" (hereafter cited as Ajke/Socobo) based on the personal account of Hans Homburger, who lived and worked in Buena Tierra from 1940 until its demise (and who remained on that land until 1967), and on an article by Franz D. Lucas, "Judíos Agricultores en Yungas," published in *El Diario* (La Paz), 31 January, 1988.

21. JDC File 1,077 (Bolivia 1939–40), report by Walter Weiss to the Refugee Economic Corporation of the Joint, September 1, 1940 (hereafter cited as Weiss Report).

22. Blumberg, "Bericht," p. 2.

23. Deanna Swaney, *Bolivia: A Survival Kit* (Berkeley: Lonely Planet, 1988), p. 143.

24. See Ajke/Socobo, p. 9. Weiss, in 1940, related that it took forty minutes on mule-back to reach the colony from this point. Other accounts expand that time to up to two hours. Clearly seasonal differences did affect the length of this journey, the rainy season extending it considerably.

25. Blumberg, "Bericht," p. 5.

26. Stern Report, p. 7; Ajke/Socobo, p. 9. Each house was about 266 square feet (81 square meters).

27. Blumberg, "Bericht," p. 7; Weiss Report, p. 7; Ajke/Socobo, p. 11.

28. Blumberg, "Bericht," p. 6.

29. Ajke/Socobo, based on Homburger's recollections, confirms that most of the colonists were secularists, but mentions that the colony had not one but three Torah scrolls, p. 11.

30. Weiss Report, p. 7.

31. Blumberg, "Bericht," p. 6.

32. See JDC File 1,077 (Bolivia 1939–40), "Notes on Discussions with Mr. Mauricio Hochschild of Bolivia," 7 February 1939; JDC File 1,075 (Bolivia 1939–40), Hochschild to Paul Baerwald, 10 May 1939; Weiss Report, p. 4.

33. See Stern Report.

34. Blumberg, "Bericht," p. 6; Ajke/Socobo, p. 6.
35. See File 1077, "Minutes of meeting between Hochschild and JDC officials at JDC office, July 28, 1939." Also, Hochschild to Paul Baerwald, 10 May and 7 June 1939; and JDC File 1078, Bonoli to Weiss, 7 June 1941.
36. Stern Report, pp. 1 and 4.
37. Stern Report and Weiss Report, passim.
38. Stern Report, p. 8.
39. JDC File 1080, Hochschild to Liebman, 2 February 1943.
40. *Ultima Hora* (La Paz), 17 February 1943. My translation.
41. Blumberg, "Bericht," pp. 3–4.
42. James M. Malloy, *Bolivia: The Uncompleted Revolution* (Pittsburgh: University of Pittsburgh Press, 1970), pp. 85–126; Luis Antezana Ergueta, *Historia Secreta del Movimiento Nacionalista Revolucionario, 1939–1943* (La Paz: Juventud, 1988), pp. 263–526.
43. Stern Report, pp. 8–12; JDC File 1081, "Minutes of meeting of 16 November 1944 between Mr. Stern and SOCOBO members, La Paz," and enclosure 3 to those minutes.
44. My italics. Yiddish original and translation of letter from "Colonia Cooperative Europea 'Piña,' " 12 July 1939, in JDC File 1,084.
45. Letter from SOPRO to JDC, 13 September 1939, in JDC File 1,084.
46. See Wertheimer, *Unwelcome Strangers*, p. 202, n. 1, and Mordechai Eliav, "German Jews' Share in the Building of the National Home in Palestine and the State of Israel," *Leo Baeck Institute Year Book*, 1985, p. 261, n. 23.
47. See Wertheimer, *Unwelcome Strangers*; Steven E. Aschheim, *Brothers and Strangers*; Leo Spitzer, *Lives in Between: Assimilation and Marginality in Austria, Brazil, and West Africa*, pp. 17–40, 73–101.

5. ANDEAN WALTZ

1. Unless otherwise indicated, translations are my own. See Johannes Hofer, "Medical Dissertation on Nostalgia," first published in 1688 in Latin and translated into English by Carolyn K. Anspach (1934), *Bulletin of the History of Medicine* 2; 376–91.
2. See Jean Starobinski, "The Idea of Nostalgia, *Diogenes* 54 (1966), pp. 81–103; David Lowenthal, "Past Time, Present Place: Landscape and Memory," *The Geographical Review* 65 (1975); Fred Davis, *Yearning for Yesterday* (New York: The Free Press, 1979); Suzanne Vromen "The Ambiguity of Nostalgia," in *YIVO Annual* 21 (1993); *Going Home*, ed. Jack Kugelmass (Evanston, Ill.: Northwestern University Press, 1993), pp. 69–86.
3. Lowenthal, "Past Time," p. 2.
4.   . . . *nur im Traum kann ich Dein Bild noch schauen,*
                Deine Stroeme, deine Waelder, Auen,
                VATERLAND!
                . . . *Qual des Heimweh's, das ich nie gekannt,*

lern ich jetzt erst schmerzhaft tief verstehen,
seit ich Dich so lang nicht mehr gesehen . . .
VATERLAND!
    F. W. Nielsen, "Vaterland" in *Rundschau vom Illimani,*
    29 December 1939.

5. Bertha Wolfinger, undated letter (1941?) from La Paz to Oruro, in my possession.

6. Bruno Stroheim, "Kleiner Emigrationsfilm," in *Rundschau vom Illimani*, 2 February 1940.

7. Schwarz, *Keine Zeit für Eichendorf*, p. 73.

8. Christopher Lasch, "The Politics of Nostalgia," *Harper's* magazine, November 1984, pp. 65–70.

9. Robert Hewison, quoted in David Lowenthal, "Nostalgia Tells It Like It Wasn't," in *The Imagined Past: History and Nostalgia*, eds. Christopher Shaw and Malcolm Chase (Manchester: Manchester University Press, 1989), p. 20.

10. Raymond Williams, *The Country and the City* (New York: Oxford University Press, 1974). My discussion in this section is informed by the work of Vromen "The Ambiguity of Nostalgia," pp. 71–74, and Lowenthal, "Past Time," pp. 20–21.

11. Maurice Halbwachs, *Les cadres sociaux de la mémoire* (Paris: Alcan, 1925), pp. 103–13; Suzanne Vromen, "Maurice Halbwachs and the Concept of Nostalgia," in *Knowledge and Society: Studies in the Sociology of Culture Past and Present: A Research Annual*, 6, eds. H. Kuklick and E. Long (Greenwich, Conn.: JAI, 1986), pp. 55–66.

12. Vromen, "The Ambiguity of Nostalgia," p. 77.

13. Davis, *Yearning for Yesterday*, pp. 31–50.

14. Egon Taus, videotaped interview. After the war, as the economic situation of the refugee immigrants improved, a number of them built houses that were clearly inspired by central European models. Many nonrefugee Germans, both those who had come to Bolivia before the war and those who arrived afterward, also built Bavarian and Tyrolean style houses; numerous examples of these can be found throughout Bolivia.

15. *Jüdische Wochenschau* (monthly Bolivia sections) and *Rundschau vom Illimani* (passim, 1939–42). For "German Hour" program, see announcements in *Rundschau vom Illimani* throughout 1939–40.

16.   *Der Wandrer, irrend in der Ferne,*
    Wo fremd das Tier, der Baum, das Kraut,
    Wo fremd die Nacht und ihre Sterne,
    Wo fremd und tot der Menschenlaut,
    Wie fuelt er sich allein, verstossen,
    Wie Jauchzt sein Herz im fremden Land,
    Wenn ploetzlicht er den Sprachgenossen,
    Den heimatlichen Bruder fand!

In Federación de Austriacos Libres en Bolivia, *Zum Dreijaehrigen Bestehen der Federación de Austriacos Libres en Bolivia* (La Paz: Federación de Austriacos Libres, 1944), p. 54. Cited hereafter as Federación de Austriacos Libres (1944).

17. Federación de Austriacos Libres (1944), p. 14.
18. For a history of the Círculo Israelita see Círculo Israelita, *Medio Siglo de Vida Judía en La Paz*. See also Schwarz, *Keine Zeit für Eicheundorf*, p. 81.
19. In August 1939 an Asociación Judía was established in Cochabamba (in July 1940 it changed its name to Comunidad Israelita, serving Bolivia's second-largest Jewish community. Officially it had five hundred registered members but in all likelihood was significantly larger. See "Historia de Nuestra Comunidad" in *Mitteilungsblatt der Asociación Israelita de Cochabamba (Bolivia): Publicación de Gala en Conmemoración de las "Bodas de Oro" de la Colectividad Israelita de Cochabamba*, Noticiario No. 29, Noviembre 1989.
20. Círculo Israelita, *Medio Siglo*, pp. 171–75.
21. Videotaped interview with Eva Markus.
22. Federación de Austriacos Libres en Bolivia (1944), pp. 9–10.
23. Videotaped interviews with Heinz and Mia Kalmar and Susi and Günter Siemons. The publication *Zum Dreijaehrigen Bestehen der Federación de Austriacos Libres en Bolivia* confirms Kalmar's recollections.
24. Heinz Markstein, 1943 letter published in *Jugend Voran: Anti-Nazi Periodical of the Austrian World Youth-Movement* (London: Austrian World Youth Movement, 1945), p. 21, and undated typed radio script, "La Juventud Austriaca hable [sic] a la Juventud Boliviana."
25. The music for the old Austrian national anthem "Gott erhalte Franz den Kaiser" (God Save Our Emperor Franz), was composed by Joseph Haydn and he then used it as a basis for the theme and variations in the second movement of his Quartet No. 3 in C Major (The "Emperor" Quartet). Much later it was used by the Germans as the tune for their anthem "Deutschland, Deutschland."
26.   *Es wird ein Tag im Osten stehn*
   Und ueber's Land
   Wird sich ein Sturm erheben . . .
   Neu erstehn wirst du, Oesterreich! . . .

   Wir wollen eining stehen . . .
   Mit neuer Kraft . . .
   Wollen dich, du heil'ges Land der Freiheit, wiederbaun.
   Neu erstehn wirst du, Oesterreich!

   Federación de Austriacos Libres en Bolivia (1944), "Hymne der Freien Oesterreicher," pp. 22–23.
27. On the relations of German political refugees in Bolivia, see Patrik von zur Mühlen, *Fluchtziel Lateinamerika*, pp. 217–39 passim.
28. Menachem Savidor, "Maccabi World Union," *Encyclopaedia Judaica*, XI, 1972. The preteen branch was Macabi Hazair.
29. See Ernesto Allerhand, Lotte Susz de Weisz, Werner Schein, "Club Deportivo Israelita Macabi y su epoca de brillo en el deporte," in Círculo Israelita, *Medio Siglo*, pp. 263–310.

30. See "Censos de Extanjeros (Judíos), 1942" (Boxes I–XIII), Archivo de La Paz.
31. From videotaped interviews with Julius Wolfinger and Alfredo Weinheber.
32. Videotaped interview with Julius Wolfinger.
33. Notes from telephone conversation with Liesl Lipczenko.

6. "LOS JUDÍOS ALEMANES"

1. For *chola* dress styles, see M. Lissette C. de Sahonero, *El Traje de la Chola Paceña* (La Paz: Los Amigos del Libro, 1987). For an ethnographic study of domestic service, see Lesley Gill, *Precarious Dependencies: Gender, Class, and Domestic Service in Bolivia* (New York: Columbia University Press, 1994).
2. *Revista de Bolivia* (La Paz), No. 21, March 1939.
3. See A. Yarmush, "Anti-Semitic Agitation in Bolivia," JDC File 1,075 (Bolivia 1939–40).
4. See *La Prensa* (Cochabamba), 23–26, 28–29 November, 3 December 1940. English translations of these articles can be found as enclosures to Milton D. Goldsmith in "Report on German Fifth Column Activities in Cochabamba," La Paz, 4 December 1940.
5. *La Crónica* (La Paz), 29 March 1940.
6. JDC File 1,076 (Bolivia 1941–44), Goldsmith, "Confidential Report on Bolivia to the JDC"; JDC File 1,075 (Bolivia 1939–40), A. Yarmush, "Anti-Semitic Agitation in Bolivia," and "Recent Letter from a Refugee, Settled in La Paz, Bolivia." Also, "Aus Bolivien," *Rundschau vom Illimani*, 5 April 1940.
7. See Herbert S. Klein, *Bolivia*, pp. 208 ff.; James M. Malloy, *Bolivia*, pp. 115–18; "Immigrant Plot Exposed in Bolivia," *New York Times*, 25 May 1939; "Bolivians Bill to Bar Jews Wins Approval: Deputies Accept First Reading of Immigration-Permit Ban," *New York Times*, 9 September 1940; "Bolivia: Refugee Racket," *Time* (New York), 30 December 1940, p. 25.
8. See the collection of Bolivian newspaper clippings (P.C. 2 322b) in the Wiener Library, London. Also see JDC File 1,075 (Bolivia 1939–40), Goldsmith, "Report on German Fifth Column Activity in Cochabamba" as supporting evidence of anti-Semitic sentiment as well as enclosures of clippings from the local press.
9. See "Bolivia: Refugee Racket," *Time* (New York), 30 December 1940, p. 25.
10. For the background of the discovery of the pro-Axis plot and President Peñaranda's expulsion of the German Ambassador, Ernst Wendler, see Alberto Ostría Gutiérrez, *Una Revolución tras los Andes* (Santiago de Chile: Ed. Nascimento, 1944), pp. 131–95, and Porfirio Diaz Machicado, *Historia de Bolivia "Peñaranda"* (La Paz: Juventud, 1958), pp. 53–65. For the renewed anti-Semitic agitation see Jerry W. Knudson, "The Bolivian Immigration Bill of 1942: A Case Study in Latin American Anti-Semitism," *American Jewish Archives*, XX, no. 1, April 1968, pp. 138–59. For a contemporary account in the Bolivian refugee press, see "Gescheiterter Nazi-Putsch in Bolivien," *Rundschau vom Illimani*, 28 July 1941.

11. Knudson, "The Bolivian Immigration Bill"; *La Calle* (La Paz), 16, 20 September, 28 October 1942; Joseph Bonastruo, "Bolivia Challenges the Jew" in *Congress Weekly*, 30 October 1942, pp. 9–10. Contemporary news accounts of anti-Semitic agitation and incidents can also be found in the YIVO archives, HIAS file, RG 245.4 XIII, 1943.

12. Klein, *Bolivia*, p. 215; von zur Mühlen, *Fluchtziel Lateinamerika*, pp. 214–15; Reiner Pommerin, *Das dritte Reich und Lateinamerika: Die deutsche Politik gegenüber Süd und Mittelamerika, 1939–1942* (Düsseldorf: Droste, 1977), pp. 250–58.

13. Knudson, "The Bolivian Immigration Bill," p. 149.

14. Goldsmith, "Report on German Fifth Column Activity in Cochabamba."

15. Reinhard Wolff and Hartmut Fröschle, "Die Deutschen in Bolivien," pp. 146–68 in Hartmut Fröschle, ed., *Die Deutschen in Lateinamerika: Schicksal und Leistung* (Tübingen: Horst Erdmann, 1979); Pommerin, *Das dritte Reich und Lateinamerika*, pp. 250–58; Hugo Fernández Artucio, *The Nazi Underground in South America* (New York: Farrar & Rinehart, 1943), pp. 202–206.

16. On Germans training the Bolivian armed forces, see Wolff and Fröschle, "Die Deutschen in Bolivien," pp. 158–61. When Hitler became chancellor, he named Ernst Roehm to his cabinet and, along with Rudolf Hess, deputy leader of the Party. In 1934 Hitler broke with Roehm and had him assassinated in the notorious purge known as the "Night of the Long Knives." For Roehm in Bolivia, see Hugo Fernández Artucio, *The Nazi Underground in South America*, p. 193; Mariano Baptista Gumucio, *Historia Contemporánea de Bolivia, 1930–1976* (La Paz: Gisbert y Cía, 1980), pp. 85–87, 96–97.

17. Fritz Kübler, *Deutsche in Bolivien* (Stuttgart: Strecker und Schröder, 1936), pp. 53–54. The Spanish translation from *La Razón* is quoted in Ostría Gutiérres, *Una revolución tras los Andes*, pp. 91–92. For another reference to this translation, see Artucio, *Nazi Underground*, p. 202.

18. Artucio, *Nazi Underground*, pp. 191–92.

19. Ostría Gutiérrez, p. 192, cited in von zur Mühlen, *Fluchtziel Lateinamerika*, p. 215 (my translation).

20. A slightly earlier edition of Artucio's *Nazi Underground in South America* was entitled *The Nazi Octopus in South America*. For a detailed examination of German pro-Nazi activities in Argentina, Brazil, Chile, and Mexico, see Leslie B. Rout, Jr. and John F. Bratzel, *The Shadow War: German Espionage and United States Counterespionage in Latin America during World War II* (Frederick, Md.: University Publications of America, 1986). For German activities in Bolivia and other South American countries, also see von zur Mühlen, *Fluchtziel Lateinamerika*, esp. pp. 214–17.

21. See Luis Antezana Ergueta, *Historia Secreta del Movimiento Nacionalista Revolucionario, 1939–43*, pp. 278–82; Klein, *Bolivia*, pp. 214–18; von zur Mühlen, *Fluchtziel Lateinamerika*, pp. 213–15.

22. The original forms of these census records, entitled "Censo de Judíos, 1939–1945" (though quite a number of immigrants were not Jewish), can be

found in catalogued but unsorted boxes in the Archivo de La Paz. Each, with photograph and fingerprint of the immigrant, contains information about place of birth, date of immigration, educational background, employment, marital status, number and sex of children, and residence in Bolivia. No summary census document compiling this information was ever produced by Bolivian officials. It was clearly in the interest of the Peñaranda government and of agencies supporting Jewish refugee immigration to minimize or be vague about the total number of refugees who had entered Bolivia. For more on the Peñaranda era, see Machicado, *Historia de Bolivia*.

23. Klein, *Bolivia*, pp. 214–15; von zur Mühlen, *Fluchtziel Lateinamerika*, p. 213. An additional component of Peñaranda's agreements with the U.S. was a settlement of Standard Oil's demand for compensation for Bolivia's 1937 confiscation of its holdings, whose terms were opposed by many of the government's opponents in Bolivia's Chamber of Deputies. In part, this group's campaign against Jews and other foreign elements in the country has to be seen in the context of a broader nationalist reaction against "foreign domination."

24. For refugee reaction to this event, see *Rundschau vom Illimani*, 2, 16 February, 1942.

25. On the blacklist, actions against German pro-Axis residents in Bolivia, and their internment in the United States, see Wolff and Fröschle, "Die Deutschen in Bolivien," pp. 161–62; Reinhard Wolff, *Die Geschichte der deutschen Vertretungen in Bolivien* (La Paz, 1970).

26. For a brilliant exploration of the many circles of complicity and deceit that enabled this Nazi immigration to occur and to sustain itself, see Marcel Ophuls' documentary film *Hotel Terminus: The Life and Times of Klaus Barbie* (1988). For Beate Klarsfeld's account of her search for Barbie, her actions in Bolivia, and her efforts to gain Barbie's extradition to France see her *Wherever They May Be!* (New York: Vanguard, c. 1975). Also see Allan Ryan, *Klaus Barbie and the United States Government: A Report to the Attorney General of the United States* and *Klaus Barbie and the United States Government: Exhibits to the Report to the Attorney General of the United States* (Washington, D.C.: Government Printing Office, 1983); Christopher Simpson, *Blowback: The First Full Account of America's Recruitment of Nazis, and Its Disastrous Effect on Our Domestic and Foreign Policy* (New York: Weidenfeld & Nicolson, 1988).

27. Videotaped interview with Heini and Liesl Lipczenko.

28. Videotaped interviews with Marek Ajke and Andres J. Simon. Others who indicated a general suspicion about Germans who had become residents of Bolivia after World War II but who had no knowledge that Altmann might be a wanted war criminal were Julio Meier, Lotte Weisz, Werner Schein, and Alfredo Weinheber.

29. Videotaped interviews with Naftali Fischzang and Salo Frischman. Most of Fischzang's long account and Frischman's as well were taped by Marianne Hirsch and me for the "Bolivia Project" of the Yale Fortunoff Video Archive of Holocaust Testimonies.

30. See, for example, Franz D. Lucas, "Wo und wie ich den Tag erlebte," in Werner Filmer and Heribert Schwan, *Mensch, der Krieg ist aus!: Zeitzeugen erinnern sich* (Düsseldorf: Econ, 1985), pp. 224–31; Renee Rosen (Renate Schwarz), *It Happened in Three Countries: A Historical Novel*, 3 vols. (New York: Carlton Press, 1979), passim. Also, videotaped interviews with Julius Wolfinger, Andres J. Simon, Renata Schwarz, Salo Frischman, and Jorge Knoepflmacher. "Acceptance Speech of 'Cóndor de los Andes' Award," Oruro, Bolivia, August 1962 (transcript from audiotape by Uli Knoepflmacher).
31. Mary Louise Pratt, *Imperial Eyes: Travel Writing and Transculturation*, (New York, Routledge, 1992), pp. 4–7.
32. Many of the people I interviewed referred to these: for example, Julius Wolfinger, Heini and Liesl Lipczenko, Heinz and Hanni Pinshower, Werner Guttentag, and Walter Guevara Arce. Also see Schwarz, *Keine Zeit für Eichendorff*, pp. 82–83; Arthur Propp, "[Auto]Biography to the end of the stay in at Sucre," unpublished memoirs at the Leo Baeck Institute, New York.

7. SURVIVING MEMORY
 1. Videotaped interview with Alex Deutsch. Heinz Markstein, also interviewed in Vienna, expressed similar sentiments.
 2. Videotaped interview with Ferry Kohn.
 3. Sentiments expressed in interviews with the author by Trude Hassberg, Liesl and Heini Lipczenko, Renata Schwarz, and Susan Gara-Frei.
 4. Until recently, *Aufbau* was published weekly by the New World Club, formerly the German-Jewish Club of New York City. Now a biweekly, its readership has declined considerably with the demise of the original German-speaking immigrant generation and the Americanization of the children and grandchildren of this generation. See *Aufbau, 20 Jahre Leistung und Erforlg. Sonderausgabe 1933–1955* (New York: New World Club, 1955); Dorothee Schneider, "*Aufbau*—Reconstruction and the Americanization of German-Jewish Immigrants 1934–1944" (thesis, University of Massachusetts, May 1975, 148 pp.).
 5. BOLIVIANISCHE IMMIGRANTEN: Für mein Buchprojekt "Surviving Memory" suche ich für Interviews Personen die in den 30er und frühen 40er Jahren aus Deutschland oder Österreich nach Bolivien auswanderten.
 6. David Lowenthal, *The Past Is a Foreign Country* (Cambridge, U.K.: Cambridge University Press, 1985), pp. 194–95.
 7. Charlotte Delbo, *Days and Memory* (Marlboro, Vt.: Marlboro Press, 1990), pp. 3–4.
 8. Natalie Zemon Davis and Randolph Starn, "Introduction" for special issue on memory, *Representations* 26 (1989) p. 4.
 9. Joan Scott, "The Evidence of Experience," *Critical Inquiry*, 17 (Summer 1991), p. 797.

PERSONAL
SOURCES

Name, place of communication, date, type of material(s)
Simon Aizencang (Eisenzang), La Paz, 25 March 1995 (videotape*)
Marek Ajke, La Paz, 16 March 1995 (videotape*)
Susana Goldbaum de Ajke, La Paz, 23 March 1995 (videotape*)
Walter Guevara Arce Jr., La Paz, July 1991 (interview; notes)
Walter Guevara Arce Sr., La Paz, 16 March 1995 (interview; notes)
M. S. de Aspis, Kfar Sava, Israel, 1991, 1993 (written communication)
Walter Blumenau, Tucson, Arizona, 26 February 1991 (memoir of cousin, Dr. Gerhard Kann; written communication)
Luisa Saperstein Badner, La Paz, 29 March 1995 (videotape)
Aron Balbaryski, La Paz, 25 March 1995 (videotape*)
Jacobo Blankitny, La Paz, 15 March 1995 (videotape*)
Alexander Deutsch, Vienna, 22 June 1992 (videotape)
Stephen Fisch, Flushing, New York, August 1994 (written communication)
Naftali Fischzang, La Paz, 16 March 1995 (videotape*)
Regi Frankl, Norwich, Vermont, 23 November 1989 (videotape)
Salo Frischmann, La Paz, 24 March 1995 (videotape*)
Walter E. Fried, Seattle, Washington, 1991 (written communication)
Max Gans, New York, New York, 26 June 1991 (interview; notes)
Susan Gara-Frei, West Nyack, New York, May 1991 (interview; notes)
Eva Renata Guttentag, Cochabamba, 21 March 1995 (videotape*)
Werner Guttentag, Cochabamba, 31 July 1991, 21 March 1995* (videotape; memorabilia)
Trude Hassberg, Bayside, New York, 4 May 1991 (videotape)

* Video interviews carried out jointly with Marianne Hirsch.

Ilse Herz, Ardsley, New York, 26 February 1991 (videotape)

Herman Hirsch, Jerusalem, 1981 (transcript of interview by Leonardo Senkman)

Marcos Iberkleid, La Paz, 20 July 1991 (interview; notes)

Hans Jungstein, Cochabamba, 1 August 1991 (interview; notes)

Heinz Kalmar, Vienna, 23 June 1992 (videotape*)

Mia Kalmar, Vienna, 23 June 1992 (videotape*)

Alicia Kavlin, La Paz, 4 August 1991 (interview; notes)

Franz "Ferry" Kohn, Holon, Israel, 14 June 1993 (videotape)

Graciela "Leli" Kudelka, La Paz, 5 August 1991 (videotape)

Heini Lipczenko, Cleveland, Ohio, 12 August 1990 (videotape; 8mm Bolivian home movies)

Liesl Lipczenko, Cleveland, Ohio, 12 August 1990 (videotape; memorabilia)

F. D. Lucas, London, U.K., (memoir and written communications)

Eva Marcus, Cochabamba, 22 March 1995 (videotape*)

Heinz Markstein, Vienna, 25 June 1992 (videotape)

Julio Meier, La Paz, 5 August 1991 (videotape*; memorabilia)

Samuel Mejer, Jerusalem, 1982 (tape of interview by Estela Gurevich)**

Claude R. Owen, St. Catharine, Ontario, 22 March 1991 (written communication)

H. Peiser, Tel-Aviv, 28 June 1993 (videotape)

Hanni Riegler Pinshower, Chicago, 10 April 1991 (videotape)

Heinz Pinshower, Chicago, 10 April 1991 (videotape; memorabilia)

Werner Schein, Cochabamba, 2 August 1991 (interview; notes)

Egon Schwarz, St. Louis, Missouri (memoirs; written communications; interview; notes)

Renata Schwarz, Teaneck, New Jersey, 2 May 1991 (fictionalized memoir; videotape)

Werner Selo, Zurich, 29 March 1991 (written communication)

Günter Siemons, Vienna, 23 June 1992 (videotape*)

Susi Siemons, Vienna, 23 June 1991 (videotape*)

Andres Simon, La Paz, 22 July 1991 (videotape)

Fiszel Szwerdszarf, La Paz, 17 March 1995 (videotape*)

Egon Taus, Los Angeles, California, 21 April 1992 (videotape)

Ursula Löwenstein Taus, Los Angeles, California, 21 April 1992 (videotape)

Alfredo Weinheber, La Paz, 29 March 1995 (videotape)

Lotte Weisz, La Paz, 29 July 1991 (videotape)

Guillermo Wiener, La Paz, 22 July 1991 (videotape)

Frieda Wolfinger, Norwich, Vermont, and Queens, New York, 23 November 1989, 21 July 1992 (videotape)

Julius Wolfinger, Norwich, Vermont, and Queens, New York, 23 November 1989, 2 July 1990 (videotape)

* Video interviews carried out jointly with Marianne Hirsch.

** In the collection of the Oral History Division, Latin American Project, The Institute of Contemporary Jewry, The Hebrew University of Jerusalem.

INDEX

Akje, Marek, 177
Algeria, 65
Altmann, Ernst, 156
American Institute (La Paz), 184
American Jewish Joint Distribution
  Committee, *see* Joint Distribution
  Committee (JDC)
American Metal Company, 111
Améry, Jean (Hans Maier), 26–27
Amsterdam, 63
Andere Deutschland, Das, 156–57
Anschluss, ix, 11–22, 26, 30–32, 35*n*,
  38, 143, 155, 206*n*25; fiftieth
  anniversary of, 8; influx of refugees
  to Switzerland after, 38, 40*n*;
  "panic emigration" following,
  60, 63
Aramayo family, 111
Argentina, ix, xv, 34, 131, 137,
  146–47, 159, 185, 189, 203*n*2,
  215*n*13; fascist sympathizers in, 172;
  Hochschild and, 112, 118; Italian
  agricultural colony in, 121, 132;
  Jewish community of, xii; political
  refugees in, 156

Army, U.S., Counterintelligence Corps
  (CIC), 175–76
Artucio, Hugo Fernández, 172
Aryanization, 17–23
Asociación Judía (Cochabamba),
  219*n*19
Aufbau (periodical), xv–xvi, 189, 190,
  197, 223*n*4
Augustus (ship), 57–61, 72, 210–11*n*8
Auschwitz concentration camp, 26,
  143, 178, 183
Australia, ix, 30, 34–35, 111
Austria, xii, xv, 3–10, 82, 186, 189;
  anti-Jewish laws in, 23; critical
  memory of, 153–56, 158, 159;
  emigration of Jews from, 24–27,
  33–35, 63; extermination of Jews of,
  46; ideal of physicality in, 96; Nazi
  annexation of, *see Anschluss*;
  nostaligic memory of, 143–52;
  refugees in Switzerland from, 38,
  40*n*, 41, 45; return of political
  refugees to, 185, 186
Austrian Club (La Paz), 141–43, 148,
  150–51, 153–56, 184, 196

Austrian World Youth Movement, 155
Aymara people and language, xiv, 96, 99, 129, 160, 161, 163–64

Baerwald, Paul, 119–20
Bammer, Angelika, 42
Banzer, Hugo, 177
Barbie, Klaus, ix, 175–78
Beer-Hoffmann, Richard, 148
Beethoven, Ludwig van, 108, 148
Beethoven: El Sacrificio de un niño (children's book), 76
Belgium, 27
Berger, John, 105
Berzelius smelting company, 112
Blade Runner (film), 183
Blau family, 6
Blumberg, Eduard, 107–9, 123–26, 129, 136, 137, 138
Blumberg, Ruth, 126
Blumberg, Trude, 108, 109, 124, 125, 131, 137, 138
Boer War, 58n
Bolivia Pintoresca (Sanden), 100, 101
Bolshevik Revolution, xii
Bonoli, Felipe, 121–22, 131–33
Braun, Otto, 117, 132–33
Brazil, ix, 34, 159, 169, 185, 189, 203n2, 215n13; fascist sympathizers in, 172; Hochschild and, 112, 118; Jewish community of, xii; political refugees in, 156
Brecher, Alfred, 149
Brecht, Bertolt, 11, 56
Brettauer family, 3
British Pacific Steam Navigation Company, 62
Buchenwald concentration camp, 57, 108
Buena Tierra refugee colony, 107–9, 121–38, 140, 147
Buenos Aires, 146–47
Bürckel, Josef, 12, 17
Burgin, Victor, 89–91

Busch, Germán, 110, 113, 117–18, 120, 167
Busch, Wilhelm, 76, 100

Caen, Herb, 141
Calle, La (newspaper), 168, 169
Canada, ix, 118, 189
Capauner, Ludwig, 124
Capauner, Marianne, 126
Catholics, xii–xiv, 6–7, 82, 99, 151, 166, 180
Central Office for Jewish Emigration (Vienna), 31
Cerro de Potosí silver mines, 112
Cervecería Boliviana Nacional, 169
Chacón, Gustavo, 168
Chaco War, 84, 109–10, 114, 117–18, 170
Chamber of Deputies, Bolivian, 167–69, 222n23
Chaparé settlement project, 119–21
Charobamba hacienda (Buena Tierra), 123, 124, 126, 132, 137, 138
Chevra Kadesha (burial society), 183
Chile, ix, xv, 66, 86, 159, 185, 188, 189, 203n2; disembarking of refugees in, 52, 61, 63, 70, 85; fascist sympathizers in, 172; Hochschild and, 112, 119; political refugees in, 156
China, 66
cholos, xiii–xiv, 96, 161–62
Círculo Israelita (La Paz), 71, 151, 158, 184
Club Amistad (Freundschaft), 156
Colegio Boliviano-Israelita (La Paz), 184
Colegio Calvert (Calacoto), 184
Colegio Mariscal Braun (La Paz), 170–71
Colombia, 50, 61, 118, 131
Colombo (ship), 69
Colonia Busch settlement (Bolivia), 110–11, 120
Communists, x, 11, 18, 156–58, 173

Compañía Unificada del Cerro de Potosí, 112
Comunidad Israelita (Cochabamba), 219n19
Comunidad Israelita (La Paz), 151, 158, 184
Condor airline, 169
Conte Biancamano (ship), 69
Crocker, Willi, 195
Crónica, La (newspaper), 166, 167
Cuba, 34, 65
Cuenca, Zuazo, 168, 169
Czechoslovakia, ix, 27, 47, 57, 63, 110, 148

Dachau concentration camp, 19, 57
Davis, Fred, 141
Davis, Natalie Zemon, 191
Days and Memory (Delbo), 191
Delbo, Charlotte, 191
Denmark, 27
Deutsch, Alexander, 94, 186
Deutsche in Bolivien (Kübler), 170–71
Deutschland, Deutschland über Alles, 155, 219n25
Diez de Medina, Eduardo, 167–68
Dinesen, Isak, 141
Dollfuss, Engelbert, 25, 26
Dollfuss Cross, 14
Dominican Republic, 34
Dornbush, Laci, 126

Eco Libre, El (newspaper), 166, 167
Ecuador, 131, 156
Edera (ship), 69
Efferoth, Hugo, 156
Ehrlich, Jacob, 18
Eichmann, Adolf, 31
Eisinger, Rosa, 12
Ellinger, Enrique, 113
Emmerich, Walter, 126
England, see Great Britain
Entjudung (expulsion of Jews), 3, 29, 30

Escuela Boliviana-Israelita (La Paz), 151–53, 184
European Cooperative Colony "Piña" (Samaipata), 138–40, 158–59
Evian Conference (1938), 40n

Federación de Austriacos Libres en Bolivia, see Austrian Club (La Paz)
Final Solution, 46
Finca Caiconi training farm (La Paz), 116, 117, 174
Fischzang, Naftali, 177–78
Ford, Henry, 168
France, 27, 50, 61–63, 65–67, 69, 71, 175, 212n23
Franco, Francisco, 62n
Frankl, Ernst, 43, 187
Frankl, George, 43, 187
Frankl, Regi Wolfinger, 43, 45, 187
Free Austria movement, 155, 186
Freemasons, 19
Freies Deutschland, 156, 157
Freikorps, 169–70
Freundschaft (Club Amistad), 156
Friedmann, Desider, 18
Frischman, Salo, 177–79, 183

Gamarra, Luis, 133, 137
García Meza, Luis, 177
Gay, Peter, 20
Gedye, G.E.R., 11, 13, 14
German Communist Party (KPD), 156–57
German Jews, xiv, 116, 156–59, 164
Germany, ix, 25–26, 47, 108, 145, 155, 189; annexation of Austria by, see Anschluss; anti-Semitic propaganda of, 167–69; Bolivia and, 169–72, 174–75; defeat of, 143; discriminatory legal measures against Jews in, 20–23, 27, 29; emigration of Jews from, 27–31, 33, 63–65, 120; and Final Solution, 46; idealization of physicality in, 96; Italy and, 52;

Germany (*cont.*)
　Kristallnacht pogroms in, 32, 35; Nazi
　　rise to power in, xii, 11, 24, 27, 46,
　　203n2; nineteenth-century
　　Romanticism in, 93–94; Poland
　　invaded by, xv; political refugees from,
　　156–57, 185; and sinking of *Orazio*,
　　71; Soviet Union invaded by, 66
Gestapo, 18, 19, 175
Gmelin, Wilhelm, 93
Goebbels, Joseph Paul, 176
Goethe, J. W. von, 88
Göring, Hermann, 17
Gottlieb, Jaime, 124
Great Britain, xv, 34, 63, 115, 145, 168,
　　187; Italian declaration of war on,
　　67; refugees in, 27, 43, 58n
Great Depression, 16, 28
Grimm's Fairy Tales, 76
Grinberg, León, 56–57, 60
Guttentag, Werner, 83, 84

Halbwachs, Maurice, 145–46
Hamburg-America Line, 65
Ha-Shomer ha-Za'ir, 94–95, 186
Haydn, Joseph, 155, 219
Hebrew Immigrant Aid Society
　　(HIAS), 65, 212n23
Helfer, Gisi, 142
Helfer, Otto, 142
Herder, J. G. von, 88
Herrera, Cesar, 166
Hertz, Ilse, 179
Hess, Rudolf, 221n16
Hewison, Robert, 145
"Hilfsverein, der," see SOPRO
Hilfsverein der Deutschen Juden,
　　27–29, 81–83
Hirsch, Baron Maurice de, 215n13
Hirsch, Marianne, 193, 195–97
Hirsch-Weber, Wolfgang, 156
Hitler, Adolf, 17, 25, 81, 84, 153, 170,
　　171, 221n16; and *Anschluss*, 13, 18;
　　rise to power of, 24, 27, 28, 30, 203n2

Hitler-Stalin Pact, 157
Hochschild, Berthold, 111
Hochschild, Mauricio, 111–13, 115–21,
　　130, 132, 134–37, 140, 167, 216n16
Hochschild, Zacharias, 111
Hochschild Company, 112, 113
Hofer, Johannes, 143
Hoffman, Eva, 141
Hoffmann, Heinrich, 76
Hofmannsthal, Hugo von, 148
Hogar Austriaco, *see* Austrian Club
Homburger, Hans, 137
*Hotel Terminus: The Life and Times of
　　Klaus Barbie* (film), 176
Huguenots, 58n
Humboldt, Alexander von, 93–94, 99
Hungary, 45
"Hymn of the Free Austrians, The"
　　(Terramare), 155–56

Ichilo River settlement (Bolivia),
　　110–11
*Ilustrativo y Informativo Material para
　　Oradores* (pamphlet), 169
Imparcial, El (newspaper), 169
Incas, xiii, 78
In den Cordilleren (May), 83
India, ix, 118
Indians, Bolivian, xiii–xiv, 82–84, 92,
　　163–64; in Buena Tierra, 125, 126,
　　129–30, 132, 137; in Chaco War,
　　109–10; children, friendships of
　　refugees and, 104–6; refugees' images
　　of, 96–101
International Jew (Ford), 168
Israel, xv, 185, 186, 187, 189; *see also*
　　Palestine
Israelitische Kultusgemeinden (Jewish
　　Community Organizations), 18, 151
Italia Line, 52, 57, 60–61, 63, 210n1
Italy, 43, 50–52, 61, 63, 65–67, 70–72

Japan, 174
Java, 118

Jewish Cemetery (La Paz), 182–84, 197
Jewish Colonization Association (ICA), 117, 212n23, 215n13
Jewish Telegraphic Agency, 13
Joint Distribution Committee (JDC), 61, 138, 139, 174, 203n2; Blumberg hired by, 109; Buena Tierra settlement and, 122, 126–31, 134, 135; Hochschild and, 113, 115, 117–21, 216n16; and ships "bound for nowhere," 64, 65
Jordan, Heinz, 94
judíos alemanes, see German Jews
Jüdische Auswanderung nach Südamerika (pamphlet), 82–83
Jüdische Gemeinde (La Paz), 72
Jüdische Wochenschau (newspaper), 146–47
Juedische Jugendbund (La Paz), 71

Kalmar, Ernst, 149
Kalmar, Fritz, 149
Kalmar, Heinz, 149, 155
Karbaum, Willi, 156
Klamper, Elisabeth, 14
Klarsfeld, Beate, 175, 177, 178
Klein, Herbert, 110
Koch, Josef, 93
Kohn, Franz "Ferry," 37, 43, 45, 159, 186, 187
Kohn, Frieda, 45, 187
Kohn, Gisi, 45, 186
Kohn, Hilde, 45, 186
Kohn, Leopold, 45, 186
Kohn, Rosi, 45, 186
Kohn family, 7, 45, 186
Kristallnacht, 8, 16, 32, 35, 38, 62, 63, 108, 155, 174
Kronberger, Adolf, 66–69
Kübler, Fritz, 170–71
Kudelka, Stefi, 142
Kudelka, Walter, 142
Kulka, Hans, 149, 169–70
Kupferstein, Rosl, 149

Labor Zionists, 158, 186
Lápiz de Sanden, El (Sanden), 103–4
Lasch, Christopher, 145
Law for the Protection of German Blood and German Honor, 21
Lebanon, 131
Liebman, Charles J., 135–36
Lipczenko, Heini, 142, 148, 176
Lipczenko, Liesl, 142, 159–60, 176–77
Lipczenko family, 196
Lloyd Aéreo Boliviano (airline), 169
Lloyd Triestino Line, 63, 69
Löhnberg, Erhart, 156
Löwenherz, Josef, 18
Lowenthal, David, 144, 183, 191
Lufthansa, 169
Lycée Français (La Paz), 184

Macabi organization, 71, 72, 94–95, 158
Maier, Hans (Jean Améry), 26–27
Mann, Klaus, 84
Markstein, Heinz, 83
Markus, Eva, 154
Marranos, xi–xii, 167
Marxists, 19, 26, 145
Masai, 141
Mauthausen concentration camp, 19, 206n25
Max und Moritz (Busch), 76–77, 80–81, 100
May, Karl, 83–84, 96–97
Meier, Julius, 83
mestizos, see cholos
Metalgesellschaft, 111
Mexico, ix, 34
Morocco, 65
Mossmann, Richard, 72
Mozart, Wolfgang Amadeus, 76, 108, 148
Multifoto, 71–72

Nantes, Edict of, 58n
National Coordinating Committee for Aid to Refugees and Emigrants Coming from Germany, 64, 65

Nazis, ix–xii, xiv, 4, 9, 26, 34, 81, 143, 153, 154, 158, 179, 185; anti-Jewish laws of, 20–23, 108, 115; in Bolivia, 167–73, 175–78; defeat of, 156, 157; and Jewish emigration, 28–31, 52; rise to power of, 24, 27, 46, 152; and sinking of *Orazio*, 71; in Vienna, 11–20, 25

Nazi Underground in South America (Artucio), 172

Netherlands, 27, 63, 83

Neumann, Heinrich, 149

New Christians (Marranos), xi–xii, 167

New York Club (New York), 223n4

New York Times, The, 11

New Zealand, ix, 34

"Night of the Long Knives," 221n16

Nora, Pierre, 183

NSDAP (Bolivian Nazi Party), 168–70

Nuremburg Laws (1935), 20–21, 27, 29, 198

Ophuls, Marcel, 176

Orazio (ship), 60–61, 66–73, 211n11

Orduña (ship), 62–63

Orthodox Jews, x, 15, 47

País, El (newspaper), 167, 169

Palestine, 27, 30, 34, 43, 131, 137, 159

Panama, 36, 50, 51, 54, 61, 62, 188

Paraguay, 34, 84, 109–10, 170

Pasternak, Josef, 149

Patiño, Simón, 111, 112

Peñaranda, Enrique, 113, 136, 168, 173–74, 222nn22, 23

Peru, 61, 112, 119, 169

"Piña" Polish-Jewish colony, 138–40, 158–59

Pinshower, Hanni, 84, 163

Pinshower, Heinz, 84, 94

Polacos, 139–40, 159

Poland, xii, xv, 45, 110, 120, 141

Polish Jews, 116, 138–40, 151, 158–59

Polo Polo hacienda (Buena Tierra), 123, 126, 132, 137

Portugal, 66

Pratt, Mary Louise, 93–94, 180

Prensa, La (newspaper), 166, 167, 169

Propp, Arthur, 55, 59

Protestants, 6–7

Protocols of the Elders of Zion, The, 168, 169

Quechua people and language, xiv, 96, 163, 164

Raczymow, Henri, 3

Radio Nacional (Bolivia), 148

Radl, Lotzi, 4–7

Razón, La (newspaper), 167, 169–71

Razovsky, Cecilia, 64, 65

Rechnitzer, Theresia Blau, 6

Reibpartien ("scrub parties"), 13–14

Reich Citizen Law, 21

Reichsfluchtsteuer (exit tax), 33

Republikanischer Schutzbund, 25

Revista de Bolivia (periodical), 165

Roehm, Ernst, 170, 221n16

Rollkommandos, 12, 16, 17

Romanticism, 88, 92–94, 99–100

Roosevelt, Franklin D., 173

Rosenberg, James N., 121

Rosenfeldt, Lizi, 9–10

Rothmund, Heinrich, 40n

Rothschilds, 31

Rumania, 151, 215n13

Rumanian Jews, 151, 215n13

Rundschau vom Illimani (weekly), 71, 126, 144–48, 156, 157

Russia, xii, 139, 215n13; *see also* Soviet Union

Sabbath, Jewish observance of, xii, 129

St. Louis (ship), 65

St. Stephen's Cathedral (Vienna), 75, 78, 160

Sanden, Walter, 99–104